**Libraries and Literature
for Teenagers**

Libraries and Literature for Teenagers

MARGARET R. MARSHALL FLA

Senior Lecturer
Department of Librarianship
Leeds Polytechnic

ANDRE DEUTSCH/A Grafton Book

First published 1975 by
André Deutsch Limited
105 Great Russell Street London WC1

Copyright © 1975 by Margaret Marshall
All rights reserved

Printed in Great Britain
by Ebenezer Baylis and Son Limited
The Trinity Press, Worcester, and London

ISBN 0 233 96604 8 ✓

To my Parents
who provided me with a happy book-lined
childhood and adolescence

Acknowledgements

For permission to quote from *The Times Educational Supplement*, Scholastic Publications and the American Library Association.

James R. Squire and Roger K. Applebee for the use of some of the tables from *Teaching English in the United Kingdom*, and the Editor, *Library Journal*, Bowker, New York for permission to reproduce the Young Adult Task Force recommended standards.

For permission to reproduce photographs: Mr Baker, Lincoln Public Library; Mrs Kate Massey, Walsall Public Library; Mr D. Bodey, Industrial Photographs; Mrs F. Winkworth, ex-John Smeaton School.

For clerical help: Miss Lillian Wong.

For information: Mrs Kate Massey and Mrs Christine Knight for information about their libraries and for their hospitality on my visits to their libraries; Miss Esme Green of Nottinghamshire County Library; the many librarians, teachers and youth leaders for their help and information during my visits to libraries in schools, colleges, institutions and public libraries; the countless librarians, writers and publishers whom I have pumped for information during formal or casual encounters.

To all these my grateful thanks and sincere appreciation are offered.

Contents

List of plates

List of tables

Introduction

This study is neither a manual of teenage library techniques nor a critical and literary analysis of literature for teenagers. Both already exist in books and periodical articles but few publications have attempted to cover the reasons for teenagers' use and non-use of books and libraries.

This is an examination of the factors influencing the teenager's attitudes towards reading and libraries, his reading needs and habits and the effect of these upon his use of libraries. By the descriptive and evaluative analysis of library practices in Britain and America it is also an examination of how publishers, teachers and librarians cater for those reading interests and library habits.

There is little value in attempting to survey the whole range of books recommended for teenagers, as evidenced in other works which have attempted it. The best have covered the field adequately for the time, the less good degenerate into a sometimes objective analysis of a subjective selection of recommended works. The intention in this study was to look at what teenagers choose to read, to examine the implications of publishers', teachers' and librarians' choice for teenagers and to assess the factors leading to the decline in reading and library use at teenage.

There is not, therefore, any attempt to list or to analyse a comprehensive range of individual authors and titles that a librarian could extract and use as a selection list. Instead the purposes, reasons, causes, aims, attitudes and objectives of both teenager and librarian are surveyed. Few librarians can stand back from their work to look at it objectively and even fewer ever try to test whether they are achieving what they intended. It is hoped that this book provides an indication of why teenagers read or do not read, how publishers, teachers and librarians succeed or fail in their book connection with teenagers, and, where the evidence points to the failure of current practice some recommendations are made, otherwise the examples given speak for themselves and may cause the reader to test his own reactions, attitudes and practices against those described.

The *Annual Abstract of Statistics* estimates that the teenage population of Britain by the year 2000, will be in the region of 5 million girls and 6 million boys; over 11 million young people as potential readers and users of libraries. The impact on libraries of such a large number requires serious study and planning to ensure that librarians are aware of the importance of knowing preferences and needs, both literary and library, and that librarians are aware of the range of possibilities for effective library service to teenagers.

There is no other book which brings together a study of the teenage reader, the book and all the types of library which serve the teenager, with an overview of current practice. The writer hopes that this book will fill the gap.

M.R.M.
November 1973

Chapter 1
The teenager's environment as it affects reading and the use of libraries

The teenager may be a hooligan, a rebel, uncouth and grubby, loud mouthed, a drop out, a loner, a gang cultist, a dabbler in the latest trends, a revolutionary, given to giggling and exhibitionism, irreligious, vulgar, inarticulate and utterly selfish. The teenager may be excessively conventional, indistinguishable from his peers, sensitive about appearance, agonizing over relationships, teetering on the threshold of idealism in philosophy, religion and social mores, seeking identity through involvement in humanitarian action for others; attempting to sift the trivial from the important.

The teenager may be one, some or all of these in adolescent years, successively or concurrently, simultaneously tugging at the apron strings, wrestling for independence from adult authority, expecting life on the mountain top and getting moments of heady elation but mainly experiencing the uneven terrain of adolescence with plains of boredom and valleys of misery.

The teenager between the ages of fifteen and eighteen is edged slowly into the legal rights and privileges of adulthood in a confused and confusing sequence. For example, one day he is legally a schoolboy, forbidden to buy cigarettes, have sexual relations, see a potentially corrupting film, ride a scooter or motor bike on a public highway or buy an alcoholic drink in a bar. On his sixteenth birthday he is legally permitted to leave school, smoke, have sexual intercourse and even marry, but not to drive a car, buy a drink or see specific categories of film. At seventeen though able to drive and smoke, marry and fight for his country he may not vote or undertake credit purchase or similar long-term financial transactions. Public attitudes towards him will differ depending on whether he is at school or a worker. Adolescent attitudes towards each other are polarized round this question too.

As the greater proportion of British and American teenagers

leave school on attaining the minimum leaving age, a great divide is created between the working teenager who has many adult privileges usually without adult responsibilities, who is normally accepted by employers on the same basis as adult employees and by parents as a working and financially contributing member of the family, and the teenager who continues at school and college where seemingly inflexible forms of control are considered necessary and the restrictive parental attitudes towards dependent children persist.

Such apparently haphazard withdrawing of restrictions or, to put it more positively, such haphazard opening of doors into legal and social adulthood take little account of emotional growth towards maturity. The increasingly lengthy period of adolescence and dependence in Western society, extended for a variety of educational and social reasons must take account of the quality of extended adolescence and its role as a period of developing mental, social and physical attributes and faculties, but must pay especial attention to the quality of the adolescent period for those, who for a number of reasons, cannot or do not wish to extend their schooldays beyond the legal minimum.

Adolescence as a period of preparation for a full life as an adult, as the nurturing of idealism allied to the constructive working towards the ideal, as the channelling of sensitivity to people, thoughts and situations, into involvement, practice and self development, is fettered somewhat by the fact that physiological and social maturity do not always coincide, and intellectual maturity is a much later and rarer development. Indeed in many instances such development appears to have been arrested at the adolescent stage, the individual achieving no further growth but running along the groove reached when formal education finished.

The quality of adolescent and subsequent life lies not so much in the physical environment as in the range of stimuli for intellectual and emotional growth in which the individual is looking for ways of testing himself and his new identity, adding to and enhancing his awareness of opportunities for progress in his peer group at home and in the community. The quality and level of such assertion has led one American writer to propound a typology of youth which qualifies the features of the disease known as 'generational gapiosis',[1] with minor adjustments for either side of the Atlantic, youth is typified as (a) alienated,

(b) committed, (c) experimenters, (d) mainstream, and (e) conservative-moving-right. While the causes of belonging to any one of those groups lie mainly in the social environment of the member, membership is also attributable to the stage of mental and emotional growth achieved; intelligence, intellect, cultural level, racial views, religious beliefs and politics may be determined largely by the local political and cultural policies and stimuli and the availability of leisure time and other resources in the community.

As a basis for stable emotional adulthood the quality of the intellectual and emotional life of the teenager in any stratum of society may be at risk as the contact with, and therefore assimilation of and emulation of, adult emotion and intellect in many contexts is increasingly rejected. The adolescent thus experiences only those of his peers or the excessively emphasized and aggressively vulgarized emotions and ideas portrayed in the media to which the average teenager is exposed or which he chooses for himself.

In all classes of society the teenager will adjust to the somatic change of adolescence, that is, the physical development with its inherent clumsiness which may cause emotional distress. Social class plays its part here in that there may be a wide variation in the age of puberty between the deprived youngster and the sheltered, well-nourished middle-class youngster. He will also make the heterosexual adjustment, acquire a mature social role through his job and become increasingly independent. Such adjustment may be late in both working class and middle class for totally different reasons; the working-class teenager leaving school at the earliest opportunity may pass from job to job, usually in pursuit of more money rather than job satisfaction before, eventually, as a result of marrying young, settling down to his felt role as an adult; the middle-class teenager adjusts at much the same time but largely because his extended schooling and subsequent starting out on a career have filled in the intervening years.

However the third adjustment in adolescence, that of personality development and self concept, which can be seen in the extremes in moodiness or idealism, is an adjustment which is the most neglected of the three in terms of aid given by parents, teachers, employers or 'authority', and the most difficult to achieve unaided. Emotional stability and awareness, not repression, inhibition or exhibition, are factors to which little attention has been paid in the social and educational organizations concerned with youth, and reading has most to offer in these fields. The social needs and satisfactions of teenagers can be seen in some of the replies given by sixth formers in a questionnaire.[2] From the boys, 'I am unsure of my abilities, afraid of failure, a person who needs many friends, full of self pity, against old people/coloured people/Jews, afraid of being physically crippled, in many ways a hypocrite, lazy, kind, generous, in love.' The girls replied with 'I am easily depressed, afraid of death, mixed up as regards my religious beliefs, shy till I get to know people, afraid of the dark, not glamorous, dithery, conscious of a desire to be popular, extremely lazy, pessimistic, moody, a snob, inconsistent, kind to animals but not to humans.'

The manifestations of physiological, sociological and psychological adolescence can be seen in the following items, and their relationship to reading and library use will be indicated later in the appropriate contexts.

1. Physical growth and change make it difficult to expect physical inactivity at a school desk during the active period of rapid growth. Allied to the increasing desire for independence this often leads to unauthorized absences from school or work and to the magnification of minor illnesses. It leads also to the recognition by some teachers and youth workers that such restlessness can be channelled into projects which require activity and aid independence.

2. Self consciousness, gauche behaviour and physical clumsiness interlink as the mental and emotional progress towards adulthood is impeded by the need to come to terms with physical change. Continual adjustment of the brakes for emotional and physical control causes frustration and occasionally collision resulting in distress or conflict and creating problems, for both adults and peers, of continuity, control and communication.

3. Growing interest in physical appearance may cause depression, unhappiness, aggression, compensatory habits, conceit, excessive expenditure of time and money on grooming and clothes for both male and female, or, particularly in older

teenagers, a studied disinterest resulting in an excessively scruffy or bizarre appearance. When linked with item 4 it appears to be especially important in some subcultures not to depart from the 'uniform' of that group, although in these cases the uniform bestows an identity upon the wearer which enables him to be acceptable to the group. In both sexes, conforming to contemporary fashion, be it suggested by the rag trade or devised by the group, assumes immense importance to the teenager.

Acne and excess weight have less importance in the sense of being acceptable but great importance to the personal and emotional state of the afflicted teenager and may affect his social behaviour.

4. Anxiety for peer approval in most young people swamps the concern for adult approval and seems to be, in some countries, capable of destroying adult authority in the home, at school and at work. Not to be different from the groups with which the teenager mixes means a great deal and springs from the self consciousness already mentioned and from the desire for an identity, even a group identity, until the individual's own personality is identifiable. The desire not to be different in terms of activity leads many young people to experiment with potentially dangerous, unhealthy, undesirable activities because to 'chicken' would mean at worst expulsion from the group, at best ridicule. Desire for approval manifests itself also in the phrase 'everyone else'. Everyone else is allowed to stay out until midnight, everyone else will be wearing a particular fashion, everyone else is going to Europe in the summer, and even everyone else has a car.

Peer approval in terms of solidarity against authority is a growing danger with similar root causes.

5. Conflict with authority in most teenagers' homes is covert if not overt over matters which spring from the desire to be independent; perhaps rules meant to be protective in the light of adult experience are considered to be arbitrarily restrictive by the teenager; perhaps a conflict of personal interests and leisure time pursuits arises, not necessarily resulting from the generation gap.

In the school world conflict arises from what the adolescent sees as increasing disparity between what is taught in school and what he sees in life, and from the earlier physical maturity of young people which causes lengthier restrictions as schooling is extended.

In the working world the often well-paid teenager finds himself with a man's wage without a man's responsibilities or a man's experience of dealing with life, and flouts authority for kicks as relief from the tedium of his chosen adult world. The same relief may well be sought in the same way by the youngster from the socially desirable suburb, who sees it as a boring, conventional, cosy cage which must be broken, or broken out of.

6. Talking and arguing rather than listening is not the prerogative only of the articulate teenager. It is likely that these manifestations occur with regularity in the home during the conflict mentioned above, despite the age-old teenage cry of 'you never listen', when parents have cut short a plea for something with a peremptory no or a 'sermon'. But talking and arguing are also common amongst friends and acquaintances in youth clubs, hanging about on street corners, in school and in the working life of the teenager. Whatever the 'argot' of the group, communication verbally is a common pastime; it is only when it must be organized, disciplined, directed, that all but the articulate few tend to become silent and embarrassed.

The methods of learning in many schools require a student to listen, although increasingly talking to a purpose under supervision is becoming a legitimate part of the educational process. Talking and arguing are both processes which enable the teenager to assert himself, to get across his perhaps shaky views on the increasing number of matters coming into his experience and conceptual range, but matters on which he will rarely really listen to others' views, as he is very susceptible to drawing conclusions without justification and to making decisions on a sudden impulse without sufficient weighing of evidence. At this age talking is also a way for the individual to find out what he does think and may be a necessary preliminary to the next item.

7. Increasing self knowledge in the later teenage years comes as a result of the greater conceptual ability and an ability to reason. Both are needed to enable the young adult to assess his capabilities and attitudes, and his personality. The average teenager may pass into adulthood before fully developing this insight, but there are some teenagers who feel they must find

themselves by opting out of their immediate surroundings and life style in an attempt to devote all their time and energy to the quest of self knowledge. Others may never achieve any measure of insight because they take life as it comes, day by day, with never a thought for their place in that life.

8. Increased awareness of school, community and world problems and of governmental, social, community and personal moral concern shows itself in involvement in social work, in concern for the deprived throughout the world, in political campaigning and in banner carrying, literally and meta-phorically, for ideals or causes of one kind or another.

It is also shown in the attitudes of many post-school teenagers and deprived young people who hold the view that the world, society, 'they' owe them a living, that they came into the world in credit and can take their rights without individual contribu-tion. The divide between those who hold these attitudes and the rest of mankind is a major feature of contemporary adolescence and a cause for concern. British and American attempts to channel idealism and awareness via a study of democracy, citizenship and social studies, builds upon the general interest but is often too passionately pressed, too unacceptably propagandist or insufficiently practical to gain the wholehearted concern of the student. The early school leaver working teenager is likely to assimilate the concern, or more probably apathy, of his workmates or to succumb to the expertly presented campaigns against specific examples of iniquity, highlighted in the press.

Idealism is there in every teenager in varying degrees of intensity and direction, but is often not revealed for fear of ridicule, scorn or betrayal.

9. Interest in the opposite sex, though placed at the end of this section is by no means the last manifestation of adolescence in chronological terms. A wide variation in the age at which such interest emerges occurs in all classes of society although advertising and commercial pressures present the idea as the norm for an increasingly early age.

The gregarious nature of the adolescent in the early years tends to relate only to the same sex but gangs gradually relax to allow friendship with the opposite sex until pairing becomes the norm. The exception in contemporary Britain, America and

Australia is the growth of gangs identified by name and 'uniform' and sometimes by territory, where girls are full members with the boys and play specific roles, but in the mainstream of adolescent development one-sex grouping is normal in the early years with progression to mixed grouping and, concurrently, occasional dating before going on to a steady relationship.

This progression may well involve all the points mentioned so far and present problems in schooling and changes in leisure-time activities. It is generally recognized that up to normal school leaving age the social environment of the child is a greater force for influence on habits and attitudes than school. Thereafter differences between the working-class teenage student and the middle class are lessened as the disciplinary and conceptual development effects of further and higher education allow the student to see the limitations and benefits of his social origins and to amend his actions and attitudes accordingly. Until about ten years ago the word 'accordingly' would have been interpreted as according to the norm of middle-class attitudes and actions as propounded by the dominant culture and by authority, not least by schools. This produced least friction and lessened the confrontations between culture and sub-culture. Today, however, 'accordingly' may well mean the adoption of a life style other than the conventional middle-class way of life and, not infrequently, produces the drop out and the revolutionary.

However, social environment begins to mould the child from birth, physically and mentally, so that any study of the effect of social environment on teenage attitude to reading, to school, to the use of leisure or any other topic, must take into account the fact that the teenager has been conditioned by his social upbringing, by class, parental attitudes and life styles, peer group activities and by the vital fourteen or so years of physical care, verbal and visual stimuli, opportunities for the development of mind, body and spirit (most of them dependent upon his social class and geographical location). He is a product of his community and is likely to remain at the level common to that community when he reaches the transition age, unless he goes on to further education.

It is therefore necessary to pay attention to the developing years which lead up to the transition years and to note those areas of social upbringing which affect the child's abilities and attitudes, in that social class is an important variable in most aspects of profiting from school, from opportunities and life. Much of the profiting is determined by the geographical location of the individual in that all urban areas have their 'good' and 'bad' districts in terms of housing, social amenities, cultural resources and educational facilities and the deprived in the first category tend to be deprived also in each of the others. Official recognition of this was shown in the creation of educational priority areas in British and American local authorities where extra help was to be directed towards the relief of substandard conditions on the premise that the social environment of the child militated against the achievement of even minimum profiting from education.

The report of a survey of the home background, health, physical and mental development of 17,000 children at birth and again at seven years of age,[3] revealed that housing conditions were a major factor in the rate of both mental and physical growth. Approximately 15% of children in England were living in overcrowded conditions, and a greater percentage in Scotland. Two-thirds of children surveyed had moved homes once or more, 13% three or more times. 17% had changed school once which indicates that moving house within the same locality was the pattern rather than moving out of the original area. This is a common occurrence in the US where geographical mobility is taking its toll in children's education.

Overcrowding precluded adequate privacy, attention, and cleanliness, caused by parental irritation, depression or aggression. Overcrowding may be the result of a large family which, unplanned, may itself be the result of social or mental inadequacy on the part of parents. Any of these factors affect the child but the combination of them which is often the case, has severe effects upon the physical growth of the child, who is more likely to be smaller in height and weight, less healthy or more prone to ill health than his middle-class counterpart. In mental growth the deprived child has a greater chance of mental subnormality and of educational subnormality and is likely to be retarded in reading and other educational pursuits because of lack of cultural and intellectual stimuli and the absence or insufficiency of conversation, discussion and parental help.

These cumulative handicaps also dominate school life and persist into teenage life in that the spurs of parental ambition and the values of peers are lacking or blunted; the leisure time activities are normally not educative in the sense of aiding formal education; the average school organization works against the less privileged in matters of school clubs, monitors or prefects and in streaming based on reading tasks. And yet such children may have seen more of 'life' before they are ten than many more privileged children will see in a lifetime. This in itself leads to the widely held teenage view that much of school life involves a direct confrontation with the attitudes and values which typify the neighbourhood.

An American estimate of the number of children generally deprived suggested that one-fifth to one-third of American children were in this category[4] and a British estimate produced a similar proportion for Britain.[5]

The general mass of the population, according to official British and American figures for the structure of the population, falls into the social class three, that is the non-manual clerical and shop workers, foremen and skilled manual workers, and class two, composed of teachers, civil servants, managers and similar occupations. These are traditional middle-class strata of society and in their geographical locations in suburban areas they may well receive the benefits of better amenities, resources and school to add to their better housing conditions.

The middle-class child is likely to have the advantages of going to many places, seeing new faces, doing more and differing things, being talked to and read to, hearing more, speaking more and responding more to aspects of life which conform to the accepted norm and which will fit him for the similar stimuli and expectations of his school life. His living conditions are more attractive, less crowded, more hygienic with greater privacy if desired and he has greater attention, both physical and mental, from his parents. His understanding of educational requirements will be greater, as will his ability to respond to them, because a wide background produces recognition which aids understanding.

However the rural area may produce children with characteristics common to both working and middle class. Many rural children are deprived socially and culturally in the sense of distance from areas of such activity though there may be local opportunities of a less sophisticated nature designed to offset this deprivation, such as youth clubs, further education classes, mail order book clubs, etc. They may be deprived educationally if the village school is unable to provide the range of methods, equipment, subjects and stimuli that the large town offers for the urban child. Physical and mental adequacy are likely to be in line with middle-class development.

Geographical influence can also be seen in Britain in the north versus south distinctions where the quality of teachers, the examination success of pupils and the numbers of students continuing into further and higher education and the amount of money spent on education decrease in a northerly direction, where the historical origins of the industrial north have shaped the way of life of the northerner along with his housing and occupation. Regional variations in Britain and America are the norm rather than the exception and inequalities in both countries are further complicated by racial distinctions.

The effect of home background on children's education was surveyed by the National Foundation for Educational Research in England and Wales[6] and showed clearly that where learning to read and reading ability are concerned the following aspects of the home were most frequently mentioned by teachers as being significant:

1. Reading material.
2. Parental interest in reading.
3. Home's encouragement in co-operation with the school.
4. Parental conversation.
5. Practice of reading to children.
6. Richness of home experience.
7. Emotional security of the home.
8. Early pre-reading experiences such as parents discussing pictures/stories.
9. Discipline and routine of the home.

The pupils' abilities or attributes in progress in reading were mentioned in order of frequency:

1. Attitude to learning to read.
2. Rate of learning.
3. Reading readiness.
4. Attitudes to school and learning generally.

5. Emotional stability.
6. General knowledge.
7. Grasp of the relationship between the spoken and written word.

Another survey found that teachers emphasized the importance of parents talking to their children and of parents displaying an encouraging attitude and concern for progress and non-material things.[7]

The factor which has greatest influence on the individual's progress at all stages and in all places, that of language, has its roots in the social background.

> Language not only serves a social function as a means of interpersonal communication but is also of crucial importance as a tool of thought. It is in this latter function that lower class language deficiences are most crippling psychologically.[8]

The inarticulate teenager or adult is no new phenomenon but the situations in which he is expected to speak have increased. The basic inability of many to find and use words lies partly in the lack of conceptual ability which precludes having many thoughts to expound and partly in an unfamiliarity with formal language. Basil Bernstein's theories on social structure, language and learning are still wholly applicable in both British and American socio-linguistic studies, and because they propound the 'cumulative deficit phenomenon' of disadvantaged youth, must be considered as a basic part of any investigation into reading and adolescents. Bernstein suggests that children from the lower strata of society will experience difficulty in

> learning to read,
> extending their vocabulary,
> learning to use a wide range of found possibilities for the organization of verbal meaning,
> their reading and writing will be slow and will tend to be associated with concrete activity-dominated content: grammar and syntax will pass them by; the prepositions they use will suffer from a large measure of dislocation; their verbal planning function will be restricted; their thinking will tend to be rigid; the number of new relationships open to them will be very limited.[9]

Such deficiencies, cumulated and compounded by other socially and culturally disabling factors, result in the maladjusted, the delinquent, the educationally retarded youngster and the illiterate early school leaver; the teenager and later the adult who, at each stage, understands more language than he can use but for whom many common words have little meaning because they are outside his range of experience and for whom what meaning there is was achieved up to two years later than for the advantaged individual.

He uses fewer words in less complicated sentence structure than his middle-class counterpart and is less able to see symbolic and conceptual aspects in the environment or in verbal means of abstraction and analysis. In effect he is limited to what Bernstein describes as 'public' language in which he can rely upon common understanding, voice inflection and facial expression, and where even these fail, a liberal sprinkling of 'you know'. The formal language which is available to the advantaged in addition to 'public' language enables him to be subtle and precise and is useful for exposition and description of abstracts and symbolism, by means of grammar and syntax, use of prepositions and adverbs and by the relationship of sentences.

Such language ability or deficiency therefore has its roots in the social, cultural and educational background of the individual and, equally importantly, has its effect upon the social and emotional behaviour of the adolescent. The ability to transform inner thought into explicit form is not only the product of education but is itself educative of the intellect and emotions. 'Personal and social adequacy depend upon being articulate, that is, on having words and language structures with which to think, to communicate what is thought, to understand what is heard or read.' The ability to articulate problems can relieve the tensions and lessen the likelihood of mental breakdown or physical expression of frustration; talking over differences or contemporary matters of concern enables young people to see better the difficulties or puts the matter in perspective, facility in spoken language also promoting facility in writing and understanding.

Language ability is displayed by many middle-class young people and encouraged by means of debating societies in school, college and youth clubs, in committee work and in verbal and written report work, but it reinforces the social differences and emphasizes the fact that much social and official intercourse is effected by verbal communication. The use of language by the majority of the population is confined mainly to conversation and simple communication. Instruction, exposition, analysis are not normally required in the working day by the mass of people and any leisure time verbalizing tends to be conversational and, with many teenagers, conducted in an argot of local, specialized and ritualistic nature.

Language needed for the expression of culture is one of the components of a subculture, culture in the sociological sense of society's actions, thoughts, behaviour, beliefs and attitudes. The inequalities of attitudes, thoughts and actions within society's culture can also be seen in the middle-class emphasis on those aspects which are also stressed in the world of education and which produce a potential academic or a potential deliquescent; for example ambition as a value, individual responsibility, cultivation of skills, postponing immediate satisfaction for long-term achievement, planning, cultivation of manners, control of physical aggression, respect for property and wholesome recreation.

Social environment is the major factor in the young person's attitude to each one of those aspects and the difference between the plus and minus lies largely in the fact that self esteem tends to be a collective product in the disadvantaged youth's subculture and an individual effort in the advantaged's.

G. H. Bantock suggests that generally schools nowhere seriously touch the cultural experiences that are likely to be the lot of most of the school population in later life and that what is done creatively in schools has no real roots in the life of the community.[10] Similarly a paper on popular culture suggested that the negative attitudes permeating beat music and pop art were an indication of this generation's abdication from the responsibility of thinking, of being committed to any idea, to any point of view or to any course of action.[11]

The three main social factors of working-class communities, extended kinship, the ecology of the neighbourhood and the local economy are not the foundations of middle-class societies but have great significance in the continuation and stability of the cultural aspects of working-class areas. The close packed nature of the lower-class neighbourhood supports the communal aspects of life where the street is the communal space and the population is closely linked with local trade and industry.

Redevelopment and rehousing has tended to break all three factors in that new towns and rehousing brought material improvement but destroyed the social cohesion and led to attempts by youth to provide it in the form of territorial gangs. High density, high rise vertical streets of development often omitted the recreational and social facilities which would have compensated for the lack of the old street space. Much of the recent activity in community development has been directed towards the provision of opportunities for leadership within the community and of projects for self development, though sociologists are divided on the matter of facilities for keeping young people off the streets and one researcher suggests that 'cafés and resource centres fulfil the social function better than canoe building, Duke of Edinburgh awards and occupational therapy.'[12]

Daniel Fader, in his attempts to get American downtown boys reading and off the street, recognized the necessity for a positive approach to the problem, taking as the starting point where the teenagers were rather than where they ought to be. By providing a reading-room stocked with attractive, easily readable paperbacks of the kind that the boys often read of their own accord, situated in the area where they lived, he proved that the boys would and did read when the restrictions of normal libraries and schools were absent and when their level of content, readability and format was relevant. He also saw a link between the use made of this reading-room and a drop of 61% in the juvenile crime rate for the area.

The popular pastimes of adolescents in contemporary society are part of the increasingly different though not necessarily inferior life style which creates an adolescent social climate, having its own norms and values, perhaps differing radically from those of adult society.

There are differences in adolescent society which are attributable perhaps to the unprecedented high level of earnings of many teenage workers, the consequent attempts at financial levelling up by the other teenagers by means of part-time jobs or increased parental aid, leading to greater possibilities of independence in material matters to back up the emotional desire for independence. Such changes have also interlinked with the opportunities for spending leisure time activity. Teenage interests come into their own or change at the point where adult influences are weakening, when teachers and parents can no longer direct or enforce the way in which leisure time should be used. Membership of youth organizations may decline, increased spending power may allow the teenager to indulge in hitherto financially prohibitive pastimes such as disco dancing or motor bike ownership. For other youngsters increased independence in leisure may take the form of pursuit of specialized knowledge or expertise in a subject field of hobby. Social differences can be seen in the ways in which teenagers spend their spare time, defined here as the time left over after the working day or the school/college day.

TABLE I   *A Schools Council Enquiry surveyed the spare-time activities of fifteen-year-old school leavers in the years leading up to the leaving year.*[13]

13–16 years BOYS	%	*13–16 years* GIRLS	%
1. TV and radio	50	1. TV and radio	54
2. Sport	43	2. Dancing	37
3. Camping, walking, fishing, etc.	31	3. Cinema	25
4. Indoor games/sport	21	4. Sewing/cookery	24
5. Being with group	19	5. Reading	24
6. Cinema	16	6. Being with group	23
7. Making things	11	7. Playing records, listening to groups	19
8. Working on bikes, etc.	11	8. Outdoor games, etc.	15
9. Reading	11	9. Indoor games, etc.	15
10. Dancing	9	10. Camping, walking, etc.	11
11. Care of animals	8	11. Shopping for clothes	6
12. Records/groups, etc.	7	12. Youth clubs	6
13. Youth clubs	7	13. Art/photography, etc.	5
14. Art/photography, etc.	4	14. Care of animals	2
15. Performing music, etc.	4	15. Performing music, etc.	1
16. Collecting/hobbies	3	16. Collecting/hobbies	1
17. Other miscellaneous	9	17. Other miscellaneous	12

The appeal of an apparently aimless, fruitless, disapproved-of-by-adults and authority-type way of spending time can be seen in the popularity grade accorded to 'being with friends', 'hanging about on street corners', in most surveys of teenagers' habits. While this habit leads to anti-social behaviour in some districts and is indulged in by some because 'there is nothing to do' in other areas and amongst other types of adolescent, hanging about means social intercourse, an opportunity simply to chat about things that interest the group. Hanging about in youth clubs is similarly an expression of the gregarious nature of the young adolescent, particularly in those youth clubs that are not formally run on a strictly disciplined full activity programme. One fourteen-year-old middle-class boy when asked what he did at youth club answered, 'I sit about waiting for youth club to finish.' Further questioned, he revealed that he looked forward to youth club and enjoyed it and that 'sitting about' was simply a constricted term for chatting to all his friends about football, girls, motor bikes, girls, adults and school, girls and girls. His schooldays and his home life were full and interesting but did not provide the opportunities for sitting about and chatting on matters of interest to him. 'Waiting for it to finish' was also telegraphese for the anticipation of the walk home with the boys or girls or both, when similar exploratory chatting and horseplay could be enjoyed.

However membership of youth clubs and similar organizations is very much the province of the advantaged youth, attracting the 'clubbable', the more socially responsible and amenable members of the population, the disadvantaged and working youth tending to congregate on street corners, in public bars and cafés, in pool rooms and any other place which allows freedom from adult supervision, constraint or interference, but enables common and communal interests to be expressed. There is no doubt, however, that large numbers of adolescents, despite greater freedom and increased spending money, cannot find satisfying ways of using leisure time. Mental inability, social inadequacy and official neglect to provide local amenities, contribute to this situation, resulting in boredom and frustration which can be most easily dispelled by anti-social activity.

There are interesting differences between the working teenager and the teenager in full-time education in the table of chief leisure activities compiled by the Central Statistical Office;[14] which relates to urban population of England and Wales, excluding Inner London.

TABLE 2 *Chief leisure activities*

	Males		Females	
Percentage of leisure periods when activity cited as chief pursuit	*Full-time education*	*15–18 single*	*Full-time education*	*15–18 single*
TV	13	18	13	22
Reading	10	2	10	4
Crafts/hobbies	3	8	11	5
Decorating/house or vehicle maintenance	1	3	—	—
Gardening	—	—	—	—
Social activities*	4	3	6	6
Drinking	2	2	1	1
Cinema/theatre	4	6	4	9
Non-physical games and miscellaneous club activities	9	10	5	7
Physical recreation as a participant	33	27	24	24
Physical recreation as a spectator	3	2	—	1
Excursions	3	9	3	6
Park visits/walks	3	2	3	6
Anything else	8	8	10	8
No answer/don't know	4	—	8	1
Total no. of respondents on sample (100%)	91	157	79	147

* Visiting or entertaining or being with friends, relatives, at parties.
Social Trends, no. 2, 1971, Central Statistical Office, HMSO, 1971, p. 65, Table 22.

After the top billing of TV and radio, social and sex differences appear in the rating of interests, most noticeably in sport and reading where the early school leaving boys put these at opposite ends of the scale and those continuing their education put them both high in the ratings. The girls, however, whether early school leaver or in continuing education rate reading highly. Sex differences in preference for the content of what is read will be dealt with more fully later.

The appearance of reading high on the lists must be treated with caution unless a definition of reading accompanies the analysis, as some surveyors mean reading only books, others widen the scope to include newspapers, periodicals, comics, etc.

The habit of reading is nurtured by the availability of books and the middle-class child is more likely to have had books in the home or been taken to the library. This is quantified in the following table showing the number of books owned by parents. In the case of 85% of fifteen-year-old school leavers neither parent had continued in full-time education beyond the statutory minimum leaving age, and in each case were in the lower levels of social stratification.

The habit of reading is rarely formed or nurtured by the school library, the habit-forming seeds having been sown, or not, in early childhood. In either case the middle class profits more, not least from the accustomed usage of books and libraries which comes strangely to the disadvantaged child meeting them for the first time when he starts school. The strange format, the obvious link with school and education, the forbidding atmosphere of many school and public libraries, the repressive attitudes of authority where book use is concerned, these are also habit forming and when, in the teenage years, the custom or necessity is no longer enforced and when other interests take over, the habit of library use declines, though the act of reading may persist in non-library type reading matter.

This explains the low figures for public library use by teenagers compared with the high rating given to reading as a leisure time pursuit.

Bryan Luckham in *The Library in Society*[15] percentaged the ages at which library membership lapsed and in the range fourteen to twenty-four the percentages were as follows:

Aged 14	18%
15	9%
16	6%
17	6%
18	3%
19	2%
20–24	20%

The two periods of great change in youth, that of the onset of puberty and adolescence and that of starting on a career or marrying and setting up home, show also in the change in reading habit. However the frequency of use was also charted and gives a clearer indication than library membership. In the

TABLE 3 *Numbers of books owned by parents*

No. of books owned by parents	Leaving age of child 15			Leaving age of child 16			Leaving age of child 17/18		
	Unskilled and semi-skilled manual	Skilled manual	Non-manual	Unskilled and semi-skilled manual	Skilled manual	Non-manual	Unskilled and semi-skilled manual	Skilled manual	Non-manual
	%	%	%	%	%	%	%	%	%
None	28	20	15	15	12	7	13	9	3
From 1–5	15	12	8	9	10	5	12	8	3
More than 5	57	57	78	76	78	88	75	83	94
Total % 100	100	100	100	100	100	100	100	100	100
Base all parents	(704)	(945)	(289)	(337)	(643)	(433)	(186)	(373)	(549)

Roma Morton Williams and Stewart Finch. *Schools Council Enquiry: Young School Leavers.* London, HMSO, 1968, p. 192.

fifteen to nineteen age range 95% of members had used the library since registering, 69% visited at least once a year, 51% at least every three months, 41% monthly and 24% weekly.

Social attitudes were charted in an American survey of middle-class attitudes and public library use[16] in which the conclusions were drawn that public library users were young people rather than old, more highly educated, from higher income families, probably professional and clerical workers, that more females than males use the library and that more users live close to the library. The deduction was that it was necessary to improve the public's attitudes to the public library by means of publicity and public relations work to encourage library use and to step up the information service to attract male users. Awareness of the public's reactions to details of organization and administration would improve the image and the service, and a knowledge of travelling facilities and distances for children and young people without their own personal transport would correct some disadvantages of the library service.

It is clear that many teenagers' attitudes to libraries spring from the library administrator's lack of awareness of his library's image or his inability to improve the image and from the refusal to recognize and cater for the social backgrounds of the local population and from the desire to maintain a high level of stock. High culture is excessively cerebral (modern music and stream of consciousness literature), excessively emotional (action painting) and excessively new (happenings, etc.) suggested Susanne Langer in a plea for the education of the emotions.[17] Perhaps this is borne out by the figures of library use[18] by the less academic socially lower early school leaver, of whom approximately one-fifth were recorded as being registered members of a public library but less than half of those being actual regular library users (taking at least one visit per month as regular). It is not difficult to see that a very small proportion of young people use the public library and that proportion is not socially representative of the population.

But attitudes are *learned* and the sources of such learning are considered to be direct experience with objects and situations, explicit and implicit learning from others, and personality development. Teenagers' attitudes towards reading and libraries

2

can be seen to have developed from the social, psychological and educational environments of the individual. The more privileged adolescent will have had direct experience with books, libraries and reading and is likely to produce a positive if not a zealous attitude; absence of direct experience produces a negative attitude in this field.

Explicit and implicit learning from others is indicated in the faithful reproduction of parents' expressed views, in the sensed fears and failures of close adults, in opinions voiced on school, education and authority, in the ways in which parents spend their leisure time, the types of reading material if any, left lying around or visibly used in the house, in the spoken views on reading and libraries and in the introduction to both by parents or relatives. In the questionnaire 'What is a good home'[19] (Appendix A) the credit results are the elements common to many middle-class and some working-class communities whereas even a small number of debit answers puts the individual in the category of deprived.

Personality development as a source of attitude is closely bound up with the two previous factors in that social and cultural deprivation may inhibit personality growth by the absence of adequate stimuli whereas the middle-class teenager will have been given opportunities for self expression and for personal growth which aid in building personality.

With such deep-rooted origins attitudes, reinforced by peer approval, are difficult to change, requiring specific efforts outlined by one researcher as follows:[20]

1. It is possible to change attitudes.
2. In order to produce change a suggestion for change must be received and accepted.
3. Reception and acceptance are more likely to occur where the suggestion meets existing personality needs and drives.
4. The suggestion is more likely to be accepted if (a) it is in harmony with valued group norms and loyalties, (b) the source of the message is perceived as trustworthy or expert, (c) the message follows certain rules of rhetoric regarding order of presentation, organization of content, nature of appeal, etc.
5. A suggestion carried by mass media plus face to face reinforcement is more likely to be accepted than a suggestion

carried by either one of these alone, other things being
equal.

6. Change in attitude is more likely to occur if the suggestion
   is accompanied by change in other factors underlying
   belief and attitude.

Such formation and change are not necessarily consecutive
occurrences and the items most applicable to those who are
trying to connect teenagers with reading and libraries are the
third and fourth where change can be affected because the
teenager is in a period of emotional and intellectual insecurity
and vulnerability and may be helped by some of the effects of
reading, perhaps in identification which is largely unconscious
but gives an understanding of people similar to the reader;
perhaps in catharsis which Aristotle saw as a release of emotion
resulting in clarifying or purifying the individual and which
Nietzsche noted as the evoking of response particularly in
tragedies; perhaps in insight, where the content of the story
encourages the externalization of the inner process. One
promoter of reading as bibliotherapy describes this as 'an
exceptional boon to achieve such new possession of one's own
self without any painful effort'.[21]

The group norms and loyalties can be seen in the acceptable
if not enjoyable class reading of a common book and group
visits to libraries undertaken in the security of the crowd but
shunned as a private undertaking when exposure to the book
or the library means

(a) it is a solitary activity at a gregarious age;
(b) the individual has to cope with the content of the book
    without comment or help from any source, relying on his
    own mental and emotional capacity when it may therefore
    become a 'task';
(c) safety in numbers in an official building, as the public
    library is, or a restrictive place, as most school libraries
    are, offsets the go-it-alone feeling in unfamiliar sur-
    roundings which have known or presumed prohibitions,
    knowledge acquired by group usage of the library or from
    the commonly held image of the library.

Attempts to change attitudes are potentially successes or failures
depending on the trustworthiness or expertise of the changer.

In the matter of reading and library use much of the cause, rather than blame, for failure lies in how high the teacher or librarian stands in the estimation of the teenager, in both status and personality.

One of the disadvantages of British and many American school and college libraries is the fact that the English or other subject teacher is also the librarian. The school student's attitude to reading and the school library may be influenced by his attitudes to that teacher and his subject, by the apparent association between the class discipline and the kinds of restrictions that teacher is likely to impose in the library also; by the visible, audible, tangible link with EDUCATION. Such a relationship may cause the student to pre-suppose, however unjustifiably, that reading and books as the English teacher teaches them are the same as the librarian sees and uses them, and that the library is an extension of the English department. However useful this might appear for the English department it is likely to undermine positive attitudes to reading in general and the use of books as tools of information in particular.

The trustworthiness and expertise of the qualified librarian in the public library is too often a matter of geographical location and local library committee policy on staffing. Availability of expertise involves the appointment of librarians who are knowledgeable by training and experience with all age groups in the population and who have specialist knowledge and experience of the needs of teenagers. Trustworthiness is unfortunately marred by the public's image of the librarian, by many librarians' inability to provide the right book in the right surroundings and by the hostile reactions of many librarians to the presence of teenagers in the library unless they conform to the quiet, studious, solitary behaviour traditionally expected of library users. The section on staffing probes this situation more fully.

The appeal of the suggestion for change and the style of presentation are certainly important in an age when there are alternative stimuli for imagination, intellect and education, and where presentation is a cut-throat competitive business. English language and literature teachers are increasingly aware of the need to change attitudes to reading and are attempting to alter methods and contents of their courses. Librarians too are paying greater attention to the means by which they promote library use and are checking the effectiveness of their services in changing attitudes as well as filling needs.

Hoggart in his *Uses of Literacy* says 'we have to see beyond the habits to what the habits stand for', and in the social environment, the emotional and cultural states of the adolescent are virtually pre-determined; the habitual attitudes and beliefs and the leisure time pursuits standing for the social advantages or disadvantages in the kinship, family life, housing, education, local amenities, language ability and mental stimuli which underlie those habits.

The factors which affect teenage reading ability and attitude towards reading and library use are the social, physical and mental foundations laid down in early years, which in the lower classes are shored up by education and social welfare but which, when the props of compulsory education and discipline are removed reveal the insecurity of the foundations. In middle-class teenagers the foundations tend to be well laid, strengthened by education and able to stand the strain when self discipline and independence are achieved.

The rich life of the mind is created by a constant flow of images, impressions and amorphous forms and such material thoughts can be tooled into shape by means of words spoken or written. Without that material, a product of childhood stimuli, there can be little recognition of meaning or response to the meaning of words. Pictorial stimuli to aid recognition have long been the norm for the growing child, and films, television and picture books are a useful medium for this purpose and it is known to be necessary for the reluctant and retarded teenage reader; in each instance the visual stimulus supporting or providing the weak or absent image.

Reading is difficult for many teenagers who have never achieved fluency because of inadequate language ability, poor schooling, lack of parental help and the common belief in working-class communities that reading books is 'doing nothing'. Reading comics and magazines is not considered to be 'reading' in the working-class world, again an indication of the attitude that education is not enjoyable and if something *is* enjoyable it is not education. Books are read in school and reading is therefore education and not enjoyable. Reading may be difficult too in the sense that many teenagers have not the encouragement or even the opportunity to read in the home, and these difficulties, added to the use of evenings for other pursuits, either leisure or study, may account for the frequently noted habit of reading in bed if at no other time. Here, in the fortunate youngster's case, he has no appearances to keep up, to impress or conform to his peers, no distraction of people or television, and the level of reading (in all but the most disciplined reader) is likely to be below his capacity, and therefore as undemanding and enjoyable at the end of the day as it is for adults who also indulge in bedtime reading.

Such habits are likely to have been sown in early childhood when a bedtime story was the norm, and one boarding school headmaster created dormitory libraries, believing that 'Reading in bed . . . is the foundation of a liberal education'. By cramming the dormitory with 'the light and not-so-worthwhile fiction' he was trying to ensure that the boys got it out of their system, enabling them to get on to the 'serious' reading.[22]

The disadvantaged teenager without a grounding in bedtime stories, and probably sharing a room with more than one member of the family is not likely to have either the inclination or the opportunity to read, although there are notable examples of adults who found relief from the overcrowding and poverty in their childhood in the ability to lose themselves in the world of make believe and who became life-long readers and often good writers against all the odds.

The effect of attitudes is usually seen in the consequent action or lack of it and when the manifestations of adolescence are related to libraries and reading, indications of possibilities for change can be seen. For instance physical size and the accompanying self consciousness, coupled with increasing mental maturity creates the viewpoint that the teenager is 'too big' to mix with the kids in the children's library or the school library, big in the sense of size to cope with levels of chairs, tables and shelves, big in the sense of being obviously different and big in the sense of outgrowing the library stock.

The need for peer approval and an interest in reading may conflict when the pursuit of the interest makes the teenager who reads and uses a library the odd one out, and may bring with it the risk of ridicule by a nickname such as 'Bookworm' or other 'derogatory' epithet.

The need for peer approval and the penchant for talking and arguing with friends conflict also with the general image of the library as a hushed, reverent place with rules and regulations and a dragon-like librarian, where the only activity allowed is book choosing. Such an image is unfortunately all too accurate in many libraries. Hanging about and chatting is not encouraged in most libraries and where discussion groups and debates are organized they are mostly interesting, relevant or intelligible only to the educated, formally articulate teenager. 'It's not for us' is an all too common reason given for not using the library and much public library activity continues to reinforce its middle-class image.

Self knowledge is a rare achievement and is often sought by the avid reader in books which increase his awareness of himself and others and which enable him to measure himself against the lives, achievements and problems of others. But self knowledge requires time for thought and either privacy or the ability to shut out the world. Most libraries are short on privacy and many teenagers shun it, but for those who do need a quiet spot in addition to bedtime reading, neither school nor public library caters adequately or separately for this need. Too many libraries require the *whole* library space to be quiet.

Interest in the opposite sex means time taken up with courting or frequenting places where there are opportunities for meeting. The library is not considered a good place for courting despite the secluded alcoves of some library designs, though making assignations to meet at the library may be more frequent where the library is centrally located in a community, as a prelude to moving on elsewhere.

However interest in the opposite sex often focuses attention on books about dating, sex and on the forms of sub-literature which are devoted to those themes. The availability of books and other media which satisfy the curiosity and need for information in those matters is an unfailing attraction in every library which is seriously trying to cater for teenagers. But the popularity of the underground movement of much literature on sexual matters, in school and colleges, and the prominence of its display in commercial channels indicate the existence of yet another restrictive barrier to add to the hostile attitudes formed by school and library. This popularity will be dealt with in the next chapter but is a factor worthy of consideration here. As one teenage girl said, the books on sex and romance that she liked to read she couldn't get in the public or school library and she couldn't afford to buy them. A fifteen-year-old boy said frankly that he liked sexy books but didn't expect the teachers to approve and bought what he could afford each week. A known interest is largely ignored by the school library, is subject to censorship by many public libraries and is hedged about by restrictions in others.

Many of the intellectual and emotional problems of youth are linked with the social environment in which they live, social inequalities producing not only inequalities of knowledge but also of sensitivity, understanding and responsiveness and these must surely have a bearing on the attitudes towards reading and the responsiveness to what is read. Failure in reading is often a failure in reasoning where the conceptual and emotional growth of would-be readers is retarded.

Cultural and emotional deprivation are not confined to the lower classes; there are many middle-class homes where lip service is paid to books and theatres, where even if the children are encouraged to read by parents, they themselves are seen with nothing more than the newspaper and the glossy magazine, and where some parents are so wrapped up in their own problems that they have no time for those of the adolescent children.

Perhaps one way of summing up the differences between the middle and lower classes is to emphasize the collective nature of the disadvantaged, in housing, clubs, gangs, large families and collective self esteem, against the individual nature of the middle class in terms of private housing, perhaps private schooling, individual effort at school and individual leisure pursuits. Collective and individual also in the attitudes towards emotional deprivation as expressed by one writer who suggested that:

> If the rank and file of youth grows up in emotional cowardice and confusion, sociologists look to economic conditions or family relations for the cause . . . but not to the ubiquitous influence of corrupt art which steeps the average mind in shallow sentimentalism that ruins what germs of true feeling might have developed in it.[23]

The abilities and attitudes of the vast majority of teenagers in relationship to reading materials and tastes are directed largely to the shallow and the tawdry, despite the efforts of English teachers and librarians, or perhaps because of them.

READING AND LITERACY

Ray Bradbury's *Fahrenheit 451* has been described as presenting

> colorful, individualistic, prideful, brave, independent book readers and word addicts as saviours of human values in a world where politically controlled television feeds infantile pap to submissive, unthinking, hyper-emotional drug dependent, low energy, marginally literate television viewers, who live only for the present pleasures. The mistake Bradbury makes is to equate print and reading with thinking and acting.[24]

It is common to find in science fiction books and films for both adults and children an assumption that print and reading must persist to 2001 and beyond because they create, strengthen and perpetuate human values and allow exploration of another's mind in eras when the soulless man and mindless machine dominates. Another writer, also with machine connections, looks at reading from the retrospective standpoint.

> It is only when we stop to consider that the vast mass of humanity, throughout human history, has not been able to read, that we realize how unusual an accomplishment it is: and we may, therefore, be led to expect that it is an accomplishment of some complexity which is bound to have an effect on the consciousness of the people which sets so high a store on the ability to do so.[25]

Some writers look at reading as the transmission of human values, ideals and ideas; most English teachers would go along with that and add the widening of vocabulary, the extending of experience and the cultivation of the aesthetic sense. Many British and American teachers and librarians see reading also as a tool by which civic sense and democracy can be shaped or enlarged. Librarians suggest that reading is a means of stimulating the imagination, satisfying intellectual curiosity and providing knowledge. What then has reading to offer the teenager of the present day and what are the effects of the varying kinds of reading?

The importance of the teenager's background can be seen in the fact that reading brings into focus those attitudes, feelings and events which the individual has already experienced. The re-organization of that experience produces the identification which is largely unconscious but which involves empathy and the recognition of similarities. Although this occurs at all ages it is particularly important at the adolescent stage when the teenager is seeking to define his identity.

Following identification the reader is likely to respond emotionally, perhaps anticipating the characters' reactions since the reader is often in possession of more knowledge of the train of events than the character. Response has the cathartic effect of releasing tension or emotion, creating an attitude towards the character or situation while simultaneously experiencing with the character. The ideal end product of identification and response is insight. In a work promoting bibliotherapy such insight is described as depending upon

> ... the nature and strength of the identification, the need of the reader to maintain his defences, the nature of the defences, the evocative power of the piece of literature and the way in which the problem is structured for him. Relevant here are not only the effective and structural properties of the literature itself but the manner in which the reader is invited to attack his reading ... intellectual awareness is not enough to effect cognitive re-organization; there must be more ... an interpenetration of the levels of experience.[26]

Cognitive reading, reflective reading is increasingly propounded as the evidence of a mature reader and the contemporary interest in teaching THINKING as a subject at school is allied to this.[27]

There are benefits from these three factors involved in reading which are useful for all readers but which again are constructive for the teenage reader in his state of uncertainty and immaturity. The increase in freedom, trying new experiences vicariously, acts as an antidote to conformity and to the often restricted life of the teenager, allowing him to see events, characters and problems in broader context and sharper perspective than would be possible in reality, in much the same way that discussion with parents of a problem may not be possible but, distanced and detached, can be helpfully explored with an uninvolved adult.

The potential of human nature is revealed in a greater variety and complexity and the reader's dreams and problems may well be shown to have been achieved, experienced and solved before, thus providing inspiration and satisfaction through the identification, response and increased self knowledge. These and other benefits are generally accepted as the product of reading but the purposes of reading have been debated for years, ranging from the acquisition of personal values and social insight; educational, spiritual and moral upliftment to the development of the ability to contribute to a dialogue with the mind of a writer. More simply, others suggest that the purposes of reading are for fun and for profit, substantiating the divisions suggested by researchers of utilitarian reading, social reading and personal reading. Reading for pleasure and for information are not necessarily mutually exclusive but they may demand different methods of reading such as scanning, skimming, studying, browsing. As the ability to vary the rate and method of reading to suit the purpose and the content is a sign of a mature reader it is important to know whether such methods of reading are taught in school and practised at young adult level. All the evidence points to the situation where English exercises purporting to encourage the skill of skimming and scanning and depth reading are often successful when applied to set exercises but that the skill is not transferred to books which are being used for information finding outside the English class. The situation is better in the United States where 75% of high schools have qualified librarians, some of whom in co-operation with the teaching staff, instruct students in library use, note-taking and reading for information; but in both countries many students in colleges and universities arrive there unskilled in the ability to vary the rate and method of reading to suit the particular purpose of reading.

Many schools which encourage the use of books for projects and autonomous learning give no help to the student from primary to high school in how to read to extract information. In England project work began in the primary school, spread to the secondary school largely for the non-academic and non-examined students and is slowly being introduced as suitable means of continuous assessment in CSE with a strong possibility of inclusion in the programme for the more academic student; but nowhere is it decreed that such a method of study requires pre-training in reading for information, with the result that indiscriminate copying of texts occurs and undigested information is presented. However, project work, though often applied to the non-academic teenage student who is likely to have poor reading ability and an unhelpful social background, has been instrumental in introducing students to varieties of reading matter, and in using those newspapers, magazines and manuals that teenagers do read, thus encouraging the skill of reading and, where the project was student-inspired or selected, giving motivation to read and enjoyment of the reading. Those adolescents who never read having found no pleasure in struggling through a story, may be helped towards a more mature use of books through guidance in project work.

The sociology of literary taste plays an important part in the motivation to read, in that tastes change. What is tasteful in classic terms may not be to the taste of the teenage reader if he is in tune with the current trends in literary taste, the generation gap being not simply an age difference but a difference of culture, heritage and sociological change.

Schücking says that:

[literary] taste is due to something other than a simple excellence inherent in the quality of the work itself; rather is it the product of a complex process in which a variety of forces – some ideological, some highly material – contend with one another and ultimately produce something that is itself far from immune to the action of chance.[28]

The teenager's taste for literature should be looked at as an escape from his linguistic limitations, his intellectual limitations, his educational deficiencies, his social limitations and his emotional uncertainties. Reading is therefore often escapism from those factors rather than escapism in the commonly used sense of retreat from reality. Whatever the level of ability, whatever the content of what is read, reading offers the teenager an escape from his limitations, and acknowledges the wider worlds within and without. Taste in the literary sense is most aptly put into its correct place in the order of priorities in C. Day Lewis's phrase, 'appetite must precede discrimination'.

The English expert on reading, Vera Southgate, suggests that:

> The improvement of recreational reading necessitates the development of a liking for reading as a leisure time activity, the ability to locate reading materials relating to one's interests and tastes and the development of more varied and more mature reading tastes.[29]

Reading in adolescence is an emotional rather than an intellectual activity and the emotions are engaged not only in the content of the book but in the activity of reading itself. This perhaps is where the book can hold its own in the face of competition for the teenagers' attention.

There are means, other than reading, of extending vocabulary and acquiring vicarious experience and it seems that in the present context of abundant opportunity for and experience of communication through non-literary channels that print and reading can make a significant contribution to the individual's ability to reflect upon and understand at a deeper level some of the ideas, information and emotions that reach him from other channels. But as critical reading comes only with maturity the emphasis must be on responsive reading where the adolescent has had some years of reading what appeals to him and sparks off a response in him, regardless of whether it is a 'good' book with worthwhile literary quality or 'acceptable' content, regardless of the level of information presented. Attempts to improve reading habits and interests will have little success until society looks on reading as an enjoyable and useful activity.

G. Robert Carlsen suggests that there are four stages in teenage reading growth.

1. . . . Young people find their satisfaction in the adolescent book: the book written especially for him, to evoke his emotions, problems, dreams and life. . . .
2. He will normally choose the popular adult book.
3. The young person starts to dip into the world of serious contemporary literature.
4. The final step towards growth in reading leads the reader to an interest in the classics: in Shakespeare and Sophocles, in Fielding and Austen, in Thackeray and Hardy. Ordinarily this stage is not reached, save it is forced on people, much before full maturity.[30]

British and American practice and experience suggest that in school such stages are not known to teachers and examiners and that few librarians are allowed to base their selection on such a pattern. Widespread concentration on the last stage is the norm.

Chapter 2
Literature in education

Much of the teenager's antagonism and apathy towards reading could be said to stem from the attitudes and pressures of those connected with the teaching of reading and the use of literature in schools and colleges, as well as from the social, psychological and educational inability to read. At the other end of the scale much of the uncertainty over what to read, which troubles some young people who want to read but do not know what to look for in the library, indicates a failure of communication between the supplier and user in the school.

The causes lie in several areas of book connection, chiefly in those schools where from the best of motives or for examination requirements, irrelevant and unreadable books, conceptually beyond the age group, are to be found in the examination syllabus or on the reading list, where the exhaustive dissection, far from enlightening the mind, creating appreciation for the work or fostering the critical faculty, frequently in all but the bright teenager and the 'natural' reader, produces a profound boredom after the initial interest in the story, poem or play, and creates a deep, if illogical, dislike of books and reading as a pastime.

The effect of the traditional teaching of English literature for most teenagers militates against the creation of long-term readers. Apt students of literature may produce success in examinations for certificates of education but surveys have shown that appreciation of that literature is only examination deep in the vast majority of 'O' level students and is of only academic interest to a large proportion of 'A' level students. The value of English literature as a subject for study is not in question for older teenagers at high school, college or university, where the application of research to literary works can be undertaken when the student's own conceptual ability will allow greater understanding. There is no question that literature is a valid subject for study; no question of teachers devising a literature syllabus that adolescents will accept rather than what they ought to have, but if the aim of education can be considered the development of wider interests, aesthetic appreciation, self sufficiency, perception, enrichment of life and preparation for a working life, or as one headteacher put it '. . . to help the young to be a little less stupid each day',[31] much of the material for study does not lend itself to the achievement of those aims.

Teachers and examination syllabus devisers appear unable to decide what are the aims of teaching, studying and examining literature at any of the age and ability levels in the secondary school. For college and university entrance the subject becomes an entry qualification or a piece of paper denoting examination success in a prescribed specialization within the subject, at a time when the curriculum should have provided a wider context of study. At this level the over-riding aim and objective of both teacher and student is the examination success necessary for continuing education, though with a good teacher there may well be additional benefits. However, it has been estimated that in Britain approximately one-third of all sixth formers (the equivalent of American tenth- and eleventh-grade students) will not gain the basic two 'A' level passes[32] and that the course leading to examination in prescribed texts at 'O' level (eighth and ninth grade) is similarly affected by drop out or failure.

Described by one English teacher as at present 'infamously short-sighted', 'A' level teaching should, he declared, 'include teaching for beyond 'A' level, equipping the pupil with interests and skills, enthusiasms and sensibilities which he will retain for the rest of his life. . . .'[33] He considered that the school, the teacher and the aim had failed if a boy left school without a love of literature and a capacity to find continuing pleasure in reading and theatre-going. Such an aim took into account the intelligence pre-supposed in boys at one of the top British schools and recognized also the variations in experience and emotional maturity which limited depth study of many prescribed literature texts.

Other aims propounded over the years include a study of texts to cultivate a taste for the cultural environment, a literary heritage, understanding a literary work or piece of fiction and evaluation of what is understood, formation of critical judgement, skill in textual analysis of structure and style, understanding the role of man in this world, and a preparation for life. Lower down the school where literature study is less restricted in the matter of texts, other aims appear to be more orientated towards vocational and student centred objectives: developing powers of comprehension, widening experience and general knowledge, encouraging response, relating literature to the student's own experience, thoughts and feelings, and lastly, the ideal over-riding aim, giving pleasure: ideal in the sense of being the perfect motivator for further reading and study but ideal, sadly, in the sense that it is rarely achieved by adolescent pupils.

A list of aims was drawn up by David Holbrook covering his expectations of an English course, both language and literature.[34] It included the ability to practise and enjoy reading, to have 'covered' one way or another at least fifty first-rate works in the secondary school years plus 'low gear' reading of poems and short stories and the memorizing of others: some discrimination on knowing reading tastes and self evaluating reading interests, and ended with the statement that the school leaver 'should feel that the celebration of possible ways of living in song, poetry, drama and other forms of literature is a primary activity of civilized man'.

Yet another objective put forward particularly for the non-examined student is the use of literature as a stimulus for creative work rather than critical study. The 'response' factor is advocated for examined students also on the grounds that such students may be proficient in memory but are deficient in response.

The purpose of literary study, bedevilled as it is in Britain by externally set and/or assessed examinations is nevertheless seen in a more liberal context below 'O' level than in American secondary schools where there is a heavy emphasis on the formal class study of content structure, meaning, form, vocabulary and classical cultural heritage.

This is seen clearly in a comparative study of British and American teaching of English.[35]

Purpose of literature study

UK Response, feeling. Pupil development.
US Comprehension, analysis, textual study.

UK   Literary history: 40% of teachers rejected this outright.
US   Literary history: 61% of teachers in favour.
UK   Greater concern for ideas expressed.
US   Greater concern for formal characteristics of literary works.
UK   39% of class time on literature study.
US   52% of class time on literature study.

The British trend towards response reading of literature has accelerated since this report was compiled and the qualified support for this treatment expressed in the study has spread to a small number of American high schools and colleges.

Logically the purposes of literary study should determine the works to be studied but this is not validated by the choice of works offered to 'O' and 'A' level pupils in Britain, although American pupils' choices are slightly more justifiable in the light of the commonly held aims of American schools.

Despite the many examining boards in Britain there is a common adherence to traditionally accepted works, so that a choice of Shakespeare play, a volume of poetry, a Victorian novel and a twentieth-century work appear as required reading and prescribed texts in each board's syllabus. As an example, the Joint Matriculation Board 'O' level syllabus,[36] 1973 for sixteen-year-old candidates offered:

1. A choice of Shakespeare's *Macbeth*   or
   Miller's *The Crucible*.
2. A choice of *Viewpoint: an anthology of poetry*   or
   Keats, *Five Poems*   or
   Poems of Auden, Graves, Larkin, Lewis, Muir, Read, Roberts, Sassoon, Spender.
3. Jane Austen's *Northanger Abbey*   or
   Hardy's *Mayor of Casterbridge*   or
   Harper Lee's *To Kill a Mocking Bird*   or
   Woodham Smith's *The Reason Why*.

Candidates were advised to 'aim at appreciating the spirit of the books, their structure and style'.

An alternative paper designed to test literary judgement and appreciation offered:

1. Shakespeare's *Richard III*   or
   Bolt's *A Man for all Seasons*.

2. Graves's *English and Scottish Ballads* or *Voices Book III.*
3. One of the following: Brontë's *Wuthering Heights*
                                    Waugh's *Decline and Fall*
                                    Golding's *Lord of the Flies*
                                    Cary's *Mister Johnson.*

At seventeen-plus, 'A' level candidates' understanding, response, critical powers, breadth of reading and ability to write clear essays on literary subjects was tested on two of the following:

1. Shakespeare's *Measure for Measure, King Lear, The Winter's Tale.*
2. Milton's *Samson Agonistes*, Wordsworth's *Prelude Book I,* T. S. Eliot's *The Waste Land.*

and at least four of the following:

3. Chaucer's *Prologue to the Canterbury Tales* and the *Franklin's Prologue.*
   Metaphysical poetry, Donne to Butler.
   Webster's *The White Devil.*
   Wycherley's *The Country Wife* and Congreve's *The Way of the World.*
   Dryden's *Absolem and Achitophel.*
   Fielding's *Tom Jones.*
   Austen's *Emma.*
   Byron's *Don Juan.*
   Gaskell's *Mary Barton.*
   Browning's *Men and Women.*
   Gosse's *Father and Son.*
   Shaw's *Man and Superman.*
   Lawrence's *Sons and Lovers.*
   Poetry of the Thirties.
   Miller's *Death of a Salesman.*
   Thom Gunn and Ted Hughes's *Selected Poems.*

The choice of any of these is usually that of the teacher not the student with consequent possibilities of teachers, reared and educated in a different era, educationally and socially, opting for the known and probably previously taught, regardless of the changes in contemporary adolescent society which influence student choice, even from prescribed lists, were such choice permitted. A vital consequence of teacher choice, necessary though it seems to be if class study is the norm, is the inevitable hostility towards certain texts, hostility based firstly on known differences between male and female preferences in literature and secondly on the less well known variations in physical and emotional development within any class of adolescents.

Attitudes to reading are influenced by social upbringing and attitudes towards the content of what is read are influenced by emotional and sex differences.

These are clearly indicated in a survey undertaken in 1970–71 of 1,000 'O' and 'A' level students in English secondary schools.[37] The findings must be looked at in the context of the more academic school pupils when assessing response to the subject of English literature. The fact that many pupils rate English literature highly above other school subjects is caused largely by the affective property of the subject comparatively and its consequent potential for satisfaction. But such satisfaction appears to hinge critically upon the choice of text as the following table shows:[38]

TABLE 4   *Pupils' expressed likes and dislikes for their GCE texts*

'O' level	Boys	Girls
Animal Farm	17:0	26:11*
Lord of the Flies	15:0	11:3
War poetry anthology	5:0	5:0
Romeo and Juliet	3:0	36:3
The Long, the Short and the Tall	58:3	28:5
The Merchant of Venice	—	22:2
Short Stories of Our Time	19:4	27:0
Nun's Priest's Tale	17:4	—
Kipling (prose anthology)	4:1	3:10*
A Tale of Two Cities	—	8:2
Strife	3:1	18:34*
A Pattern of Islands	8:3	5:0*
Great Expectations	23:10	18:0*
Macbeth	17:10	41:5*
The Pardoner's Tale	8:7	7:21*
Twentieth-century short stories	2:2	3:0*
Keats: selection	4:5	22:6*
Wuthering Heights	9:11	38:2*
Henry IV, Part I	59:62	14:3*
Conrad: four stories	—	6:18

'O' level	Boys	Girls
Rhyme and Reason (poetry anthology)	12:46	5:17
The Warden	7:27	0:1*
Poems of spirit and action	1:4	0:2*
De Coverley Papers	1:5	1:1*
Cider with Rosie	—	0:3
Book of narrative verse	0:4	1:2*
Pageant of modern verse	0:12	4:6

The criterion for listing is set at 3:1 approximately for or against a particular text. Where only one sex reaches this level, or a reversal of preference takes place an asterisk is used. The first figure in each case is for liking, the order of texts being determined by the boys' ratio of likes to dislikes.

'A' level	Boys	Girls
R. Graves: *Poetry Selection*	—	14:0
D. H. Lawrence: *Short Stories*	12:0	—
Tess of the D'Urbervilles	9:0	—
A Passage to India	6:0	16:0
Macbeth	5:0	2:1*
Keats: *Odes*	3:0	5:0
Hardy: *Selection of Poetry*	2:0	6:1
To the Lighthouse	1:0	18:2
Dr Faustus	21:1	3:1
Othello	19:1	40:3
Henry IV, Part I	11:1	1:0
Prologue to the Canterbury Tales	9:1	2:3*
The Old Wives' Tale	11:2	27:2
King Lear	21:4	11:0
T. S. Eliot: *Poetry Selection*	9:2	9:3
A Portrait of the Artist as a Young Man	8:2	8:5*
Joseph Andrews	7:2	—
Antony and Cleopatra	7:4	9:1*
Peacock: Three Novels	2:1	1:5*
Donne: *Poetry Selection*	8:6	11:1*
The Clerk's Tale	1:2	1:15*
Comus	1:5	0:6
Framley Parsonage	1:5	0:6
The Canon Yeoman's Tale	2:12	0:2
Paradise Lost, Book I	1:6	8:9*
Paradise Lost, Books IX, X	1:7	—
Middlemarch	1:7	6:3*

'A' level	Boys	Girls
Bartholomew Fair	1:8	—
Microcosmographie	1:9	—
H. James: *Short Stories*	1:10	—
Emma	0:3	11:1*
Culture and Anarchy	0:4	0:5
The Courtier	0:9	0:5
Bacon: *Selections*	0:11	—

The large differences in absolute numbers of expressed likes/
dislikes is largely explained by the relative popularity of
different examining boards among the schools used.

The situation becomes more tolerable for the student who is
examined for the Certificate of Secondary Education (CSE)
where a greater effort has been made to consider relevance to
the pupil's contemporary needs and interests and to his mental
ability. Although the CSE is an alternative to 'O' level GCE
and is normally taken by the less academic students, an experiment undertaken in 1969 in which grammar school pupils
were entered for both examinations in each subject, produced
the discomforting information that many students who passed
GCE failed CSE.

An analysis of CSE set books[39] found that the CSE Boards
recommended between them:

(a) 50 plays, including Anouilh, Bolt, Brecht, Goldsmith,
Willis Hall, Miller, Moliere, Priestley, Shakespeare, Shaw,
Thomas, Ustinov, Wilde and Williams.
(b) 124 novels including Allingham, Austen, Bradbury,
Conrad, Dickens, Forster, Fitzgerald, O'Henry, Heming-
way, Innes, Joyce, Lawrence, Orwell, Shute, Sillitoe,
Steinbeck, Sutcliff, Tolkien and Wyndham. A measure of
agreement was seen in the works common to a number of
the boards, e.g.

Orwell's *Animal Farm*	10	Boards
Wyndham's *Day of the Triffids*	8	,,
Golding's *Lord of the Flies*	7	,,
Brontë's *Jane Eyre*	7	,,
Twain's *Huckleberry Finn*	7	,,
Dickens's *Great Expectations*	6	,,
Shute's *A Town like Alice*	6	,,

(c) 37 non-fiction works including Laurie Lee's *Cider with Rosie*, Grimble's *Pattern of Islands*, Heyerdahl's *Kon Tiki* and Maxwell's *Ring of Bright Water*. Though many of these titles were condemned by the surveyor in his article, as of second-rate worth, the list goes a long way towards providing works which have some relevance for the teenager, some bearing on his ability to respond and yet provide the meat for critical evaluation at whatever depth is required for examination.

The introduction of CSE Mode 3 giving students and staff an element of choice, and the opportunity for assessed course work has opened up the possibilities for interesting developments in range of choice, method of study and form of assessed work.

One experimental approach to this new freedom was devised in a Welsh school.[40]

We do not believe in the efficacy of a separate literature paper to stimulate the right kind of reading. . . .

Library lists are provided throughout the school course. From these and other books read during the English course, the candidates will be asked to submit a list of recent reading. The list must contain at least 8 books plus a poetry anthology chosen from those made available to them. Not more than 2 of the books may be class readers and the list must contain 3 fictional and at least 3 non-fictional books. Candidates must be prepared to discuss the books in their lists with the teacher and sample discussions could be taped for external moderation. Reading aloud to an audience of short suitable passages of prose and/or verse from books on their own list. Candidates should be given the passages in time to prepare them and will be assessed primarily for their understanding of the text.

This approach is much more likely to make the reading and the study enjoyable and useful in the fulfilment of short-term and long-term aims, and may contribute to a desire to read in post-school years. In such a flexible course and in the non-examined courses the suitability of works is judged by their capacity to evoke response thus providing the enjoyment necessary for promoting further reading, the motivation for studying the initially chosen work and the mental attitude required for creating an assessable end product.

David Shayer in his book *The Teaching of English in Schools 1900–1970*, says:

> The literature must be relevant, that is, it should preferably be contemporary, and should contain scenes, situations and characters which the pupil can recognise as being part of his own world, and if it deals with the kind of 'problems' which adolescents are likely to experience . . . then so much the better. Rather than testing the pupil against the text, the text is tested for its suitability, relevance, entertainment capacity, against the pupil, and will be rejected if it fails to fulfill the functions required of it. A criterion for selection might well be, does the novel or poem help the pupil 'to live'? rather than asking whether the work is an important part of the Great Tradition, deserving study as a landmark in the cultural heritage.[41]

American research into the attitudes of teachers concerning the place of contemporary novels and plays in the senior high school curriculum[42] found that teachers favoured the use of contemporary mass media extensively in teaching contemporary works and were using paperbacks rather than school texts. In spite of censorship which is a continuing problem in American schools, controversial themes and expense, teachers felt that they were teaching works that should be taught.

Paperbacks were also used for CSE choices and non-examination students in a Yorkshire high school, where eighty individual paperback titles were made available for selection, including *Billy Liar, The Long, the Short and the Tall, The Loneliness of the Long Distance Runner, The Pearl, The Old Man and the Sea, High Wind in Jamaica* and *To Kill a Mocking Bird*. Thus some of the people involved in teaching literature have recognized that range of choice is necessary, change in examination method is rewarding and recognition of the acceptability of paperback versus hardback is influential. As the Advisory Officer for the National Association of Teachers of English put it: '. . . how much of whatever sensitivity or discrimination about literature they have supposedly learned in order to pass the examination carries on into their reading, and their living, afterwards?'[43] The answer is assuredly, very little, if the statistics of public library use, book buying and reading tastes have any validity, and he was speaking only on 'A' level students.

It would therefore seem sensible for examining boards to include a range of texts which allows for obvious differences; for teachers to select those texts which have common appeal for a mixed class or to allow independent student choice from a range which caters for the variations in stages of emotional development and preferences determined by sex. An alternative possibility, explored by the 1,000 responses team, discovered that any suggestion of segregation into single sex classes for literature study was firmly dismissed by the students.

It is not easy in the co-educational system to select works with a common denominator for male and female students but it is long recognized that motivation and relevance are key factors in learning and it is unrealistic at the present time and with the present level of attainment of much of a school's teenage population, to expect that the average pupil can demonstrate more than acceptance that the work must be studied.

The method or standpoint adopted for studying or teaching literature varies from school to school ranging from the structural examination-required 'consideration of style, aptness of description, sense of atmosphere, imagery, symbol, unity, imaginative insights . . .'[44] and the American stress on factual content, literary history, technical analysis of structure, plot, character and language; through the formal but flexible class study of a wide range of books on a theme or genre basis to the individual's in-school reading, determined by his interest and ability levels, self selected with guidance from enthusiastic and knowledgeable teachers and school librarians.

A study of the use of class readers[45] established teachers' ratings for class sets of books as:

essential	56%
very important	21·3%
of some importance	19·1%
not very important	3·0%
detrimental to good teaching	0·0%

Of approximately 250 titles of books reported as used for class work approximately thirty-five were written with children and young people in mind, all of which contain the qualities which make them good reading and worthy of study, and it is significant that in a table of pupils' reactions to some of the books used in class, the most favourable reaction was to one of the children's books, *Family From One End Street*, which received a 91·4% rating from secondary modern pupils, against a 56·3% rating for the *Road to Wigan Pier*. On the whole most books chosen for class use were considered too long, too dull, too out of touch with the present, too often more suitable for boys and too discouraging in appearance with dull format, small print and poor illustration.

The investigation concluded that '. . . it could be that the great diversity shown is a sign of health, of a great deal of initiative and experiment. It could also be that none of us knows enough about what kind of books our children ought to be reading at any particular stage, in terms of their own growth and development.'[46]

A questionnaire answered by fourteen- and fifteen-year-old students in thirteen representative grammar and secondary schools revealed the student preferences in this matter.[47] Asked would you rather

(a) read from class reader;
(b) choose from small selection;
(c) choose from library

the results were:

		(a)	(b)	(c)
Grammar School	Male	12·6	23·6	55·1
	Female	10·7	31·1	47·4
Secondary Modern	Male	12·8	34·0	51·0
	Female	12·3	36·0	50·7

The long-established custom of class readers in Britain and America requires the purchase of class texts in sets, selected by the teacher as worthy of study, or the use of texts because they happen to be in the stockroom. Less formal methods include reading aloud in turn round the class, the teacher reading aloud, reading silently, reading the set text partly at home and partly in class, each method followed by class and/or group discussion with the teacher prompting. There are obvious dangers in some of these methods in that the good readers will

get to the end before either the teacher or the poorer reader and
may be bored and frustrated at having to wait for the others,
and the less able reader, who is further humiliated at displaying
his lack of ability in reading aloud, will probably not do the
home reading and may well never reach the end of the book
in silent class reading. In each case the book may have no
appeal or message for the individual. Different novels read by
any of these methods may get over the last problem by the
teacher reading, provided he reads well and has chosen a book
that stands the test of reading aloud and one that can catch the
interest of each type of reader; this may well be the only
redeeming feature of class readers.

Following reading, various forms of discussion have been
tried to enable students to think critically and put into words
their thoughts on the book read. One teacher of eighteen-year-
old engineering apprentices, who were compulsorily studying
on day release from industry at a college of further education
and who had all left school at fifteen, found that he was justified
in reading aloud to the class rather than teaching literature in
the traditional way, on the grounds that his 'unqualified
readers' were totally impervious to reading and literary
criticism, but, stimulated by a good story they could extend
their area of consciousness by discussion.[48]

In another case a group of teachers attempted to test literary
response by tape recording fourteen- and fifteen-year-old pupils
talking about *The Day of the Triffids* and produced some
valuable deductions from the exercise as to what goes on in the
student's mind when evaluating literature. The team detected
four main levels of talking about literature:

1. Putting oneself in the character's position.
2. Treating character and incident as if they were real.
3. Being aware of the novel as an artefact, an expression of an
   author's intentions.
4. Discussing the novel as existing in its own right as a 'virtual
   experience'.
   . . . for adolescent pupils, talk at the more direct and naïve
   levels of response may well be a necessary preliminary to
   talk at the more 'distancing' levels.[49]

This accords with the description of what takes place in reading
mentioned in Chapter 1, the identification, catharsis and

insight. The team concluded that most full class discussion in schools starts off at the wrong level, at 3 or 4, thus excluding the less able student who must have 1 and 2 before he can approach 3, and probably severely hampering even the able teenage student.

It seems, therefore, that the less able adolescent student in many schools is at a disadvantage in the choice of textual content, its format and its treatment in class, thus ensuring that the already large proportion of students who get no personal pleasure from reading will receive neither corporate pleasure nor educational benefit from literature study. Books which are too old and too advanced for even the more able students will continue to discourage the pursuit of reading as a source of pleasure.

A more recently introduced approach to literature study is the theme treatment involving related literature and materials showing thematic relationships, music and art forms, an approach which an American research[50] concluded improved the class/teacher rapport but did nothing to improve either sensitivity or written expression. Some British schools have introduced integrated studies incorporating English and social studies or English and history or, as in one school, English, history, economics and social biology, making extensive use of team teaching, multi-media and the library. The dangers in this were stated by an educationalist who wrote:

> In the teaching of literature, for example, it seems to me that many of our more progressive teachers have escaped from the prison of the classical text into the miasmic marsh of the socially meaningful extract; and they have substituted for arid intensive study only ill defined and inconclusive extensive study.[51]

This is a fear voiced by those who deplore the potential stress on the factual content of fiction, but which is dismissed by others who genuinely seek to relate the values, ideals and experiences offered in manageable proportions through fiction to reality. Indeed this belief in the efficacy of fiction in integrated studies has for many years been demonstrated by history teachers who have used in class or have set home readings from historical novels. The comprehensive work called *Handbook for History Teachers*[52] includes a section on historical fiction and its use in teaching history. Such thematic use in this subject is also building on the known liking for historical novels of many girls.

The thematic approach is library centred or reading based. 'It does need books in quantity, disposed on library rather than stock room lines. The teacher who sets out on this kind of approach without a helpful school librarian, or without a librarian at all, or who fails to make clear the scale of library use entailed by whole classes reading a dozen books a year each, is asking for a breakdown. . . . Those who have tried library-centred methods have found normal allowances sufficient, so long as the local public library is prepared to help schools systematically.'[53]

Student preferences have been measured in many ways involving surveys, questionnaires, observation and direct questioning, and all methods draw very similar conclusions as to the reading preferences of teenagers, so that the example on page 62 can be taken as representative.[54]

Most of these rankings correspond with the preferences already indicated in the table on responses to GCE texts, and the top placing of humour right through all grades in secondary schools should give teachers and librarians food for thought, although an American book[55] compiled by one of each makes the plainly truthful statement 'we can never expect them to think of books as a source of fun if they never encounter a book that is fun to read', a statement made in connection with books in school.

Students' reactions to aspects of literature have also been tested, one example being that of violence.[56] The researcher selected five passages depicting violence from works by Joyce, Dickens, Laurie Lee, Brontë and Fleming and submitted them to thirteen- and fifteen-year-old classes to ascertain reaction at the two age levels. He discovered that the older pupils showed a more interpretational approach but that all had difficulties with both comprehension and identification. Majority placings determined by enjoyment scores put the passages as follows:

1. Dickens 2. Fleming 3. Joyce 4. Lee 5. Brontë

Enjoyment of horror, mystery and violence is also demonstrated in the high ranking given in the comparative British and American table, second only to humour.

TABLE 5   Reading preferences in rank order

	All		Boys		Girls		Form 4 Grade 10		Form 5 Grade 11		Form 6 Grade 12		College bound		Terminal	
	UK	US	UK	US	UK	US	UK	US	UK	US	UK	US	UK	US	UK	US
Detective and mystery	2	1	3	5	2	4	1	2	2·5	4	3	5	2	4	1	3
Adventure	3	2	2	1	5	5	3	3	4	2	4	2	3	2	4	4
Romance	5	3	11	12	1	2	5	5	5	5	11	4	7	5	3	2
Humorous	1	4	1	2	3	1	2	1	2·5	6	1	1	1	1	2	1
Science fiction	4	5	4	3	4	8	4	6	8	8	2	8	4	7	5	6
Sports	8	6	5	4	10	12	8	8	8	8	12	11	10	9	6	7
Poetry	12	7	12	11	9	7	12	12	12	11	9	10	12	12	12	10
Biography	9	8	9	7	8	3	10	4	9	3	7	3	8	3	9	5
History	6	9	8	6	6	6	6	7	6	7	5	6	5	6	8	8
Current problems	11	10	10	9	11	9	11	10	11	9	8	7	11	8	10	11
Science	10	11	7	8	12	11	9	11	10	12	10	12	9	12	11	12
Other	7	12	6	10	7	10	7	9	7	10	6	9	6	10	7	9

n = 4,301 British and 16,089 American students

Reactions to feminine characters in literature have also been tested.

A survey to ascertain the actual effect of reading programmes on students[57] attempted to determine the effect of feminine characters in the literature used in high school English classes, on the students who read and discussed the works. The influence of set books on changing thought or behaviour was shown to be less than the influence of books chosen and read independently of school. 29% of boys and 35% of girls felt that at least one book set for school English had produced a reaction and *To Kill a Mocking Bird* was mentioned most.

The survey of the students' own choices showed that 46% of the girls and 34% of the boys felt that their choice had changed their thinking, *Gone with the Wind* and *The Bible* being the most frequently mentioned.

A varied assortment of women characters were accumulated from the English programme texts, most of them either passive and insipid or vicious, very few of them were considered by students to be worthy of emulation, admiration or respect; Juliet, Scarlett and Hester gaining most votes from boys and girls. The most telling percentages, however, are those which reveal the preferences for male characters by both girls and boys. Girls admired 475 women and 773 men while boys mentioned 824 men and only 65 women. The surveyors concluded that while girls sometimes identify with male and female characters, boys rarely identify with women in their book characters.

Early conditioning to the sex roles in life is largely responsible for such differing reactions and the survey suggested that the treatment of female characters in books for children and adolescents and in the books set as study material only emphasized and furthered this conditioning.

An interesting and stimulating conclusion resulting from this survey is one that is mentioned in my introduction, that in the mobile society of today when families are often smaller and isolated from their kin by distance or dislike, when adolescents are treated as a distinctive and separate brand of human being, the opportunities for knowing adults closely enough to identify attributes and to test themselves against the models, are few enough to require a much closer look at the books adults offer to adolescent readers.

It is evident that the adolescent in school wants vicarious satisfaction from his reading material but is prepared to probe for that satisfaction if there is sufficient motivation, other than examination success, motivation lying mainly in the area of elemental human emotions.

New approaches to teaching, new social and political pressures, new testing methods have influenced the current 'response' element of literature study which has benefited the less able student, who is as capable as the more able of responding to feelings and situations. The stark difference between the able and the supposedly less able students in school in *enjoyment* of literature classes[58] is a result of this recognition of the place of literature in the average student's life and in the consequent choice of book and teaching method.

Do you enjoy literature classes in school?

Grammar school %			Secondary modern school %		
Male	Yes	41·5	Male	Yes	61·5
	No	58·6		No	38·5
Female	Yes	62·8	Female	Yes	73·6
	No	37·2		No	26·4

It is likely that the small proportion of pupils in the secondary modern school who did not enjoy literature classes were hostile or apathetic for reasons unlike those of the hostile or apathetic grammar school students; reluctant readers being much less common amongst the able, and retarded readers a rarity.

> Reluctance is the symptom and not the disease. Reluctance like retardation is a matter of degree. There are degrees of reluctance which extend from revulsion to simple indifference ... revulsion, repulsion, resistance, reluctance, disinterest and indifference. . . . The reluctant reader has to be brought to the position of being susceptible to influence, re-orientated to reading and re-motivated.[59]

Teachers of literature and English in both Britain and America have found different ways of influencing and re-orientating their pupils; sometimes motivating them to read for information as a prelude to reading for pleasure, as in a British school where a class of leavers discussed problems and questions about life after school, made notes on common points and were sent to the local public library reference department for the rest of the term to find answers. The reference library staff found the exercise fruitful and the students discovered means of finding information, reading widely and using books in a way which would normally have been beyond them, and which would enable them in later life to pursue knowledge and to gain pleasure in finding knowledge.

In the USA a teacher faced the fact that the classics and literary works prescribed were reasonably mind building for the college-bound youngster but were sleeping pills for the job-bound youth.[60] He cancelled English classes for three days and held a book fair of 2,000 books in attractive jackets on hundreds of subjects and many levels of ability and interest. The pupils browsed, and bought or read at random and discovered for the first time books which began where they were rather than where the teacher thought they ought to be. After the fair the majority of these disadvantaged teenagers were reading at least one book a month, many far more. Borrowing from the school library doubled and the interest continued with the Teenage Book Club (Scholastic Publications). Pleading for teachers to listen to the children, this enlightened teacher said, 'Let us search out the books which, as Robert Lawson has put it, will give these kids the chuckles, the gooseflesh, the glimpses of glory.'

Such promotion of reading provides the influence, the re-orientation and the re-motivation for the reluctant and retarded but teachers of literature are discovering that teenagers of all emotional, physical and mental levels will respond to promotional techniques, given the relevance, the availability, the accessibility of books and the right conditions for reading.

Teachers and librarians who have failed to make themselves the readers they want their students to become cannot on the whole expect that the absence of evident stimulation and reward from reading will lead teenage students to seek reading as a rewarding activity. Promoting reading for pleasure rather than as an examination subject, a teaching aid, an English exercise or as a verbal test is considered an unheard of luxury despite the now recognized fact, that if it came first, the rest would be facilitated.

Many English rooms and departments have what amounts to classroom libraries, collections of novels and paperbacks from

3

which the students may choose under varying conditions. Some paperback collections are there to encourage further, and more varied, reading. Some are there to aid teaching in connection with themes and are changed termly. Some form branch libraries from which pupils select in the same manner as from the school library, that is with complete freedom of choice but involving the student in keeping a loose-leaf record of his selections with comments.[61]

Daniel Fader's experiments in promoting reading in school are widely known but necessitate here a brief outline of his basic premise which is that saturation in terms of availability and accessibility has a beneficial effect:[62] saturation by putting the books in *every* classroom and diffusion through *every* teacher, not just the English teacher. The selection of 1,000 paperbacks for this programme was amended over the years until an acceptable distribution of types of fiction was reached by taking careful note of the reading preferences of the supposedly unreachable, unteachable boys in the penal institution in which Fader was working. Action stories formed 40% divided between adventure, science fiction, spy, war, and detective books. The rest was made up of non-fiction ranging from paperback scientific and technical works to the books dealing with what every teenager wants to know about sex. It was found that gradually the interests changed from the sole interest in cartoon books to a more demanding range of reading matter and it was realized that this expansion came from the obvious and stated needs of the boys 'who have learned to like to read'.

Book talks by school librarians cause a mixed reaction in American schools but have scarcely been tried in Britain, since full-time school librarians are themselves scarce. Young adult librarians and children's librarians in both countries commonly talk to groups of teenagers in schools, taking copies of new books, possible selections, interesting and unusual fiction and non-fiction. In one British secondary school for educationally subnormal children, weekly story hours are given by the writer and some of her students to selected second- and third-year pupils aged from thirteen to fifteen, who respond spectacularly to the fairy stories they never had in their disadvantaged childhood and to the stories and excerpts which relate to their adolescent needs and interests in their contemporary surroundings. Talks to sixth-form or tenth- and eleventh-grade students are common and again the writer has found interest amongst such students, the arts and the science-based alike finding identification in the books written for teenagers, especially the students who admit to not reading or to disliking reading as a leisure time pursuit.

Book clubs in schools are common in the USA and increasing in Britain, in both cases largely through the enterprise of Scholastic Publications, a commercial organization which encourages children to buy paperbacks in order to discover the pleasures of reading and owning books. The book clubs made up of classes or groups of children in a school, are categorized by approximate age, e.g. See Saw Club for the nursery school/playgroup age, Lucky Club for the five to eight, Chip Club for the eight to eleven years old, Scoop Club for the eleven to fourteen age group, in Britain, with the addition in the States of TAB (Teenage Book Club) and Campus for senior high school and college students, the American clubs being sponsored by Scholastic Book Services.

A monthly newsletter for each member of the club is sent to the school with a teacher's memo giving fuller details of the books available. A choice of approximately twenty books is given each month, all the titles having been selected by the editorial staff in co-operation with educationalists and librarians, from the range of children's book publishers plus some specially commissioned and published by Scholastic Publications and available only from the company. What the company provides through the school bookselling agencies is dealt with more fully in Chapter 4 where the teenagers' choice of book purchase is discussed. The British company is expanding rapidly as the increasing interest in books and the growing concern about reading standards direct attention to all aspects of book provision. Though some local education authorities do not allow book clubs to operate on school premises on the basis that trading is not a suitable venture in school, many others find that the enthusiastic teachers who operate the bookstalls, unpaid, have discovered willing and keen readers amongst previously unwilling-to-read children, when a choice of attractive paperbacks is available for browsing through, for spending pocket money on and for taking home to show the family.

Very few bookshops in Britain stock an adequate range of children's books and very few schools or colleges are near enough to any bookshop to make book buying possible, so that when the book club magazine arrives with news of books available or when the book stall is open in school breaks, a complete range of young people through age, ability and interest is represented. The American extension of the range into the college level is extremely successful and is being considered for introduction into British schools at the higher secondary, sixth-form college and colleges of further education stages. The quantity of fiction specifically for teenagers is small by comparison with that in the States but it is increasing. Less attention has been paid to forms of subject reading material in which teenagers are interested, such as biographies, sex, sport and the leading hobbies, which figure largely in the American paperback selection for the Teenage and Campus members. Most teachers, librarians and educationalists consider their book funds inadequate for teaching and library purposes and are anxious to promote reading by any means available. Most have been surprised at the way in which young people will spend money on books when the books are placed before them and at the increased interest that arises from a constant flow of books in the school, the opportunity to buy and the pride of ownership.

The differences between the British and American use of book clubs can be seen in the following table as can the clear preference for the public library over the school library in the

TABLE 6   *Sources of books obtained in the previous month as reported by British and American pupils*[63]

Source	No. of books borrowed		% of students using each source		Average no. of books per student	
	British	American	British	American	British	American
Public library	10,549	43,142	57·9	58·5	4·2	4·6
School library	6,159	26,420	51·5	59·6	2·8	2·8
Paperbacks	5,581	24,634	55·1	59·5	2·3	2·6
Home library	5,458	18,843	49·9	48·3	2·5	2·4
Friends	3,906	11,590	46·0	43·2	2·0	1·7
Book clubs	193	3,000	2·7	7·8	1·8	2·8
Teacher	1,678	no data	23·3	no data	1·7	no data
Other	728	2,666	6·8	5·2	2·5	3·2
Total	34,252	130,295			8·0	7·9

British n = 4,301   American n = 16,089

average number of books obtained per student. The high proportion of students buying paperbacks is also indicated and
will be explored more fully in Chapter 4.

There are possibilities for change in the educational approach
to literature in schools, in the feasibility and development
studies of the Schools Council which is co-ordinating working
parties on a common system of examining at sixteen-plus and
in the deliberations of both the National Association for the
Teaching of English in Britain and in the National Council of
Teachers of English in America.[64]

Such change and indeed, those areas of development already
under way, require changes in the teacher also.

> There is a fairly widespread view that we must cater more
> than we have in the past for individual needs, that children
> should read widely in the literature that interests and excites
> them, and that our role is to provide a rich and varied
> reading diet for their nourishment. All this means extending
> vastly our own knowledge of what is available in the field.[65]

Many colleges of education make it their business to provide
courses in literature for specific age categories, either as an
examined option or as an ancillary non-examined course;
many education authorities and higher education establishments offer short courses, weekend schools and summer schools
on books for children and young adults. Some school librarians
specifically liaise with the teaching staff in updating the latter's
knowledge of contemporary books and some public library
services attempt to provide an information service to teachers
by means of book lists, individual bibliographies and exhibition
collections of children's books, both static and mobile displays.

The School Library Association in Britain and its equivalent
in America offer guidance and information through their
services and their journals, in addition to the courses and local
branch activities which are designed to help teachers to keep
up to date in the book and library world for children. The
attraction of courses and the different national preferences can
be seen in Table 7.

It appears that an attitude to *all* reading can be conditioned
in school particularly by the analytical treatment of works of
fiction, producing in many students, particularly in those who
are not 'readers', the feeling that reading is a chore.

TABLE 7 *Courses of greatest interest and value to teachers*[66]

Rank	Course	% of teachers responding British (n = 143)	American (n = 1,331)
1.	Practical methods of teaching English	90	71
2.	Literature of adolescents	86	72
3.	Speech or drama	82	65
4.	Advanced studies in curriculum	79	69
5.	Literature of periods	74	85
6.	Close studies of single works or authors	71	83
7.	Literary criticism	62	85
8.	Teaching of reading	57	69
9.	Literature surveys	49	65
10.	Literary genre	47	72
11.	Intermediate or advanced composition	43	82
12.	History of the language	35	67
13.	Structure or generative grammar	33	71
14.	Traditional grammar	10	39

It seems sensible to accept the thesis propounded by many teachers of examination-type literature that the majority of pupils up to sixteen and seventeen are not, on the whole, capable of practising literary criticism and are not enthusiastic about critical analysis of set books. Two American studies of this aspect concluded that judgement of the quality of prose might be an independent skill apart from emotion, or it might even be a product of maturity, and that courses of study in literature designed to promote reading appreciation had little influence on it.[67]

It ought to be a safe assumption that those who choose to study literature after that age do so knowing what they are doing and that they bring to that study an eagerness to ponder, savour and analyse and that such students would also be readers, but the assumption is unsound. Indeed there is a noticeable absence of readers amongst student teachers and student librarians, both being educated for professions which subscribe still to the belief that 'reading maketh a full man' or that reading is the mark of the educated man, and both committed to the promotion of reading.

Comparisons between Britain and the USA reveal that Britain is moving towards responsive study of a variety of books and is attempting to change the currently abrupt transfer from such liberal study in the early teens to the close analysis of set texts for 'O' and 'A' level examinations, by introducing CSE Mode 3 type literature study. In the USA there is still a definite emphasis right through the grades for close textual analysis, looking for the how rather than the why in a small number of carefully censored texts. It is possible that this difference in purpose and method of literary study is the cause of differences in reading habits between the two countries, American teenagers and adults reading less than British teenagers and adults. This is partly explained by the greater amount of homework in American schools, leaving less time for personal reading and partly by the attitudes towards voluntary reading engendered by the critical dissection of set texts and the emphasis laid on vocabulary and syntax.

TABLE 8   *Time spent reading outside school by British and American pupils*[68]

Type of reading		Percentage of students responding					
		less than 1 hour a week	1–2 hours	3–5 hours	6–10 hours	more than 10 hours	no response
Assigned reading outside school	British	18·0	31·0	32·0	12·2	4·7	2·1
	American	5·7	16·5	43·0	25·9	7·4	1·5
Reading (unassigned personal reading)	British	10·3	25·2	36·6	20·2	6·6	0·8
	American	20·6	29·8	31·8	11·5	4·8	1·5

British n = 4,301   American n = 13,291

A middle way is achieved between emphasis on uncritical reading of a variety of literature and the close textual analysis of set books, by the critical interpretation of responses to character, plot or mood. While this would not satisfy the American teachers of literature who believe that the study involves a study of origins and literary structure, it offers an organized, disciplined, cognitive alternative to the current affective approach used in England for non-examined purposes.

The promotion of reading in school is beset with problems and it has been suggested that neither teachers nor parents are the best people to say what is good for young adults to read.

'Another adult with a less vested interest in the result (teachers want examination results, parents want signs of emergent adult behaviour) may be the best mentor, and who better placed than the librarians?'[69] Undoubtedly school librarians in the USA try to fulfil this role and the few in Britain, at present prohibited by lack of clerical and other assistance from giving time to reader guidance, recognize the importance of this function. Teachers too, while anxious to build up class-room collections, are increasingly aware of the value of the library and librarian in the promotion of reading in all subjects and at all levels of ability; though a large proportion of teachers and the majority of the authorities providing the finance are reluctant to accord the librarian and the library the status of the all-pervasive collector and disseminator of information. They still cling to their interpretation of him as an aide to the English department. The attitude of the teaching staff is the second crucial factor in the formation of the pupil's attitudes to reading and the library.

Chapter 3
Libraries in educational establishments for teenagers

Whatever the terminology used to describe the school's centre for source materials and information, whether it be simply library, the term employed throughout this study, or educational media centre or resourceteria, the fact remains that changes in education are changing the usage made of school libraries. Theories of learning, technical inventions, curriculum reform, all necessitate a larger quantity and a wider range of information sources. The project/topic/discovery method in Britain and the United States can combine the latest in content and media; team teaching and integrated studies have called for technology in the classroom; independent learning has moved up from the primary school and down from the university to early teenage where assessed work entails extensive use of the library's internally and externally available resources and where the teaching staff must be aware of the availability of material in order to advise on the feasibility of the project.

But not all schools have adopted these methods and there are many schools where some subjects or some of the staff retain the examination set book, text book, chalk and talk methods either from necessity where the examination board insists or from the teacher's inclination. In large comprehensive schools where many pupils are pursuing different courses or approaching a field of knowledge in differing ways the more academic students are given the least scope to deviate from the confines of the text and the memory work of written examinations and the less able are encouraged to explore and exploit and develop individual approaches to a chosen subject. The problems of the teaching staff and librarian alike lie equally in finding a way of liberalizing either the curriculum or the methods of arriving at knowledge so that the examination confined student may develop his self directed abilities, and in enabling the less able student to make the most of his opportunities for semi-autonomous learning by instructing him in how to find information from a variety of sources. Far too many teachers allow pupils to embark on projects with little idea of how to use a book to find information and no knowledge of other media or sources, a skill, which if taught from primary school onwards, would enable students to learn a great deal more, faster and with more lasting effect before arriving at college. Most college students are unable to make notes adequately and have only a hazy notion of how to extract information.

How much do secondary school students read and why the need to look closely at the school library's role and services?

A monthly breakdown of the typical teenage senior pupil who is devoting a large portion of his life to education is given in one study of student reading.[70]

> He devotes 15–16 hours per month to reading for homework outside the classroom.
>
> He reads almost six books (other than text books) in whole or in part each month for school work, two of which he gets in the school library and four in the public library (these six books are in addition to reference sources consulted briefly). He spends 14–15 hours per month in libraries looking for materials, consulting references, reading books (part of the 15–16 hours of reading time mentioned above). $\frac{1}{3}$ of this time in his school library, $\frac{2}{3}$ in the public library.
>
> In addition to the 15–16 hours of reading for school work, he spends 9–10 hours per month reading for personal interest or amusement.
>
> The 'free' reading time is devoted primarily to newspapers and magazines, although the high school student goes through 2–3 books of his own interest during a year (the books about equally distributed between material he finds at home, paperbacks he buys or borrows from friends, and books from the public library).

However the use made of the school library by the teaching staff also inculcates negative attitudes towards the library and reading. The extremes are epitomized in a teacher's remark that pupils should not be given much time in the library because 'they'll sit there just reading'[71] and in a headteachers' comment that 'the greatest value of the resources centre is that within school it has been an agency for curriculum innovation and teacher development'.[72] Between these two extremes lies

a variety of interpretation of the role of the library and a variety
of attitudes which affect the pupil's use of the library, conse-
quently colouring his attitude towards it. The negative attitudes
emphasize the purposes other than reading or information
finding to which the library is put.

MISUSE

The library is frequently the place to which students are only
directed if it is raining in the lunch break thus compelling pupils
at their most active stage of growth to be physically still and
quiet for yet another hour in the school day and making an
imposition of being in the library. Rather than cram two classes
together if a teacher is off sick, it is common for the teacher-
less class to be sent to the library, usually without any set work
and under the supervision of the librarian if there is one or a
senior student who is trying to study. The library thus becomes
a place to fill in time.

It is considered a suitable punishment for wayward pupils
to be sent to sit and read a book in the library and is thereafter
a most acceptable punishment if the student likes reading or a
prison if he doesn't. As there is a strong correlation between
misbehaviour in school, social background and academic
achievement, it is more than likely that the miscreant is not
good at or interested in reading, the punishment thereby
confirming yet again his dislike of books and libraries.

The library is used as a classroom when space is limited
elsewhere thus restricting the proper usage, undermining its
role and distorting its image as a service agency over and above
subject department categorization and outside the jurisdiction
of the teacher. Because it is neat and clean and has an aura
either of hallowed ancient learning or up to the minute
progress, depending on the school, the governors' meeting is
likely to be held in the library which is displayed with pride
as a status symbol when showing visitors round the school,
visitors and staff equally unaware of the fact that if the library
was doing its job properly the place would be full of students
and less full of books.

Architects of schools are rarely aware of the functions of a
school library and tend to place it either in an inaccessible part
of the campus, necessitating a lengthy walk often between

buildings, or in such an accessible place that it is virtually a corridor. Both locations militate against the effective use of the library by pupils and build up an antipathy towards it.

Less negative than the above restrictive practices but equally common, is the practice of allowing the library to be used during class hours only by the senior students for private study, regardless of the fact that many senior students are studying from texts and may not be using the stock of the library, only its tables, its chairs and its quietness. The student who has come up through such a school will never have had the opportunity of freely using the school library except in the short lunch break if he felt so inclined and may well leave school with a minimal knowledge of books and libraries and a belief that libraries are only for the senior academic student types. It is not unknown for the students who become seniors to wish to preserve this time honoured 'perk' and to resist the infiltration of juniors into the library.

One other attitude-affecting item must be mentioned here, that of the dull, uninteresting and uncomfortable appearance of many school libraries, not conducive to encouraging pupils to stay once they are allowed in, with little to catch the eye and start a pupil off on the joys of browsing and almost nothing to enable him to visually locate what he wants; not enough table top space to allow him to spread materials around him and with the room arranged in such a way that the logical order of the stock is sacrificed so that the supervisor can see what everyone is up to. Visual appeal has long been noted by the ad men and by promotion experts as the basic attraction but is conspicuously absent in many school and other libraries.

Most of these negative attitudes are found in schools where there is no full-time librarian and where rigid control is thought to be necessary to preserve the stock from indiscriminate use, possible damage and, it is thought, probable theft. Long-standing indifference to the library on the part of many teachers has not only caused missed opportunities for pupils to use the school library but has bred indifference in the pupils also. It is not surprising therefore that apathy, indifference and hostility are apparent in student attitudes. Differences in student attitudes occur also as a result of the student's own background and aspirations, which vary between those who intend to leave at sixteen, those who are staying on for further schooling, those who are destined for vocational courses and those intending to go on to higher education.

POSITIVE USE

Positive student attitudes towards the library spring from positive teacher and librarian attitudes and can be achieved in schools which must retain the traditional teaching and examining methods. However the move towards assessed course work and independent learning has emphasized the library as an integral part of teaching, a source for the teacher and student alike, for the whole class, for the student working in a chosen field, for the messenger sent from the classroom to find information, for the individual's personal interests and recreational reading.

In much the same way as many universities and vocational colleges have continuous library instruction in the relevant subject areas so more subject teachers in schools are incorporating the effective use of the library in their subject field into the teaching programme. It was suggested earlier that a teacher seen to be reading was a good advertisement for reading, similarly the teacher seen to be using the library for his own purposes or with a student produces a co-operative attitude. Positive attitudes springing from satisfaction with the library service are the responsibility of the librarian. The attraction of the library is minimal if the students' needs, interests and preferences are not catered for.

There is often a dichotomy between the English teacher's and librarian's attitudes towards books.

> High school teachers' reports of the reading interests of their students differ more from the students' own reports of their reading interests than is the case in the elementary school. . . . Secondary teachers seriously underestimate reading interests in the social studies. The tendency of high school teachers to see students' interests in terms of their own field of specialization undoubtedly accounts for some of the discrepancy between their reports of student interests and the reports of the students themselves.[73]

The librarian's view emanates from his over-all view of the

stock for all subject disciplines and for the other information needs of the students and staff.

SELECTION

The selection of materials is basically geared to the school curriculum taking account of the fact that the subjects are studied from, for example, the ages of thirteen to eighteen and that the subject stock must cater for the conceptual, mental, interest and reading ages between those chronological years; the merits of one medium in getting across the subject matter better than another medium; the known use to which the work will be put and its potential use; the amount of duplication required, based on the known use, and the importance of material for subject staff in each subject field.

Perhaps the biggest change required of a school library with new methods of learning is the opening up of previously self contained units of knowledge, formerly easily confined within the Dewey classification but now involving multi-disciplinary stock, less easy to classify but filling the need for a work which looks at many related aspects of a given topic. Selection of these works complements and supplements basic subject stock and facilitates inter-disciplinary teaching and resource based learning.

General reading and recreational reading for the teenage student are important selection aspects in that these are the areas of strongest personal motivation and interest and may well attract the reluctant reader. A nationwide survey of reading interests and informational needs of high school students in the States[74] revealed that the social sciences, including history, were important reading interests as were biological and applied sciences; most of the science interest centred on automobiles, space travel and medical matters. An indication of the information students would like to ask about is given in the following percentages:

Major areas of social science	28%
Personal and social adjustment	20%
Vocations	9%
Religion, recreation, philosophy	43%
Psychology, arts, maths, money, literature and languages	10%

The survey makes the point that there is not necessarily any link between (a) the subjects students want to read about, (b) the subjects on which they want to ask for information, and (c) the subjects they do reference work on.

> Thus reading interests are not identical with informational needs as youth see each of these. . . . For example, problems of personal and social adjustment are not predominant in either the reading interests or reference behaviour of youth, but these concerns show up prominently in what they would ask about. . . . It would seem that if an interest is strong enough it will show some response even in unlikely circumstances.[75]

The importance of the school stock containing material to cater for the general subject reading, the reference work and the information requirements is not to be underestimated, though the last area is the most often neglected when funds are scanty, the priority going to the curriculum orientated works.

There is a common core of such books which would seem to lend itself to some form of co-operative inter-loan between schools, thus freeing some of the limited bookfund and allowing students a much wider range of stock. One such scheme was explored recently after a feasibility study to discover overlap, quantity, title diversity and availability. It was suggested that the core titles were those listed in the Senior High School Library Catalog. The general conclusions were that the large quantity of duplication suggested co-operation and that title diversity of unique holdings indicated a range of titles amongst a number of schools that no area public library could hope to maintain.[76] While this might be a viable proposition in the States the situation in Britain is different in that libraries in most schools in Britain are nowhere near the size or standard of American school libraries and, more importantly, many take part in a co-operative arrangement with the schools service of the public library, whereby schools service stock is loaned and exchanged regularly to the schools to complement and sup-plement the school's own stock, to cater for temporary subject needs and to provide individual titles on request. This allows the school to concentrate its bookfund on the permanent curricula needs, on basic reference works and multi-media.

PAPERBACKS

The question of selecting paperback or hardback is a perennial problem for the teachers and librarians who must decide. Studies have confirmed over many years that a paperback has the psychological advantage of being, unlike the hardback with its educational connotations, visually attractive, smaller and therefore apparently less demanding, and is more easily portable. Many school librarians facing the lack of interest of teenage students have taken Daniel Fader's viewpoint that 'now children need now books' and supply much of the stock in paperback, maintaining that larger quantities can be bought in softback than hardback, more students will read them and that though the paperback will wear out more quickly, the primary object of having books – that they should be read – will be achieved.

School librarians also approach the promotion of reading via paperbacks in other ways. Some have a paperback collection of fiction and general reading for which no records are kept and for which the loan system involves only a date stamp on the back cover. The money saved on the non-recording for what amounts to approximately ten issues of a title can be spent on replacing it, the only necessary record being the indication to the student of the date due for return.

Others have attempted to relieve the pressure on the curricula stock fund by encouraging the head of school to channel other funds into the creation of paperback collections in the leisure areas of the school or into the classrooms, thus relieving the library of recreational responsibilities or at least decentralizing the recreational stock while retaining functional control.

Other librarians and teachers have set up a paperback-selling area in the library, with an agency from the local bookshop or from Scholastic Publications, so that students' non-curricula interests can be catered for, thus again supplementing the stock and the bookfund, though not opting out of the responsibility for lending to students who cannot buy.

Some schools buy paperbacks and then have them strengthened and laminated, thus preserving the advantages of the format while lessening the disadvantages, but this treatment is usually reserved for the more expensive paperbacks, usually non-fiction works, some of which appear only in paperback.

At least two schools of thought can be found over the shelving of paperbacks in school libraries; that which favours the integration of this format with the hardback stock on the grounds that discrimination will only emphasize the supposed differences between the two and, more positively, that students see the whole range of material if shelving is integrated; and the viewpoint that believes that segregation of paperbacks into racks and free-standing spinners is less likely to frighten off the reluctant reader, who can go straight to the visually attractive and easily accessible material without difficulty. Segregation of format in this instance may also facilitate the arrangement of the library into quiet and noisy areas, in that the greatest amount of movement will be concentrated into the area where the paperbacks are shelved, thus leaving most of the library for quieter study.

PERIODICALS

Much of teenagers' interest reading is done in the periodical format and many schools are discovering, slowly, that the library stock of periodicals is non-existent for interest reading and very inadequate for subject use. The school librarians who have made use of teenagers' known preference for magazine type presentation of information have consulted with subject staff to select relevant subject periodicals and have consulted representative pupil sections to obtain a consensus of opinion on the choice of general and recreational periodicals. There is often a very low correlation between the periodicals actually preferred by the students and those provided by the library. This is borne out in many studies, one of which demonstrated the very wide interests of teenagers which were not reflected at all in the magazines available in the school libraries surveyed.[77]

Many of the magazines represented in each of the libraries ranked low in student preference and many magazines high in student preference lists were not in most of the school libraries. Although *Life*, *Post* and *Time* were found in most school libraries half the schools did not stock the next rankings, *Seventeen*, *Look* and *Sports*. The effect of bad or non-representative selection of periodicals is to deter still further those pupils who can be reached through their only reading matter, magazines, and to underline the traditional viewpoint that reading is an academic exercise and that information can be found only in books. The average and bright students also need both the subject and interest periodicals for up to date subject information and for recreation. Stimulating the average pupil and particularly the early school leaver can be done by appealing to the preferences he already has, those of his personal interest and his liking for magazines. While such stimulation may never lead to deeper reading, it nevertheless maintains literacy, provides information and makes reading enjoyable for those sections of the teenage school population who equate reading with English literature classes and heavy hardbacks.

Consultation with staff and students and a joint assessment of what is available, perhaps based on the appropriate guides such as the ALA's *Periodicals for School Libraries* and Bill Katz's *Magazines for Libraries,* and in Britain, C. W. Waite's *Periodicals for School Libraries* and *Willings Press Guide*[78] would produce a list of needs and preferences from which priorities would emerge to fit the periodicals funds available.

Similarly newspaper subscriptions are curiously limited in many schools. British schools in particular are backward at including even one newspaper in the library, though occasionally the sixth-form centre and the staff will set aside other funds for newspapers for their respective common-rooms. Many schools follow the policy that if you can't have them all you don't have any, otherwise political bias would be shown; some argue that everyone can buy a newspaper and that the students see newspapers at home, therefore the school does not need to spend its scanty funds on what is commonly available. These views ignore the value of the newspaper as a tool of information on current affairs, on social studies, on financial matters and as a vehicle for language and reading practice. (The use of newspapers in class plus copies in the library is described later in relation to work with teenagers in a penal institution, but is occasionally found in normal schools, and the sections of newspapers read by teenagers is discussed in the next chapter.) However commonly available outside the library, with whatever variations of title and interpretation of news, the newspaper is by no means read from cover to cover by teenagers in their own time, and for the library's purposes, is a medium of information.

NON-PRINT

Other material of relevance to teenage interests thus motivating them to use it, is the audio-visual content of the school library. Although few schools in Britain or the United States have full-scale multi-media centres many schools are cautiously dipping a toe into the relatively unknown waters of educational technology and audio-visual media; cautiously because it is new, it is expensive, it is fragile, it is potentially time consuming and space consuming, it requires different treatment, it needs a specialist to keep its hardware in working condition and, in some teachers' views, it has yet to prove itself as better than print.

Once again the teenagers' known interests and abilities can be utilized here to aid use of the library's store of information. Many students are familiar with record players, cameras, cassette players, movie projectors and slide viewers in their own homes and their youth clubs. They have been brought up on visually presented information and opinion through the television and cinema screens. They are, on the whole, far more adept at handling the hardware than their teachers and far more used to assimilating information from audio-visual media than their teachers or parents. Many school libraries which have information in non-print form allow it to be used by the teaching staff in the classroom but not by students anywhere, others have arranged the library in such a way that the use of the hardware in the library is facilitated, sometimes in wired up carrels or booths, sometimes in an adjacent room, sometimes in the main area of the library with suitable noise and vision control. Some have removed non-print material altogether from the library and have concentrated it in a separate non-print unit, others have left the non-print material with the teachers who have acquired it over the years in subject departments and have centralized the hardware. Whatever the location it is rare to find a school which allows the students to borrow or use for reference this material in the same way as the print material.

Some senior students have circumvented the restrictions by

arranging that records be bought from the proceeds of fines in the library, the records to be freely available to the senior students.

Increasingly educationalists recognize that one piece of knowledge can be achieved by a variety of methods and that ability to learn by any one medium varies from pupil to pupil. It is generally agreed that non-print material and the library availability of the hardware to students can aid both independent learning for senior students and group and project work for the early teenage pupils, not in isolation from other media but as one part of the library's total stock of sources of information.

Certain categories of teenage student need to be considered when selecting material, for example the backward, the immigrant, the early school leaver and the career seeker. These categories are largely neglected in the selection of stock in many schools despite the existence of large numbers of students in each category.

THE SLOW LEARNER

The backward student or slow learner may be in a normal class in the bottom stream, in a remedial class or in a special school for educationally subnormal children, and in any of these situations he is likely to be one of many such students with too few teachers who are prepared to go beyond the usual view that because Johnny cannot read he doesn't need to have access to a range of books or to use the school library. In Britain the range of easy reading books (other than reading texts) for teenage retarded readers is increasing and librarians are able to identify those normal books which contain the qualities needed, plenty of illustration, large clear print, short words and sentences, humour and relevance, and to extract them as occasion demands from the general stock.

Librarians are also aware that many backward readers, the majority of whom are boys, are interested in non-fiction subjects and are, again, identifying normal non-fiction with the right qualities for use by slower pupils. The recreational magazines play their part here too in that they contain most of the qualities required plus the advantage of being familiar in out-of-school life.

Some analysis of what publishers and writers produce for slow readers is given later; it is sufficient to say here that there is now a wide enough range for every school to provide reading material in the library to cater for the abilities and interests of the most backward. The staff and the time to adequately guide these students is the secondary problem. The primary objective is to get the stock that will attract them into the library. One London school librarian recalls seeing a tough fourteen-year-old boy she knew to be a backward reader apparently absorbed in an erudite periodical. On surreptitiously glancing behind the periodical she discovered it was hiding a child's fairy story book which he was evidently capable of reading but which he would have died rather than ask for or be seen openly reading. This librarian wisely refrained from commenting to the boy, knowing that he would never set foot in the library again if he knew his choice had been noticed.

The question of whether to segregate the easy reading material arises here. Some school librarians integrate it, relying on lists or the librarian to help the student or teacher to locate it; some shelve separately, labelling the shelves Easy Reading or Easy-to-Read Books and may well wonder why few students are to be seen there except in remedial class visits when all are directed to these shelves. Others, and the writer subscribes to this view, believe that the solution is to have an unlabelled rack or shelf section on to which are put a number of attractive paperbacks, easy to read books with the right chronological age content and some age-relevant magazines, with maximum visual impact by placing all the items front cover outwards rather than spine. Most students will gravitate immediately towards this section, thus allowing the slow reader the face-saving opportunity of finding something he can look at or read without advertising his disability.

SELECTION FOR MULTI-RACIAL SCHOOLS

The ethnic composition of the school will have a bearing on the presence and amount of stock required to cater for the multi-racial students and the immigrant. Much has been written about the difficulties of attempting to integrate the immigrant into the nation's way of life, culture and customs, while simultaneously attempting to preserve his cultural heritage, religion and national customs. In the States the long history of immigration and the contemporary concern about racial bias in books for young people, has produced practical and documentary evidence of the need to pay attention to the ethnic origins of young people. In Britain, where multi-racial schools are relatively new, teachers and librarians are attempting to ease the assimilation into British ways mainly through remedial teaching, at the same time looking for means of providing reading and information relevant to the pupils' origins. Few schools in Britain have libraries which reflect the interests, concerns and backgrounds of the immigrant or of the coloured British. An increasing quantity of good quality Caribbean literature is available and there are a few books set in the British multi-racial context. The problem of insufficient Indian and Pakistani literature in translation remains and a few schools and public libraries stock a small selection of such national literature in the original language.

The necessity for material for project work on the countries of origin of these students has also been recognized and school libraries are attempting to stock up on suitable accurate, non-biased books and materials which aid such projects and can be used also for 'Black Studies'. A British school librarian, noting the enthusiasm with which sixteen-year-old second generation West Indian girl students read and passed around one book about black teenagers in Britain commented that

> . . . most of these books tend to portray a multi-racial society from the point of view of its 'Problems' – with an unmistakable capital P. Race-riots, the black child trying to find acceptance by a white gang, the tensions of a black/white teenage romance – all these make high drama in the stories. While some of the situations are true to life, there is a danger that if we get too many books like this they will help to perpetuate the idea that multi-racial communities are fraught with tensions and explosive situations. The black child will still be unable to see himself as a perfectly normal and acceptable member of the community.[79]

The backward reader, the immigrant or non-white student and the early school leaver tend to be one and the same all too often.

EARLY SCHOOL LEAVER

The early social environment, the non-attainment at school, the pull of the pay packet are contributory factors to the category of the early school leaver and the drop out. The raising of school leaving age (ROSLA or The Extra Year) created a potentially useful opportunity for teachers to make school relevant to the leaver and many education authorities set up ROSLA units in order to pay special attention to the usually hostile students, frustrated in their desire to leave school at the earliest opportunity. Other education authorities took the chance to create a situation where all students could take the sixteen-plus examinations, where previously those below sixteen had left school with no certificates. Others developed non-examined courses designed to enable the student to achieve independence in the adult working world. The same situation in the States produced similar action by teaching staff and after the antagonism of the students affected in the first year of change, the extra year became, to the oncoming students, accepted as the last compulsory year of the school period rather than the extra year.

However the effect on the library of changes in curriculum and methods of learning for the ROSLA students, was to produce a need for very widely ranging subject matter, much of it in the technical and commercial fields which had hitherto been a minor part of the stock and which had been considered the province of the College of Further Education or the trade school to which, in Britain, the apprentices or young workers might go for day-release classes such as woodwork, metalwork, cookery, typing, book keeping, which have minimal need of library books; to social studies in which group or individual project work was done in matters of social importance, where the resources of the library was vital, and to the 'liberalizing' activity of reading, much of it undertaken by the English teacher in the form of short stories and excerpts and some independently using the library's stock.

The majority of early leavers are reluctant or retarded readers though as society changes and more middle-class teenagers are dropping out of full-time education at the first opportunity, the proportions of readers and minimal readers may change. The school library, therefore, is vitally concerned to aid these students while they are at school as it is unlikely that they will ever go to a public library after leaving school. School librarians recognize that a different standard must be applied to such students and to be realistic about their needs and abilities the library must go more than halfway to meet them, by providing plenty of magazines, newspapers, humorous and exciting paperbacks, good quality comic books with their easy to read balloon talk or onomatpœic, explosive words, plenty of bright attractive books on their leisure time interests such as motor bikes, cars, grooming, sex, pop music and sociological subjects, on the premise that the mind will be stimulated – a basic consideration when most early school leavers go into mindless jobs – interests may be furthered, literacy will be maintained and the leisure time pursuit of reading may be created. For most reluctant and retarded readers in teenage these are considerable achievements, as considerable, given the comparative circumstances and backgrounds, as that of the more academic teenager who is through teenage books into adult fiction and serious non-fiction.

A further category mentioned previously is that of the career seeker.

CAREERS MATERIAL

Some schools have a careers room staffed by a careers teacher who may or may not be full time in that sphere depending on the size of the school. One such British school is Filton High School, Bristol, where 1,500 students need no encouragement to use the careers library in a suite of rooms. The headmaster suggested five basic needs for an efficient careers library:

1. A large enough area for display to present . . . an overwhelming amount of literature attractively and intelligently.
2. A discussion room where vocational ideas can be quietly explored by all the interested parties in the decision-making process.
3. Easy communication between 1 and 2 so that, while privacy is possible, accessibility to the careers counsellor is obvious.
4. A waiting-room arranged to encourage browsing, to

enable parents to feel at home and thereby play a full part in the proceedings.

5. An administration base for the careers staff and somewhere to house the equipment necessary to run the department.[80]

The Filton careers library has a bench for audio-visual aids so that pupils can use, individually, the filmstrips, slides and tapes on aspects of jobs. Most large schools now pay serious attention to the counselling aspects, but some keep the material in the main library as a separate collection.

Some schools have a collection of careers pamphlets in the school office; some leave the responsibility to the local youth employment office; some liaise with a local authority careers department as at Chester where a careers library operates during normal office hours in the Youth Employment Service. It is used by early school leavers, by senior students, by parents and by a growing number of people, older and younger, who are seeking an alternative career. The clientele indicates the usefulness of placing this library in an organization which is open during the school holidays and is accessible to non-school people interested in a new or a different career.

In each type of careers library the contents cover factual and fictional careers literature, directories, government and company pamphlets and broadsheets, college prospectuses, youth employment circulars and varying amounts of audio-visual material. In every case students make considerable use of the facilities.

STOCK EDITING

One of the failings in many school libraries is in the lack of stock editing and the failure to weed out the obsolete stock. This is one of the causes of student apathy in library use. Many libraries, particularly those run by teachers rather than librarians, contain large proportions of stocks which are out of date, inaccurate, damaged, dirty, no longer applicable because of curriculum change, or no longer suited to new methods of learning.

Reasons given for failure to revise the stock vary: lack of time, lack of subject knowledge adequate for removal of subject stock, the shelves would be empty if stock revision were done, the tooled bindings look good, the sixth edition of *Encyclopedia*

Britannica will have to stay because there is no money for the
latest edition, these books might come in useful one day, I
didn't know there was a new edition of this book, there isn't
the money to replace discarded stock.

One head of a science department in a large school was
asked by the librarian to weed out science books from the
library shelves, concentrating on the out of date works. After
doing so he then asked the librarian who was preparing to
throw them out if he could have them to store in his department
cupboard in case he might need them again.

Weeding out and replacement of audio-visual material
whether centralized or decentralized in the school is often
neglected, resulting in information or a visual approach which
is out of date and in film and records which may be damaged.

Surveys attempting to uncover reasons why students do not
use the library, have revealed over and over again that although
the main reason is lack of a range of stock to suit each subject
need and each level of ability, the second reason is nearly
always that what is in the library is not up to date. The British
and American standards for school librarians both recommend
a replacement figure of one-third per annum, and one-sixth
for rebinding, but this is rarely achieved.[81]

LIBRARY SERVICES

The services offered to the teenager in the school library may
be much the same in practice as those offered to him in his
earlier years by the school and by the public library though the
reason for them may differ slightly. The justification for a much
wider range of services is based on the rate of growth of
information, changes in education, the curriculum, the learning situation, the development of non-book media and the
objectives of school education.

LOAN SERVICES

Even a service as basic for libraries as the loan service varies
from school to school, with some schools insisting on reference
only because of shortage of stock, lack of duplication, persistent
theft or damage, or, in a few instances, total lack of awareness
of the role of the library in the student's education; others set

up short loan collections in the style of most universities so that works in constant demand can be shared fairly without massive duplication.

Variations in loan rules and procedures are justified by type of stock and by supply and demand, but overnight loan, short-term loan, semi-permanent loan (to staff), classroom loan, paperback loan, inter-library loan and normal loan may all feature in the well planned and used school library. Students are aware then not only of the importance of methods of loan which ensure availability but also of the relative time uses of various kinds of material.

Certain charging systems will yield useful information about aspects of loan and reading interests of students, many schools using a system which requires the reader to put his name on to the book card or conversely the book information on to the reader's card, thus at a later date if required, providing some indication of what a particular student reads or what range of students uses a particular book. The usefulness of such information in selection and guidance cannot be underestimated.

REFERENCE SERVICES

The reference service requires the stock to be separated into, for instance, quick reference works and others, the former including yearbooks, directories, indexes, general encyclo-paedias, atlases, etc. where reference is made for a specific bit of information, the others covering the definitive works, the encyclopaedic subject works, the rare, the valuable, the single copy works in subject areas, a representative copy of the standard works, etc. While the quick reference works are frequently sited near the entrance and the librarian's desk, the other reference stock is usually shelved in the study areas of the library though some libraries integrate it with the lending stock, identifying it with, for instance, an R on the spine. A reference only school library, apart from recreational fiction, will facilitate project work and research at the various levels of the student body in that all the stock is always available, but is disadvantageous in limiting such work to school time only and ignoring the subject interests of students who would extend those interests out of school.

INFORMATION

The information service is less well organized in schools and practically non-existent in schools without a school librarian full time. The selective dissemination of information (SDI) common to specialist libraries and many higher education institutions, even where directed only to the staff, is not found in many schools, and the information requirements differing from reference needs as indicated earlier, are largely inadequately met, if at all. Sources of information available through outside contacts, such as the old boy network, other information services and well publicized organizations, are rarely contacted on student request or to meet student information needs, though occasional use is made for the staff's information.

In many British and American schools the most basic tool for obtaining information, the telephone, is lacking in the library, to say nothing of Telex. Questioners are often recommended to ask at the public library or are told to wait a few days until the librarian has a few more enquiries which she can deal with at one time on the school secretary's telephone, or simply given a 'don't know' or 'information unobtainable' answer.

Much of teenage involvement and interest is fleeting and urgent as in younger children, but may develop more depth and longevity if sustained by information to feed the interest. Many of the assignments have a short time limit for delivery and the speed with which information is obtained for the project can make or mar the content and quality of the finished piece of work. Even with instruction few students have the time, the ability or the knowledge of information sources to plumb the depths adequately. It is interesting to note that one of the first visible differences that a professional librarian makes in a school library previously run by a dedicated teacher unskilled in professional librarianship though experienced in library techniques, is the development of an information service, and one of the best public relations ideas and practices for the average teenage library user is the successful acquisition of a piece of information, perhaps hesitantly and doubtfully asked for and speedily and accurately obtained for him by the librarian. Thereafter confidence grows and the student is less hesitant and more interested in the informational role of the library.

However, information should also be obtainable in pre-digested form via abstracts, annotated lists, bibliographies and published digests although there are at least two schools of thought on this. One body of opinion holds the view that part of the student's education is to develop his abilities to find out for himself starting from zero; another body of opinion believes that life, time and school are all too short to go the long way round if there are valid short cuts available, and that how the student assesses and uses the information and knowledge he has is more important than in what form he obtained it. Both viewpoints are exemplified in the true story of the school class in the library, looking for information on deer. One boy, turning to the correct volume of an encyclopaedia, was admonished by the teacher for using an encyclopaedia on the grounds that it was too easy to find the information.

A good example of a pre-digested information or guiding to information for the student can be seen in the following resources guide produced by the full-time librarian at a fourteen to eighteen upper school. This shows the student examples of the range of ideas and materials, and while not confining him only to those listed, enables him to save time by directing him to specific Dewey numbers and authors.

TABLE 9   *John Smeaton High School*

LEISURE

A Resources Guide

Introduction   Key: RC = Resources Centre

The general number for Leisure is 301.5. Those books could be a useful way of approaching the topic.

Locke, A. *Thinking about Leisure*	301.5
Roberts, K. *Leisure*	301.5
Thomson, I. *Leisure*	301.5
Woolner, A. H. *Work and Leisure*	550

1. *Personal Leisure and Use of Time*

Here are some words to look up for material on personal leisure. If you use the catalogue, you will find books, tapes, etc. on the subjects. If you want a less detailed picture, look up some of the words in the encyclopaedias.

(a) *Athletic pursuits* e.g.

Athletics	796.4
Trampolining	796.47
Rugby	796.333
Volleyball	796.325
Netball	796.32
Cricket	796.358
Football	796.33
Games	790
Cycling	629.2275
Golf	796.352
Gymnastics	796.4
Hockey	796.355
Swimming	797.2
Nature study	574
Rambling	796.51

(b) *Handicrafts* e.g.

Metalwork	669
Origami	7455.54
Cooking	641.5
Hobbies	790.2
Sculpture	730
Ceramics	530.4
Toys	745
Chess	794.1
Pottery	738
Coin collecting	737.4
Embroidery	746
Gardens	635
Jewellery	391.7
Music	780
Flower arranging	745.92
Photography	770

(c) *Activities outside the Home* e.g.

Aggression and	573
Violence	301.153
Brass rubbing	754.45
Pets	636
Astronomy	520
Camping	796.54
Canoeing	797.122
Cinema	791.43
Dance	792.8

Festivals	791.6
Folk songs	784.4
Jazz	785.42
Pop music	784.3
Music	780
Charities	361.02

Some materials you may use in this section:

BBC 'Inquiry' Programme. *Man – the aggressive animal*	301.153 Tape RC
Knight, Maxwell. *The Young Field Naturalists Guide*	
Gettings, Paul. *You are an Artist*	700
Ashton, E. T. *People and Leisure*	301.5
Jones, E. *Work and Leisure*	301.5
BBC. *How to Visit a Picture Gallery*	708 Filmstrip & Notes RC
Davies, J. *Taking up Cruising*	797.1
Burgess, C. V. *Discovering the Theatre*	792
Bystrom, E. *Printing on Fabric*	746.6
Carnick, P. *Motorcycle Racing*	629.2275
Bagg, C. *Ideas for Clubs and Societies*	371.8
Brummond & MacKay. *Entertainment*	790
John Smeaton School. *Mining Folk Songs*	784.7 Tapes & Notes RC
Gammonds & Clayton. *A Guide to Popular Music*	785.4
Frasor, P. *Punch & Judy*	791.53
Williams, G. *Instructions to Young Collectors*	790.02
Houston, P. *The Contemporary Cinema*	791.43
BBC 'Inquiry'. *Pop & Life*	784.3 Tape RC
Cave & O'Malley. *Living with the Mass Media*	301.54
Myers, R. H. *Music, Song & Dance*	780
Gammond, P. *The Meaning and Magic of Music*	780
Mabey, R. *Behind the Scene*	784.3
John Smeaton School. *Cinema*	791.43 Folder RC

2. *Local Leisure Patterns and Activities*
You could look up names of the various localities, e.g. Yorkshire, Lincolnshire in the 942.7 shelves also.

Towns and Town Life	711.4

Some useful material would be:

Graven, A. B. *Victorian & Edwardian Yorkshire* (also historically useful)	942.74

Yorkshire Naturalists Union. *The Naturalists' Yorkshire*	942.74
Chander, C. *Everyman's Book of Ancient Customs*	394
Hoskins, W. G. *Provincial England*	711.4
Healey, S. *Town Life*	711.4
Moss, P. *Town Life Through the Ages*	711.4
Hartley & Ingilby. *Life & Tradition in the Yorkshire Dales*	942.74
Emmett, I. *Youth & Leisure in an Urban Sprawl*	301.4

3. *Resorts and Population Movements*
Words to look up:

Countryside	631.27
Environment	574.5
Festivals	791.6
Holidays	391.426
Sea	

Helpful materials:

John Smeaton School. *Holidays*	394.26 Folder RC
BBC 'Inquiry'. *Holiday Making*	394.26 Tape RC

Also local studies of resource areas:

'Wish you were here' 4. *Beside the Seaside*	394.26 RC
'Wish you were here' 7. *On the Continent*	394.26 RC
White, R. J. *Life in Regency England*	942.18
Williams, E. N. *Life in Georgian England*	942.17
Quennell, M. *Everyday Life in Roman and Anglo-Saxon Times*	942.01
Pictorial Charts. *The Development of Crafts*	745.5 Charts & Notes RC

4. *Leisure in History*
For leisure of certain eras, look for the words of the era, e.g. Elizabethans, Victorians, Romans. Some books you might use are:

Rowell, G. *The Victorian Theatre*	792
Cootes and Snellgrove. *The Ancient World*	930
Workman, B. K. *They Saw it Happen in Classical Times*	930
Tull, G. K. *Early Civilization*	
BBC 'History in Evidence' Series	942 Tapes RC
Page, R. I. *Life in Anglo-Saxon England*	942.01
Danes, J. D. G. *English Life Part I*. People of the Past Series	942.01

1. The Library, John Smeaton School, Leeds.

2. Children and Staff in the Career's Library, Fitton High School, Bristol.

Burrell, R. E. C. *How the Romans Lived*   930
Briggs, Asa. *Victorian People*   942.18
Cecil, R. *Life in Edwardian England*   942.19
Batsford, B. T. *Life in Elizabethan England*   942.15
194 Shakespeare's London   942.15 Filmstrip RC
197 Shakespeare's London   942.15 Record RC
Wilson, J. D. *Life in Shakespeare's England*   825
Ashley, H. *Life in Stuart England*   942.16

It is often propounded that in the after school years in library and information services there are aids and guides and personnel at hand to cut through the undergrowth of unnecessary material and to guide directly to appropriate sources and that only the academic, college or university research student will use all the informational finding skills expected of every thirteen to eighteen student in school in the absence of an information service.

FACILITIES

Apart from the aforementioned services there are facilities which the student may be able to use in the good school library. While every effort is made to enable students to use the book stock, obstacles are often placed in the way of easy access to non-book and non-print material, the latter particularly.

The library may well hold non-print stock but not the equipment to even scan the material or to view or hear properly. The well organized and equipped library facilitates access to the material through identification and location catalogues or indexes, access to the content of the material through the hardware, perhaps located in special carrels or wired booths, and access to out-of-library use by means of classroom or home loan with suitable safeguards for either. Some school librarians instruct students that the world of learning and knowledge is theirs for the taking while arranging facilities in such a way that the world is only in an open book, not in any other medium. Others believe that the content of the medium is more important than the form and their multi-media catalogues and integrated resource materials are designed to promote access to information regardless of its package.

As an increasing amount of student work results in an end product itself in multi-media form, in folders of material,

4

textual, illustrative, taped and filmed, access to similar media will not only provide knowledge of facts and encourage comparison but may also produce familiarity with the media which will enable the student the better to understand the requirements and the technicalities of the media, and to decide which medium is the most suitable for conveying his knowledge.

Other aids to student work provided by some school libraries are the photocopying and reprographic facilities, usually for a small charge, whereby students may photocopy within the limits of copyright anything copyable needed for assignments and projects. The American practice of typing assignments is most uncommon in Britain but there are schools in both countries where one or more 'silent' typewriters are available for student use in the library.

In Zindel's *The Pigman*,[82] John and Lorraine are in the library at Franklin High School, using the librarian's quiet typewriter to record the events which led up to the death of the pigman, although the librarian believes they are typing a book report for English homework. The library is nearly empty because it is seventh period study and only the unfortunate students who have to stay for eighth period are around. The kind generosity of this fictional librarian is no doubt based on something similar in Paul Zindel's experience but the use of a typewriter at the whim of the librarian is more common than the availability of such machines as an accepted part of library use.

Students might also 'wish to communicate their ideas in non-print formats . . .'[83] so that the availability of hardware and permission to use it must be linked with the availability of photographic and reprographic facilities for student use, the aural/visual privacy required being catered for in future school library design.

KITS

A service provided by some libraries in schools where methods of work are becoming more individualized, is that of collecting multi-media information into kits or packs, sometimes after consultation with subject teachers, so that the student can ask for or select from the open access kits the pre-selected body of information on a particular area. These kits are not to be confused with those sometimes created by the teaching staff in multiple copies, where worksheets and duplicated materials are housed in, for example, clear plastic folders and each pupil in a whole class works independently of his fellow students but on the identical material. Library packs are usually created from duplicated copies and photocopies so that though the copies may be confined to that subject pack the originals are still available for use in other subject fields for individual loan.

All these facilities are particularly useful below sixteen in the years before the rigid requirements of examination boards restrict the pupil's field of interest, when the library should be the means of opening up new areas of knowledge by a variety of means to enable the student to explore the range of materials, and after sixteen, to enable staff and students to widen the approaches to the possibly rigid syllabus and to encourage independent learning in preparation for college and university. The extensive and correct use of all these requires also some instruction in their use and application.

LIBRARY INSTRUCTION

A library facility frequently lacking is the library classroom or tutorial area in which class or individual library instruction can take place without disturbing the other library users. Neither American nor British schools have adequate space at present to consider such a facility as in any way a priority when normal classroom space is at a premium, so that where library instruction does take place it is usually in the library itself. It has already been emphasized that when the library is used as a classroom for non-library teaching, the role and function of the library are seriously endangered and this can happen also where library periods throughout the day affect the casual usage, the privacy and the resource based learning students.

The purpose of library classes as practised at present cover one or all of the following:

1. To create an awareness of the range of materials available.
2. To inform the student of services available internally and externally.
3. To familiarize the student with the physical layout of the library, and arrangement of stock.
4. To indicate those facilities which help him to get at the

knowledge stored in whatever form, through catalogues, indexes, bibliographies and hardware.

5. To suggest ways of quickly achieving information from the media by using the contents list, the index, etc. in the book.
6. In co-operation with the subject staff to draw attention to particular areas of the library and the stock pertinent to a subject field.

The library period takes many forms. Most students dislike library instruction and find it boring or difficult to understand, particularly the classification and cataloguing aspects unless it has been given at primary school when it is more digestible because presented in simple form at the acquisitive age. The role of the library is undermined by the frequent practice of timetabling library classes in English periods, again, reinforcing both teachers' and students' narrow views of the library's function and confirming the generally held opinion that the library is an adjunct of the English department.

The use of the library for silent reading is a useful activity if sufficient leeway is given to allow for the variations in interest and activity in a class of students. The writer has been present in many schools during library periods in which fourteen- and fifteen-year-old pupils were marched into the library by the teacher, given two minutes to choose any book from the shelves, ordered to sit down with whatever was in the hand at the expiry of the two minutes and told to sit and read in silence until five minutes before the end of the period when the book was to be returned to the shelf or to be taken to the counter for loan recording. The lucky and the prepared students were quite content and were soon engrossed but the majority turned over the pages in desultory manner for the period or sat with glazed eyes and book open at page one for the whole time, leaving the library empty-handed.

In other schools students were able to spend the whole period coming and going between shelf and table, browsing at will amongst books and periodicals and making a much more considered choice of book borrowing, very few leaving the library without fiction or non-fiction for school or home use. Few adults, with the added years of knowledge, experience, and mature taste, could choose a book in two minutes flat and expect to read it to order, but many students are regimented and restricted in this way at a time when interest is precarious and taste just developing.

To surmount the problem of instruction at secondary age when it is frequently viewed as yet another boring class, some librarians attempt to instruct by using library games and for younger teenagers this is often acceptable.

Others use audio-visual means, tape slide presentations relating to the library or how to use an encyclopaedia or a catalogue, with the intention that these presentations can be used at any time by any student or group of students apart from the time-tabled class instruction, films both home made and bought or hired, tapes made by students under librarian supervision and videotape instruction, all of these usable either in the library or in the classroom, by student, teacher or librarian. These have the added advantage of being acceptable to teenagers who are attracted to the movement and the medium.

Too many librarians, for reasons of time and space, offer only an introductory session in the first year at secondary school which is little more than a guided tour of the library though some misguidedly attempt to compress into a short talk or lecture what it has taken them as librarians years of education and experience to learn. Thereafter it is expected that teachers and students will ask for help but many teachers are themselves not library-minded and only the keen library users will make the effort or overcome their shyness to ask.

The most effective library instruction is that which is carried out as an integral part of the teaching programme in each subject field, where it is related to the actual subject as it is being taught, stemming from the practical need for knowledge rather than separated into a theoretical exercise in a separately timetabled library period. But it requires the wholehearted involvement of the teachers who inspire the classroom motivation by choice of topic or project, who, with the librarian in the library or classroom will encourage students to volunteer information on which aspects they have chosen and why, and elicit the nature of the needed information. Having discovered what the students need to find out, the librarian can indicate the range of tools for extracting it, either previously collected together for the purpose or left *in situ* but pinpointed verbally and with a duplicated sheet of locations, etc. The experience of using these tools is the vital part of the learning, epitomized in the old Chinese proverb, 'I hear and I forget, I see and I remember, I do and I understand.'

The actual usage of the material for planned and discussed information-finding, needed for subject projects is difficult in the forty-five-minute period obtaining in many secondary schools, but where school heads have recognized the usefulness of integrated, resource based studies, the timetable has been adapted to cater for block timetabling to enable longer periods to be spent in library use. This is valid educationally in that a change of position, location or activity is all that is needed to sustain interest and learning over periods longer than the normal forty-five minutes. The classroom based teaching, followed by discussion on information needs, followed by finding the information provides a variety of methods of teaching and learning which, together, are likely to produce more knowledge, in a more interesting way and with long-term effect on the use of resources. In the follow up to these methods the librarian may display all the media itself and comment, with the help of students, on the usefulness or otherwise of the items from the point of view of content, both textual and illustrative, indexes, accessibility and other factors.

The educational validity of this approach is summed up by Martin Rossoff, who in an article described it as aim, motivation, presentation, development, drill and summary, the approach used in most teaching,[84] and in his book, *The School Library and Educational Change*[85] suggests that the library lesson for class projects is demonstration and dialogue.

Enabling every class to participate in this way raises problems of librarians' time and library space and these are all too often solved by limiting access for the more able classes and leaving the way clear for the less able. While this is probably reluctantly decided upon, it must be clear that some of the schools who impose this answer to the problem do so on the grounds that the more able are also at present more tied to examination texts and in theory have less need of the library; others justify their decision by suggesting that the able students are more likely to be able also in using books and libraries in their own time. Whatever the grain of truth in these reasons there is strong evidence that the less able pupil will benefit from library classes.

Indeed the fourteen- and fifteen-year-old students who play

hooky from school are often to be seen in the local public library, sometimes passing the time in newspaper and magazine reading, sometimes engrossed in book reading, usually non-fiction. There is something to be said for allowing the less able and the truant a considerable amount of latitude in the day's timetable to legalize the kind of browsing and undirected learning that accrues from his illegal visits to the public library, and much to be said in favour of a library class which encourages him to channel his interests and subject requirements in a more purposeful way, the retarded reader being particularly helped by guidance in the non-print aspects.

In the ideal situation the secondary school student will have received at primary school instruction in the parts of a book, the basic services of a library and the layman's use of the catalogue, enabling the secondary school librarian and teacher to concentrate on visits to the library which have been 'planned by the teacher, expected by the librarian and understood by the student'.[86] The time needed for this level of instruction and guidance is unfortunately spent largely on the technical and clerical staff and some of it is in fact done by pupil helpers.

PUPIL LIBRARIANS

Many schools mobilize students into a work force on a volunteer or rota basis to cope with the processing, shelving and issuing of stock and with controlling. This could be viewed as a means of denying the librarian the proper staffing establishment necessary for efficient service, a form of labour which allows the authorities to get, at no expense, more assistance in the library. Alternatively it could be viewed as a means of encouraging responsibility on the lines of the prefect system so that the library monitors or student librarians become the elite and the powerful at the same time exercising self control and qualities of leadership and fulfilling a useful function. A third possible aspect is that of participation, that the presence, on a voluntary or a decreed basis, of students willing and able to help in the promotion of reading and library use, is a form of co-operation which ought to create the right links between teaching and learning and between staff and student.

Most student volunteers for library work are themselves keen readers who are interested and enthusiastic about their library duties. They derive both skill and knowledge from many of the routines and even the mundane aspects of cutting up newspapers and mounting illustrations are found to be rewarding. But the most useful aspect of student helpers' participation lies in the selection of stock. The necessity for asking students what their needs and preferences are has already been mentioned. The next step is to involve the student in selecting to fulfil those needs.

Occasionally a library committee exists where students and staff are represented, both categories being expected to read reviews, to suggest titles, to comment on others' suggestions. There are schools where students are encouraged to suggest titles and where library lists of new acquisitions are displayed after informing the original requesting students that the books are now in stock. Only a few schools involve the students on a less systematic basis but with a greater degree of personal involvement. In these the latest works are obtained on approval and individual students are asked by the librarian to take whatever catches their attention and to read and comment on the suitability for inclusion in school library stock. One such school in America[87] enlisted the aid of a pupil who read and evaluated at random a selection of books coming on approval from publishers. When this proved to be useful to librarian and pupil the scheme was extended to other boys and girls in the seventh and eighth grades who take four books at a time and after reading, return them with a brief comment on each. The reliability of the evaluation has proved to be acceptable, having been checked against published reviews of the works and against other student comment.

In some instances there were differences of opinion over books recommended by teachers and other adults but heartily disliked by the student evaluators. Only if the student recommended the books were they bought for the library. This system affected only a part of the total stock selection and was operated by keen readers rather than a range of students covering each ability level, nevertheless it was noticed that apart from the assistance it afforded the librarian in getting through the reading of a large number of books during the selection stage, the reading of the participating students was strengthened; their motivation increased partly as a result of the prestige attached to this kind of student help; the link between staff and student in communication was vastly improved and the students' sense of responsibility was deepened as they realized that their selection report meant their decision on the inclusion of a book in their school library.

Some incorporate the previewing of books into the English class where students write a report or review as part of the English studies but this again allies the library openly to the English department and makes a subject out of what should be a co-operative venture between librarian and student. A wide range of students can be involved to cover all levels and subject fields, thus dispersing comfortably amongst many what might be a burden if concentrated on a regular few. It is usually found that the students who choose to or agree to undertake this selection responsibility, do the job with speed and enthusiasm and with commendable awareness of the criteria required, qualities expected of any book selector.

This form of pupil aid is obviously more valuable in indirectly encouraging reading and producing book knowledge than the more usual negative form which requires senior students to be on duty at stated times in order to control possible mis-use of the library; neither form has any difficulty in finding volunteers.

It is obvious from current practice in British and American school libraries that insufficient use is made of the library, the neglect largely stemming from teachers' and students' ignorance of the purpose and range of the library. Most are unaware that there is more than one book or one medium of information in a subject field, that books can be used in differing ways for differing purposes and that what is not in the school library can usually be obtained elsewhere. Most teachers do not adequately liaise with the librarian in preparation for both short-term and long-term projects and most students, because use of the library has been doled out in measured spoonsful like medicine, have a negative attitude to libraries. When access to books and information is made difficult students will stick to their textbooks or glean information from unreliable sources leading to low marks in grading homework and examinations and smothering the development of wide reading. An American work, *Better Libraries Make Better Schools*,[88] epitomizes in its title one half of the effect of libraries, the other half being better library use makes long-term readers.

Noting a difference in requirements for main school students and those for senior students some schools create a library for each, raising problems of duplication of those materials which are common to both and a problem of restricting the bright main pupil who might otherwise have benefited from the more advanced stock intended for the senior pupils and similarly curtailing the availability of less advanced stock intended for the less academic senior pupil. However, sixth-form libraries are increasingly popular in British schools and their requirements are similar to those in other establishments attempting to educate the older teenage student, in that there is usually a common element which makes for common reading needs and common use of the library, providing clearer terms of reference for the librarian.

SIXTH-FORM COLLEGES, SIXTH-FORM LIBRARIES, SENIOR HIGH SCHOOLS, ETC.

The age level of sixteen to nineteen obtaining in sixth-form colleges or senior high schools implies a fairly common level of maturity in that students have chosen to stay on at school and have achieved a common standard of education. In most cases such students have a common aim, that of college or university entrance. The lower age range in Britain may be re-taking CSE or 'O' level examinations while embarking on the 'A' level course, and the older age range may be pursuing scholarship work for university entrance, so that the range of stock in the library must cater for the sixteen-year-old average student at a broad level of knowledge to the nineteen-year-old bright student with a specialist depth knowledge.

As in the schools with sixth-form centres and sixth-form libraries, these types of student require a first-class library of texts, critical works, reference works, detailed books, up-to-date non-book materials, specialist periodicals and a wide range of audio-visual materials.

A detailed analysis of libraries in the sixth-form colleges of an English county in 1972 revealed a sad state of affairs in both stock and usage, the latter an obvious comment on the former. In one college of 600 students these deficiencies were found:

1. The fiction stock of 960 volumes was assessed as needing 95% replacement or rebinding. The stock included five complete

sets of Dickens's works and two complete sets of the Waverley novels.

2. The 800 literature section of 2,000 volumes needed one-third replacement or rebinding and about 300 should not have been in the currently used shelves but needed relegation to the stack.
3. In the social sciences section about one-sixth was unusable and there was a great deal of omission.
4. In the pure sciences 90% of the stock was below sixth-form standards.
5. In the 600s technology section there were 200 volumes of which only 62 were suitable and in good condition.

In the other sixth-form colleges in the county all the libraries maintained non-fiction stock for reference use only and all had inadequate reference books. One college listed as its only encyclopaedia the 1956 *Oxford Junior Encyclopaedia*.

In mitigation it must be said that none of the colleges had a professional librarian; in each case a teacher had responsibility for the library, in most cases an interested teacher but with insufficient time or knowledge. Insufficient money was also a factor, the book fund being £400 of which £300 was for books, £30 for periodicals and £70 for binding. The intention behind the survey was to assess the situation so that quantities of books could be determined in order to supply them from the public library stock, integrating college and public library stocks in the county, a policy which pertains to several public library systems in Britain and which is discussed in the section on public library service to teenagers.

COLLEGES OF FURTHER EDUCATION

The student body at colleges of further education in Britain and similar establishments in America is composed of people aged sixteen-plus and is made up of:

1. Teenagers attending full-time courses.
2. Teenagers and mature students training by part-time day or evening classes.
3. Teenagers in unskilled work or apprenticeship attending day-release classes from industry and commerce.
4. Teenagers and adults pursuing recreational courses.

The courses themselves vary from General Certificate of Education subjects for students, some of whom failed them at school and who prefer to go on to college rather than re-sit at school, some of whom left school before the leaving examinations and, recognizing their lack, return to full-time education courses or take the certificate subjects at evening classes after work, and those who preferred to do an 'A' level course in college atmosphere rather than at school.

The vocational courses such as those for catering, nursery nursing, secretarial work and hairdressing are at a mostly practical level unlike the advanced colleges which may offer a degree. Other courses involving business studies, science diplomas and certificates attract the students who have already achieved school leaving certificate standards as a prerequisite for entrance to the courses. Many of the courses are of one-year duration leaving little time for extensive study or coverage of a subject.

The day-release classes are composed of teenage workers most of whom left school at the earliest opportunity, many of whom are deficient in basic reading and writing skills and some of whom would rather not be at college even one day a week.

The leisure and interest classes mainly in the evening attract teenager and adult alike. It is obvious from these examples that the range of abilities, level of knowledge and objectives of courses is very wide and that the two major items common to all students in colleges of further education are that they are all over sixteen and almost all are there because they have chosen to be. Another item which is commonly found is the retention of textbook teaching for nationally awarded certificates of competence in the theoretical and practical vocational fields.

All these aspects affect the necessity for reading and the use of the library. It has been estimated that at least 30% of colleges of further education students are non-readers in the sense that they read nothing outside their formal studies and even then craft apprentices are likely to read only in their technical journals.[89] So much remedial work is required for sub-literates that one teacher has recommended that the steps in remedial English are:

1. At first dissociate the idea of reading from the idea of books.
2. Stress the more practical uses of reading in connection with the student's own practical interests.
3. Start by exciting interest with ads, TV announcements, racing news, football results, signs, tickets, etc.[90]

The relevance of the periodical and interest stock is demonstrated here as is the necessity for a selection of subject material covering the whole reading ability range. In fact the librarian who commented on the non-readers found that he had to compile readability lists on, for instance, aeronautics for the day-release students from the local aeronautics factory, listing material in encyclopaedias and children's books as well as the more technical and specialist material.

The effect of practical and textbook courses is slowly diminishing as the project methods infiltrate into further education and as liberal studies programmes attempt to widen the student's areas of knowledge.

The library's difficulties centre round the enormous range of subjects and levels required to cater for the needs of several thousands of day and evening students, many of the teenagers being functionally literate though reluctant to use those skills and most of whom view their time at college as providing more freedom than school and as a means to a vocational qualification or expertise which will enable them to get into the working society as quickly as possible.

However, the imaginative tutor librarian finds that there are many areas of the loan, reference and information services which attract these teenagers into continued use for general or technical reading and just a few into recreational reading. The writer, faced with a day-release class of seventeen- and eighteen-year-old motor mechanic apprentices, booked for a library period by the liberal studies tutor largely because he could not cope with their studied disinterest in liberal studies and their exuberant and loud rejection of anything unconnected with either girls or cars, won the class over by starting the session with items from the *Guinness Book of Records*, picking out those connected with cars and motor bikes and speed records, beginning with the world's most expensive car with its mink-covered floorboards and sonic steering. Immediately arguments and betting took place on other records in the motor world and some of the technical aspects were disbelieved until shelf searching at 629 confirmed them. This led to an interest in borrowing some of the books on cars and while milling round the relevant shelves, the students on the fringe of the crowd discovered the 610 section at which were shelved books on their other interest – sex. It was interesting to note that though these boys happily took their chosen motor books through the proper loan channels, *What Every Girl Ought to Know About Sex* was illegally removed by them (though it was returned each time equally secretly to its place on the shelf). The students' apparent embarrassment at revealing to a female librarian or to their mates, their desire to read such a book, involved the circumvention of the library's charging system and though this was known to the librarian it was discreetly ignored in the interests of encouraging the young men to read what obviously interested them. Duplicate copies were obtained and thereafter a path was beaten from the door to the shelves at the 600s, one of the several aspects of library promotion where it may be better to bend the rules to promote reading, under close but discreet surveillance, than to enforce the rules and lose the readers.

Another side-effect of using the *Guinness Book of Records* with these students, and more expected than that resulting from the close shelf proximity of 614 to 629, was the moving on from that book of reference to other works of reference on the quick reference shelves. The students had apparently never come across *Who's Who* or the *Dictionary of Slang* when they were at school and derived an immense amount of pleasure and information from both, reading snippets out to each other and guffawing loudly over the hobbies of the eminent and over the juicier slang words.

Such an introduction to the library led on to co-operative sessions of guidance and instruction for students who were totally anti-library previously. Similar results were obtained with the teenage girls on the secretarial courses, where the initial approach to library instruction was through the *Guinness Book of Records'* fattest woman in the world's measurements, leading to appearance, grooming and fashion.

The information side of the college library's function requires a quantity of outside contacts with trade and industry, with local national information centres and with specialist and public libraries, in order to cater for the needs of staff and students.

As with school students some of the information requested is not necessarily linked to subject studies though some have an indirect origin. Three typical queries were, on questioning the enquirers, unconnected with subject studies, but in the interests of building up confidence in the library and the librarian, required answers: What does a Lakeland terrier look like? What is the basic ingredient of lipstick? I belong to an amateur pop group, who should I contact to get a disc made? All these questions were asked by students who did not normally use the college library and the last question was asked by a sixteen-year-old student who had been turned out of his class for misbehaviour. All three students were highly delighted with the answers, none of which were within the library's scope normally and two of which had to be obtained from external sources.

It could be suggested that the library of a college of further education is the last hope for attracting the semi-literate teenager in full-time education and the working teenager in part-time education before they slide into non-use of books and libraries in adult life, and that the librarian's responsibility is therefore greater to devise ways and means of encouraging interest and use of the college library and to provide a much closer link with the public library for post-college use.

Some library authorities in Britain have developed integrated services and stocks for colleges in their areas thus making available larger quantities of material and rationalizing subject stock in a given geographical area. Such links must be utilized to encourage library use after college.

It has been suggested that teenagers in educational establishments after the school leaving age are there by choice but some teenagers find themselves in institutions of another kind certainly not of their choosing, either by reason of behaviour or because of some physical or mental handicap.

PENAL AND DETENTION INSTITUTIONS

Here the library has a remedial function in that statistically, many of the law breakers are educationally backward and semi-literate. The educational role of the library is thus to the fore.

As in other residential institutions, the leisure function of the

library is important but particularly so in a Borstal or correctional school where other amenities for free use of leisure are
limited. Well to the fore in the role of the library is the element
of rehabilitation where the library must supplement and complement not only the normal educational programme but aid
the social adjustment of the individual who is in the care of the
institution. However these roles are only marginally touched on
in the majority of libraries in such establishments, a situation
springing from a number of factors. The reading level of many
inmates or trainees is low for the sociological and educational
reasons stated in the first chapter, thus providing the problem
of selecting appropriate material for the age level, both fiction
and non-fiction. The practices in British and American correctional institutions differ somewhat in the amount of general
education and the amount of trade training slotted into the
day's timetable. In America, most of the correctional schools,
training schools and penitentiary education programmes are
geared to remedying the failure of previous attempts at general
education, with a certain amount of training in a useful trade
added to the curriculum.

In British Borstals and local authority schools for young
people in custodial care, the greater part of the day is spent in
work such as building, printing, farming or catering with short
spells of classroom work in English, science and mathematics
and evening sessions of social studies, with a very short leisure
time for any chosen activity. The difference this makes to
reading and library use cannot be underestimated as Daniel
Fader realized and recorded in his book *Hooked on Books*,[91] his
account of the saturation of a training school with paperbacks.
While his experiment was successful in producing readers from
both retarded and reluctant disadvantaged youthful readers
and was copied by a number of similar institutions in the States,
not all such schools achieve or have attempted to achieve those
results. Nevertheless it is true to say that in general, libraries in
such American institutions are much more advanced in policy
and practice than their British counterparts. Indeed while
none in Britain has a full-time qualified librarian, many in
American have, and the Association of Hospital and Institutional Libraries produced its Objectives and Standards for
Libraries in Correctional Institutions, emphasizing the difference in the stage of progress reached in the two countries.

It recommends nine areas of service which should be operating in the library:

1. Reading guidance.
2. Information and reference.
3. Inter-library loans.
4. Booklists and bibliographic information.
5. Recreational reading.
6. Educational reading.
7. Discussion groups.
8. Listening groups.
9. Exhibits and publicity.

These areas are covered in any good library service but are particularly noted as needing to be stated for the library services in penal institutions, in which emphasis on reading guidance to the individual is necessary to fulfil the remedial, the educational and the rehabilitative roles in the library.

Again the implementation of these recommendations is extremely rare in Britain and certainly not widespread in the States. The lack of a full-time librarian implies the presence of teacher or officer who 'looks after' the library either as a required part of his duties or out of the goodness of his heart in his spare time. In neither case is it possible to approach any of the recommended services as the technical aspects of librarianship demand all time allotted for library duties.

In many British institutions the Education Officer has nominal if not actual responsibility for the library and may delegate the day-to-day running of it to one of the teaching staff. Overcrowding in most detention establishments leads to the use of the library for non-library purposes as in schools, but the use may also be rigidly dependent upon its requirement for subjects or upon success in the remedial reading class. The shortage of free time allows the keen reader the opportunity of choosing books for recreational reading but little time to read them before lights out, and does nothing to encourage the less keen, the apathetic, the disinterested or the hostile.

While it is a rule that every detention establishment shall have a library and every offender shall be allowed to have library books and exchange them, little is done to encourage the inmates to benefit from this rule except in the few cases where the library is run as a branch library by the local authority

public library service. Most prisons and detention establishments in Britain have at least a loan service of books exchanged
regularly and a request service to cater for book needs that
cannot be supplied internally. Some 66% take advantage of
this co-operative service. In some instances the *per capita*
allocation from the Home Office is used by the public library
for stock for the institution, in other cases the public library
provides a service to the institution as part of the normal
service to ratepayers and educational establishments within its
boundaries, leaving the *per capita* allowance for internal
purchase of library requirements.

As the financial arrangements vary, so the standard of
service and type of service vary throughout the country. This
is so for libraries of all kinds but assumes great importance when
the young offender who has probably had a deprived environment all his life meets yet more deprivation in the establishment
which, though denying him freedom as a punishment, denies
him also the opportunity or the encouragement to widen his
knowledge and his imagination through free ranging amongst
a large selection of books and magazines. This restriction is
partly the result of the long held view that leisure reading is a
pleasure and therefore out of place in a punishment centre, a
view which is still evidenced in the Standing Orders for prisons
which states that library books are a privilege for which all
prisoners are eligible and then goes on to withdraw that
privilege should there be a serious abuse of it.

Part of the problem lies also in the attitude in institutions for
young offenders, rather than in prisons for adults, that because
of poor reading ability the library cannot be extensively used, a
view persisting largely through teachers who, as in ordinary
schools, fail to see the potential of the library. Where such
teachers are also in charge of the library it is not surprising that
the inmates cannot make use of the library, as the stock is likely
to be irrelevant to their needs in the lack of magazines, easy to
read teenage books, colourful pictorial non-fiction and audio-
visual materials.

The libraries with close links with the public library fare
somewhat better in that selection may be better geared to
needs, using the professional librarian's knowledge of suitable
stock and the greater resources of the back-up system, though
there may still be a deficiency born of the public librarian's

belated recognition of the importance and usefulness of periodical and non-book materials for semi-literate and reluctant reader teenagers.

In one north of England institution for 250 boys aged fifteen to eighteen the library, in 1973, housed two periodicals and approximately 1,000 books of which 300 were on loan from the public library. The rest were tattered, obsolete, unsuitable in content for age and ability ranges and demoralizing in terms of presenting a dull unattractive physical picture of the library. This library under the control of the Education Officer is administered by a part-time English tutor with clerical help from a sixteen-year-old inmate, trainee is the term used. This can be compared with a similar establishment in America where under the supervision of a full-time librarian the library, in 1970, stocked 6,300 titles, 125 periodicals, 100 filmstrips, 300 records, 100 slides and the audio-visual equipment, and distributed large numbers of paperbacks to each of the twelve cottage living units or houses in the institution.

Daniel Fader again points the way with his successful experimenting with paperbacks. By making 1,200 original selections of paperbacks he thought suitable for his young offenders (selected from *Paperbacks in Print*), 500 were read and 700 ignored by the boys, leaving him with a core collection of 500 works known to be readable in the teenagers' terms. These he bought in multiple copies and they have formed a basic collection for many such institutions and high schools. In addition he arranged with a generous daily paper for 100 copies of each day's newspaper to be donated so that saturation of acceptable and suitable reading matter was effected, availability being backed up by time and encouragement to read what was available.

Compared with libraries in many British institutions for detention this is highly enlightened. Far too many in Britain are used as extra classrooms and open for book reading or choosing for an hour or so in the evening. In one Borstal in Britain this situation existed but a trainee who did the clerical work was in the library all day carrying out these duties. As he already had a trade he was not required to do the trade training in which most of the boys were involved. Literate enough to laboriously copy out the title page information on to catalogue cards and to operate the charging system he also increased his literacy by the continual use of his reading ability both in his clerical duties and in the inevitable browsing he was able to do. He was familiar with the reading interests of the trainees who did borrow books while he was on duty three evenings a week and was able to recommend not from his own reading but from the comments of the trainees on the books they read. In his pre-Borstal days he had bought two or three paperbacks a week but had not thought of using a public library on the grounds that he did not think they would have the sort of book he would like, and from the descriptions he gave of the violence/sex/war/blood and thunder titles he mentioned he was undoubtedly right in his belief. However, during his time as 'librarian' he had perforce graduated to light thrillers and cowboy stories and to easy non-fiction.

Of 250 boys in that Borstal, 100 had borrowed a book within the previous two weeks, seventy more had looked through the colour supplements, the only things that interested them in the library, and several had asked for a book to be obtained for them, one such request being promptly turned down by the governor who, as in most such institutions, has the right to censor library books. The request was for a book on antiques; the requester was in Borstal for stealing antiques; the governor knew that the offender was trying to update his knowledge of antiques to keep in touch for his later activities.

Approved schools or community homes for 'delinquent' boys in Britain operate the kind of system whereby boys, who have got into trouble partly because they came from deprived backgrounds with no home or family controls, are provided with a house system boarding school environment, a shorter than average school day to accommodate trade training, a programme of re-socialization activities and an active policy of education at the individual's pace and for his needs, with individual attention.

One community home of ninety boys exemplifying this structure uses its open plan classroom/library block and integrated day studies to fulfil these provisions. The library is part of the open plan teaching area and houses approximately 1,000 books of which 700 are on loan from the local public library. The *per capita* book fund from the local education authority is totally inadequate hence the small number of permanent stock volumes owned by the school. A newspaper allowance from Home Office funds enables the library to take three daily papers and three periodicals, two of the latter related to the trades pursued by the school, *Motor* and *Farmers Weekly*. *Angling Times* reflects the fact that fishing is a nation-wide popular pursuit with boys of all ages and backgrounds and this periodical is eagerly read.

The library is open during school hours with no restrictions and no supervision, although the English master responsible for the library is at hand because of the open plan arrangements. As a boy needs a book for subject study or reading period he gets it for himself and he charges it by taking it to the English teacher. The only restriction on the use of the library is the fact that it is not open in the evenings as the teaching area is locked up. There are small collections of easy reading series and schemes in each classroom for the use of any boy, and a graded collection to which boys are directed for remedial reading practice, the latter involving perhaps 50% of the inmates.

Aged twelve to seventeen and ranging from IQ ESN or 50 to 70, to IQ 135 the boys require all the works listed below but this library contained only junior fiction normally found in a children's library, a poor selection of non-fiction and four different sets of good encyclopaedias. A handful of adult novels completed the stock. No easy reading books or colourful information books, no teenage novels and no paperbacks. This was perhaps the fault of the public library which does not itself stock paperbacks and which has no organized library service to schools. The loan collection is simply selected from a central stack and delivered to the school once a year.

Despite these disadvantages some of the boys read. What some of them had read before entering the institution and in some cases brought with them is described in the next chapter.

The reading needs of boys in detention institutions differ from those of girls in similar reformatories, partly because of the greater proportion of non-readers amongst boys and partly from the known differences in likes and dislikes for subject content between the sexes. But young offenders of both sexes should be able to find in the library:

1. Picture books, both fiction and information works.
2. Easy-to-read books for teenagers.

3. Teenage novels.
4. Adult novels.
5. Easy-to-read non-fiction in conceptual level.
6. Relevant to age and interest non-fiction.
7. Instructional works in the sense of how to play the guitar/
   football, how to do first aid or make-up, etc.
8. Discursive but simple works on sex, drugs, politics, social
   issues, etc.
9. Biographical works on current personalities and relevant
   people through the ages.
10. Magazines for teenagers.
11. Subject periodicals in relevant fields of knowledge and
    interest.
12. Audio-visual materials.
13. Quick reference works.

Where possible such stock should be in paperback to utilize
the known attractions of this format and to capitalize on the
known fact that many teenagers, thought to be poor readers,
do buy paperbacks and read them. The library should attempt
to start where the inmate is rather than where it is thought he
ought to be.

Treatment of offenders in penal and detention institutions
has been defined as – what we do for, what we do with and what
we do to the inmates.[92] The roles of the institution's library
incorporate all three areas of treatment.

PHYSICALLY HANDICAPPED

There are other teenagers who because of some handicap are at
a special school. For those unable to use the public library or to
attend any school, public library services arrange to take the
service to the housebound, the term usually used in Britain
and America, although some authorities devise their own
terms such as Pittsburgh's service to the 'shut-ins', or sometimes
make arrangements through the schools service of the public
library.

The majority of residential schools for the handicapped have
libraries although very few in Britain have a full-time librarian.
Many have loan services from the public library, particularly
those in county library areas, and enjoy the periodic visits of a
professional librarian responsible for schools in the district.

One boarding school for severely handicapped children aged five to eighteen catered for approximately seventy children of whom thirty were in their teens. Most were educationally retarded but by no means mentally backward, indeed many were highly intelligent and socially sophisticated perhaps as a result of meeting a great many people and receiving individual attention, and had similar interests to the physically able teenager. The educational retardation is caused by the physical handicap which requires continual hospitalization, treatment periods and therapy all of which severely reduce the amount of time possible for schooling to say nothing of the reduced concentration resulting from continuous pain and suffering. Most of the teenagers were incontinent, part of illnesses such as cerebral palsy, muscular dystrophy and spina bifida, and this alone causes disruption of both schooling and play. All these young people were classed as educable and all were mobile, either unaided, aided by sticks or able to propel wheel-chairs.

The library was dispersed into classroom collections so that books were immediately physically accessible though all could use each collection if desired. The books ranged from picture books for the youngest through a varied selection of attractive non-fiction for potential use with the small classes, to children's fiction for the older child, but there seemed to be something lacking. On talking to the few older teenagers (children with some of these handicaps die before reaching their late teens) the writer became aware that many of them had a paperback tucked into the wheelchair or lying on the table beside them. Paperbacks were not provided by the public library loan collection nor by the school and these had been obtained during the holidays or brought to them by visiting parents and friends or borrowed from some of the teachers.

Conversation revealed that the paperback format was more convenient to handle when handicaps made it difficult to hold anything heavy and was more portable when moving anywhere was difficult. But more importantly, the paperbacks they were reading were the popular titles of light fiction for adults and teenagers and both boys and girls were anxious for more. The resident teachers and the visiting librarian from the public library which supplied a loan collection regularly, were surprised at this information and both promised to supply more paperbacks at a more adult level than previously. These keen readers were all teenagers who were not born with their handicap and had therefore had normal schooling and achieved a high level of reading ability before being incapacitated by an illness such as muscular dystrophy or multiple sclerosis.

When few of the teenagers at such schools will live to be adults and when those who do will not reap the full benefits of adulthood, one of the library's services should be to provide the imaginative experience and the proxy experience and mental escapism from the physical shackles.

The Association of Hospital and Institution Libraries, of the American Library Association, produced a list of books for and about the handicapped, called *New Horizons*[93] which covered such handicaps as leukaemia in Carson McCuller's *Clock Without Hands*; mental retardation in Pearl Buck's *The Child Who Never Grew*, and Dale Roger's *Angel Unaware*; paraplegia in Terry McAdam's *Very Much Alive*; poliomyelitis in Sholem Asch's *East River* and June Opie's *Over My Dead Body*. The list was intended to be a reading list for those interested or concerned with an individual aspect of physical or mental handicap, a guideline to those serving the handicapped, a potential checklist for librarians who wished to include the subject matter in public or special libraries and an indication of the works potentially useful in bibliotherapy with those afflicted by the particular handicap.

No doubt all librarians who have connections with service to handicapped teenagers would benefit from perusal of the list or better still, reading a representative selection. This would do much to dispel the widespread habit of thinking of and speaking to handicapped teenagers either as if they were deaf and stupid or as if they were small children.

HOSPITAL SCHOOLS

For long stay hospitalized children up to school leaving age hospital schooling is provided in Britain by local education authorities. The teenage patients receive schooling relevant to their age and ability and a library supports the teaching, sometimes providing also for recreational reading interests. Additional to this stock, many hospitals have a central library, a trolley service round the wards perhaps organized by the

RWVS or the Friends of the Hospital or sometimes as part of the public library service of mostly recreational reading matter for short stay and long stay patients alike.

Many American hospitals for children and young people have library clubs with organized activities and have developed the audio-visual aspects of the library to cater for the audio-visual methods of teaching employed in the hospital teaching programme. Most British hospital schools have collections of books run at a distance by the local public library with voluntary assistance from teaching staff.

SCHOOLS FOR THE MENTALLY HANDICAPPED

Ranging from mentally subnormal to severely and grossly subnormal the teenagers thus handicapped range also in the degree of physical handicap accompanying the mental disability. Many with brain damage also have physical impairment.

The education and care required also varies, from day schools for those who can live at home and are educable and boarding schools for those who for various family reasons must have residential schooling, to hospital schools for those who cannot be looked after at home and need special care. In most of these schools the mental age rarely exceeds ten and the average mental age of the teenagers is around five. In such schools there is likely to be a handful who can read simple books after prolonged and individual instruction from a reading scheme but the majority will not achieve even the basic skill, but may be able to use pictures in books for recognition and verbal description.

Books in the conventional sense then are often unsuitable in content and form for the mentally handicapped teenager. Just as small children may throw their books and toys around so the mentally handicapped teenager with his greater size and strength is likely to treat books without consideration, and those with a physical handicap also may well compound the damage to books. Books with substantial text are no use, even for reading aloud to the pupils, as their concentration level is on average little more than five minutes and even then a visual stimulus is necessary. Books with few words and clear bright pictures are more useful but a number of objects on the page will distract all but the most advanced of such pupils; the others will glance at the page, stab at the only recognizable object in the picture and rush on to another page, without the eye-searching over the crowded picture common to normal children. The exception to this is in non-fiction picture books where a street scene or a country scene is often lingered over.

The simple reading schemes for young children are in common use in most special day and boarding schools and large brightly coloured simple picture books on informational subjects are of greater value than story books or story picture books. The appeal to the imagination and the emotions of story books for the normal child is usually lost to the mentally subnormal teenager, the only response being a passing interest in the rhythm of the words and the voice, rather than in the story. Only a few can manage to read and understand the conventional story written for the normal young child. More can manage the simple information picture books for the young, such as the Ladybird first books, but the majority need strong board books with a simple colour illustration and a single word on each page. Such books are rare.

Many schools and hospital units house their books in the individual classrooms with a small central library, in much the same way as infant schools, though the condition of the stock is likely to be poor. The size, shape and strength of books for young children are rarely able to withstand the small child's handling and do not withstand the teenagers' use. One of the desperately needed requirements of such books for the mentally handicapped teenager is a format and system of binding which disintegrates less quickly on usage. However many of these points can be exemplified in the Meanwood Park Hospital School for the Severely Subnormal, in Leeds. Children who cannot live at home and are not educable in day schools are hospitalized and receive schooling and special care, formerly under the health authorities now under the education authorities.

Ranging in age from five to seventeen and in disability from severely subnormal to grossly handicapped, the children spend the day in classes of about ten, with a large amount of stimulation, physical, mental and visual. The multiple handicaps of some of the children preclude movement so they are placed on airbeds, inflated plastic shapes, hammocks and swing beds which react to their slightest movement and which are continually set in motion by the staff. Rattles and tinkling mobiles and other audio-visual stimuli are placed so that each child has some form of mental and physical stimulus during the day.

The kinds of books required for the other children and teenage pupils were described by the teaching staff as non-available at present and they make do with the nearest approximations on the book market. Their specific requirements can be listed as:

1. Strength: rag books do stand up to the throwing, chewing, scrubbing, tearing habits but the pictures are not very clear. Board books come apart usually on the first handling, leaving a set of board pictures which crack when thrown about. The pictures can be scraped or licked off. Ordinary books do not stand a chance and comics, magazines and newspapers are totally unsuitable for all but the most advanced or the most docile.

   What is required is a plasticized rag book which would give strength and clarity of picture, or a greatly strengthened board book which would not leave its binding at first use, with plastic or polythene covering or treatment which would prevent scratching or licking off the contents.

2. Visual aid: many picture books for small children are brightly coloured and depict scenes and objects familiar to the children. However the hospitalized mentally handicapped teenager needs picture books with a single picture on each page, preferably of one object and that object to be associated with the only life the pupil knows, that of the hospital, so that instead of words like mother, postman, telephone or dog, the relevant objects and words would be for example bed, nurse, hand, swing. The pop-up books available on the commercial market are found to be useful if kept out of touching range, a strong cardboard pop-up would help here.

3. Tactile quality: one teacher suggested that books with different materials to touch would be of great value or with the paper or board raised or ridged to create a tactile surface. If this were allied to the picture and word so much

the better. A few book publishers and commercial firms in Britain and America have produced 'touch' books but not of the strength and simplicity required for mentally handicapped readers.

4. Content: apart from the single illustration to a page book with its mainly visual appeal there is a need for simple information books on the day-to-day encounters with life common to such children. Increasingly book publishers are creating information books for the young but relevance to the normal child is non-recognition to the institutionalized child. Humour as such is not part of the mental ability of most subnormal children where it concerns verbal humour but one sixteen-year-old boy said he liked the 'monster books' which his teacher reported later to mean the Dr Seuss books. This boy was one of the three who could read simple books at this school.

On the whole what reading skills there are, are directed to the business of getting through life as independently as possible so that the words needed in daily life with other people and to aid independent use of public facilities, are required in books. The teaching staff often produce them on flashcards and posters but the addition of colour and print and the book form is thought to be necessary. As Mr Robertshaw, the Meanwood Park Head Teacher commented, all teachers of the subnormal know what is needed but so far no commercial firm has philanthropically come forward with the answer to these needs, and philanthropic it would probably have to be since the cost of producing the items would be many times more than for a normal picture book.

Libraries and literature for such teenagers must be looked at in a totally different way, the conventional library and the conventional book having little relevance or use in the context of the mentally handicapped. The printed word and the picture book cannot be viewed as escapist entertainment or enriching the imaginations but must be seen as a means of keeping the mind stimulated, enlarging the vocabulary and advancing the teenager's ability to recognize objects and words.

At seventeen mentally handicapped teenagers go to workshops or back home or to carefully chosen jobs or into an adult mental hospital, where, apart from in the latter, it is unlikely that the world of books will touch them and whatever reading skill was achieved may well lapse for lack of promotion and stimulation. The few however will continue with dedicated parents' support, and public and hospital libraries should make it their business to serve by advice through the schools service on which of the published books come nearest to the needs, by the provision of appropriate books through the hospital service, by continual pressure on publishers and education authorities and research bodies for the creation of a suitable format and content of book for the estimated 50,000 pupils in special education for the subnormal in Britain, of whom half come into the category of severely and grossly mentally handicapped young people.

SCHOOLS FOR THE VISUALLY HANDICAPPED

Many libraries for the use of the visually handicapped have developed collections of books on tape, cassette and record, in addition to the Braille stock and the series of large print books, produced largely as a public service rather than for commercial profit by a small number of firms and organizations in Britain and America, such as F. A. Thorpe (Publishing) Ltd who produce the Ulverscroft Large Print series for adults and young people, the National Library for the Blind's Austin series, the Jennison series in America and the Library of Congress Division for the Blind's books.

Students at special schools for the visually handicapped are familiar with the hardware for their reading experiences and have open to them all the stories now available on record and cassette for sighted people and the tapes of broadcasts, particularly schools broadcasts, for use instead of non-fiction subject books.

The National Library for the Blind provides a loan service to institutions and to individuals and some schools take advantage of this for specific items and for temporary additions to their permanent collections. The Royal National Institute for the Blind has a Students' Tape Library from which postal loans can be obtained, and, resulting from the Nuffield scheme, the British Talking Book Service for the Blind.

Obviously libraries in schools for the blind are different from those for sighted students in the proportions of non-book materials to printed matter. They are different also in the shortage of 'reading' matter suitable for teenagers. The teenage novel is not yet available on record or cassette and the talking book titles are predominantly adult as are the large print series, the dozen or so titles in the Ulverscroft series for ages eleven to fifteen catering mainly for the younger end of this range. It is recognized that some partially sighted young people are able to use normal print books by holding them much closer to the eyes than the normal distance. There is a degree of accommodation which the young eyes retain which decreases with age, so that the partially sighted teenager will have the two areas of book provision open to him where the older person must rely on large print alone. Nevertheless librarians need to be aware of the special stock and the special problems relating to this disability.

Alison Shaw's *Print for the Partial Sight*[94] describes her research into the medical/optical/technical problems and Landau and Nyren[95] produced a bibliography of large type books in print, commendably *in* large type, for use by both sighted and partially sighted.

Most public libraries now stock a selection of large print books and offer the normal record library services, but few offer tapes and cassettes for normal use and certainly not many loan to special schools through the schools service. Many librarians are not aware of national services nor offer advice on how to obtain the software and the different sources for obtaining hardware for the visually handicapped to enjoy a 'book'. It is fortunate that staff in schools for the handicapped are usually knowledgeable and can get the benefits from the organizations offering help but it is a matter for concern that the individual blind reader would not automatically get information or help from his local public library.

While at school the visually handicapped teenager is offered the most relevant material it is possible to find but there is only a small amount of printed matter put into Braille. Reading ability in Braille is as variable as in print so that a range of Braille books is as necessary to practise fluency as high interest low vocabulary books are to the sighted teenager struggling with print. Because of the shortage of material in Braille the teenager is deprived of newspapers, periodicals, comics and the teenage novels available to the sighted reader. Such deprivation is caused by the cost and time taken to convert print to Braille and the fact that the small quantities required make such conversion a commercially unprofitable business. The majority of schools for the blind and partially sighted buy everything that is produced for reading with such a handicap, but everything in this connection amounts to a pitifully small collection and much of that may not be geared to the reading ages. Many young people were born blind or with sight defects, some as a result of maternal illness, usually producing physical as well as visual handicaps; some were rendered blind by accident or disease in childhood or adolescence. In either case there will be the same variations in reading ability engendered by intelligence as in the sighted child, and in both cases there is likely to be a difference of two to three years' achievement caused by a slower rate of education, possibly by hospitalization in some cases, and by the time needed to learn Braille. It is estimated that a fast Braille reader will achieve a reading speed of about 160 words a minute but the average is around 100 which is a little less than a normal reading-aloud speed and about half a sighted reader's speed. However when comprehension of a given passage is compared the achievement is equal.

One of the problems of books for the visually handicapped teenager, especially for those who were previously sighted readers, is the availability of books of interest in simple Braille. The difficulty of learning Braille requires the same kind of simple readers as those used in sighted remedial classes. To facilitate this a number of such readers have been converted to Braille, for instance the Windrush, Onward and Forward series. The Inner Ring series is now available in Braille pamphlet form and all are published through the Royal National Institute for the Blind.

A British example of a residential school for visually handicapped teenagers is the Henshaw School at Harrogate, catering for sixty to eighty secondary school aged children from various parts of the country. Most of the students are less able in educational terms and many suffer from some physical disability in addition to their visual handicap. The library, looked after by one of the teaching staff is a visually attractive room with widely spaced double sided island stacks as well as wall shelving. It houses approximately 1,000 volumes, which because of the large size of Braille volumes take up most of the available stack space which would accommodate double the quantity of normal print books. Tables and chairs to seat a class, normally about ten to a class, are in the other half of the library, thus creating a necessary physical distance from the shelves to allow free unimpeded movement.

As instanced for all such schools, the stock is composed of all the Ulverscroft Large Print series titles for young people, all the Rylee Clear Print classics, some of the Harrap Large-Type series of the classics and most of the Ladybird books because of their fairly large and clear typeface and simple illustrations. The rest of the stock is in Braille fiction and non-fiction titles, both children's and adults' bought from the Royal National Institute for the Blind and the Scottish Braille Press in Edinburgh, books borrowed on a termly basis from the National Library for the Blind, Braille reference works such as the *Oxford English Dictionary* and the Bible, and a number of Braille music scores, published by the RNIB.

The periodicals subscribed to are:

> *Argosy*
> *Braille Sporting Record Weekly*
> *Trend*
> *Home Help*
> *Trefoil Trail*
> *Fleur de Lys*
> *Jack and Jill*
> *The Braille Library Bulletin.*

All of these are British except *Jack and Jill*, an American magazine produced in the Braille edition of Voluntary Services for the Blind Inc. in association with the *Saturday Evening Post*, and all are in Braille. Of these the two most popular were *Trend* which was read by all the girls and most of the boys, and the *Sporting Record Weekly* which many of the boys enjoyed.

The book stock was arranged by title and the teacher librarian had put a Braille strip on the spine of each volume to facilitate quick identification. Sample authors were Charteris, Douglas, Stewart, Ransome, Nesbit, Amis, Austen, Shute, McVicar, Huxley, Greene, Cronin, Power, Sigal. Much of the non-fiction was of recreational interest rather than for subject study, mainly because of the dearth of the latter in Braille.

3. Children using the Career's Library, Fitton High School, Bristol.

4. A corner for relaxing in the Teenage Library, Walsall.

5. Teenagers using a quiet corner in the Teenage Library, Walsall.

However science, agriculture, history, hobbies, sport, travel and biography were represented.

The charging procedure involved simply clipping the reader's name card to the catalogue card, a visual task done by the sighted teacher in charge of the library.

Much material housed in classrooms is freely available to staff and students, for instance the Inner Ring readers and some of the easy reading schemes for teenagers, in Braille editions but considered more classroom than library material. Similarly tapes of broadcasts are kept in the relevant subject teacher's room. Records are housed in the music teacher's room as is much of the Braille music but the discs cover other subjects as well as music and the BBC schools broadcast records are centralized in this collection.

On talking to a group of students, aged fifteen and sixteen, it was clear that all were keen on reading and spent some of their leisure time reading, many preferring to read in bed but often prevented from so doing by others in the shared bedrooms. All were aware of the importance of reading widely and all were actually conscious of their deprivation in the matter of pop magazines, girls' magazines, sports literature and light reading. Most of the books converted to Braille are those considered worthwhile or 'good' thus providing a continuously heavy diet unrelieved by the relaxing 'trash' most people need from time to time. These teenagers avidly read *Trend* and the girls particularly liked the horoscope, while the boys lapped up the pop information. Such interests and reading needs are part of the 'growing through' to adulthood and this example serves to emphasize the importance of a much wider range of reading matter for the visually handicapped. This school has an arrangement with some prisoners at a local prison whereby having taught them how to use a Braille machine a number of print items are converted into Braille for school use. This arrangement suffers from the potential gaps in service when the Braillists are liberated, although it has been found over a few years that it is not long before the Braille machines are working again – with the same operators!

The school does not work closely with audio materials such as talking books, cassettes and tape recordings for class and individual use, largely because of the nature of the students' physical disabilities and their educational ability. However

5

the half dozen or so other residential schools for the visually handicapped in Britain do maintain quantities of such material and the related hardware and much of the learning takes place semi-autonomously by these means.

It is clear that the small amount of reading matter available in Braille and large print further seriously handicaps the teenage reader with a visual handicap, and that much of the entertainment value of reading is denied the teenager who cannot cope with high quality literary books; much of the information value of reading is absent when there are so few non-fiction works available, and much of the grasshopper reading done by the sighted teenager in magazines, newspapers, broadsheets, paperbacks and books is impossible for the visually handicapped, not because of his handicap but because of the lack of such material in Braille.

The disadvantages and omissions apparent in library service to teenagers in educational establishments are:

1. The lack of full-time professional staff.
2. The shortage of clerical help.
3. Meagre book funds.
4. Unsuitable stock, further reducing the effectiveness of funds.
5. Unsympathetic teaching staff.
6. Cramped accommodation.

While the appointment or guidance of a qualified librarian would do much to dispel some of these disadvantages, little can be done to remedy the financial limitations and this situation has led to the setting up of community colleges, community schools or joint public library/school library arrangements which have the advantages of integrating the resource in terms of finance, space, staff, stock and service, providing an adult association which is more acceptable to the teenager, housing the school, the youth centre, adult education and community leisure activities on the site with one library catering for all. One such community centre, purpose built is the Abraham Moss Centre in Manchester, originally the Cheetham/Crumpsall Project, where the following are all on one site under one roof or linked at each floor level by corridors.

1. School for ages twelve to fifteen.

2. College of further education sixteen-plus.
3. Youth centre.
4. Arts and social block.
5. Sports centre.
6. Old people's centre.
7. Short stay residential block for young people.
8. Shopping centre.
9. Library and resource centre for the school, college and community use but staffed and serviced by Manchester public library system.

Such a composite arrangement allows a closer contact between school, home, further education, evening classes and leisure activities, educational and recreational opportunities for people of all ages, the creation of a centralized greater quantity of books and other resources suitable for each section of the community than would be possible in separately organized libraries and, relevant to this study, allows a continuity of library use which may counteract the tendency to drop out of public library use in the early teens.

Many community colleges and joint provision schools throughout Britain demonstrate that a better and bigger range of sources is made available, benefiting particularly the schools, that more professional expertise and guidance is available producing a better service and a greater usage. Young people who, previously, would have shirked the effort to go to the public library or the school library use the community service because it is, in addition to their school library, also a place where they spend their leisure time at youth club or sports centre.

While such utilization of buildings, staff, stock, and money avoids duplication and is more economical in many aspects it is unlikely to become the norm until current school and college buildings become obsolete or people group themselves into communities facilitating such community ventures.

It seems, therefore, that the practices and disadvantages described so far will persist unless the solutions of qualified staff and more library funds are implemented. However certain trends are visible which inspire the hope that they may become widespread in the service to teenagers. It is clear, in British and American schools in general that there is an increasing use of the library for research/topic/assignment work as part of the learning programme. It is clear too, that much of this work is undertaken with inadequate prior knowledge of how to set about such work, how to use the library's resources, how to extract information from internally and externally available material or how to present the information thus amassed and recorded in digested and appropriate format.

Increasingly subject teachers are coming to realize the importance of library instruction, in general terms, in the context of an individual school and in specific areas. The need for coverage of wide areas of knowledge on topic work and the amount of instruction required has led to the recognition that a teacher running a school library in his spare time is no longer able to effect an adequate library programme and that full-time professional librarians are essential to administer and promote library use. The combination of the two professions, teaching and librarianship, ought to produce a dynamic information team dedicated to the promotion of learning and knowledge by every means possible or suitable, and in a few schools such teamwork exists, where curriculum development involves the teacher and the librarian, topic and examination work inter-connect them and the student and where feedback from each of the three is used to amend or expand both teaching and library practices and services.

This is the library as the servicing agency in the school, complementing and supplementing the subject teaching. The second role of aiding reading as an activity not specifically related to a subject class or a required programme, is still unclarified in most schools. Relegated to low priority because, as discussed earlier, it is considered too pleasurable to be education or too recreational to merit serious allowance of time, the general tendency is to suppose that non-required reading comes under the umbrella of the English department if it is in fact anybody's business, and that recreational reading is the public library's job. The tendency the other way, is for librarian or English teacher to draw up a long list of fiction, *x* numbers of which must be read and reported on in a given time, thus providing the keen reader with a helpful focus on probably worthwhile books while daunting the apathetic, hostile or incapable.

It is possible to sugar this pill by adding a bit of spice to the young teenager's undertaking of this task in the form of a game such as a space journey where the reader must surmount various hazards on his journey to the moon before making a safe landing and claiming territorial ownership. This has been done by making a reading list and log book card combined, from which the reader chooses a required number of books, satisfies the librarian he has read them, by discussion, and is recorded in the log book as having reached a stage or surmounted a hazard in the journey, after which he can go on to read the choice from the next stage. The first reader to reach the moon by this means wins a prize and readers who complete the journey receive a badge. This, with variations, has been successfully used in public libraries and schools and gives

1. some motivation for what would otherwise seem a dull task to many students;
2. a sense of achievement to those who reach any of the stages; and
3. whatever educationists say about the competitive element in schools, an element of a race to the moon for those who wish to view it that way.

Obviously the student who reads fastest and with comprehension will be first to the moon and the end of the reading list, but for many, getting there at all will be satisfying because it is achievable in digestible portions or stages, an important aspect of the psychology of education and learning which seems to be left out where teenage reading is concerned.

Most of the sociological and psychological components of adolescence are ignored or trampled upon in libraries in educational establishments, except for the special schools for pupils with some physical or mental disability where individual attention to all needs is the norm. Components such as the drive towards independence, the idealism, the sensitivity to people, thoughts and situations in many teenagers, the self development or the development of an identity, the exploratory nature of adolescence, these are the areas which could be enhanced, strengthened and aided by a more sympathetic attitude to use of the library, by a positive encouragement to use the library by freeing it from the petty restrictions of time common to many schools and college libraries, by making available sufficient quantities and types of material to support needs, interests and tastes and by allowing sensitivity and identity and reaching out to grow in the explorations and discoveries possible in a happy combination of free and guided use of books and libraries.

Chapter 4
What do teenagers read?

Public library and school library surveys of reading tastes and habits have normally concluded that there is a stage in early teens when reading and library use lessens or ceases. Occasionally a survey ensures that the questions asked cover reading material other than books, a necessary emphasis in the light of the definition of reading held by many, though possibly itself suspect when so many young people call magazines books. As indicated in Chapter 1, newspapers, magazines and comics are often not considered reading, this term being reserved for the hardback or school book.

The conclusion that teenagers do not read is therefore only half a truth; book borrowing from the libraries undoubtedly declines and regular reading of books is not the norm but there is ample evidence that most teenagers use the skill of reading in several forms and at varying levels above and below their actual or school classified reading ability.

It is important to know what teenagers read when they are not under compulsion from school or the influence of parents and teachers, the clearest indication tending to be shown in the reading matter on which teenagers are prepared to spend their money. Time and again surveys and personal experience of talking to teenagers show that a large proportion buy paperbacks, books and magazines every week. Some, particularly the boys, are reluctant to reveal what they buy because they think they might embarrass themselves or the enquirer in discussing the sexy magazines and 'dirty' books; some are pleased to reveal their buying preferences because of deep personal interest in the content; few can articulate the reasons for their preference beyond a chance attraction, 'I just liked the look of it' or 'it looked interesting' forming the usual unpressured response.

However, one print medium outstrips all others in the reading popularity polls, that of the newspaper. Statistics show that most young people read at least one newspaper every day but it must be stated that there is little element of choice in which newspaper is read when statistics also show that the newspaper is most often that taken by the parents. Nevertheless the choice to read or not to read is there, and the whole range of this age group demonstrates that it does read both national and local newspapers, available in the parental home and bought by the individual teenager. The British have a greater choice of daily paper than the Americans, there being many national and a few local morning papers in Britain against no national and hundreds of local papers in the States, though in the American local papers coverage of news is national.

There is an overwhelming preference for the tabloid press rather than the quality papers and an unmistakable and persisting vote in Britain for the *Daily Mirror*, a paper with a large pictorial content, short news items, broken columns and light human interest presentation. Second and third in most polls come the *Daily Express* and the *Daily Telegraph*, confirming the national adult preferences also, but significant in that the latter maintains its place through the readership amongst teenagers over seventeen, with the implication that such readership is in further and higher education, achieved probably by virtue of social background and the influence of parents who themselves read the *Daily Telegraph*, an influence already outlined in the first chapter.

The newspaper preferences follow from the social pattern and the reading ability of the age range and though other people's papers may be glanced at, borrowed or exchanged, the indications are that newspaper readers read the papers which mirror their politics, social interests and attitudes and which provide the news and entertainment in form found assimilable by the reader. When much of the population has left school at the earliest opportunity with a reading level barely capable of coping with the school leaving examinations but adequate for magazines and comics, it does not come as a surprise to note that on the evidence of many surveys in both Britain and America, over 90% of teenagers read newspapers daily, around 80% of whom read a popular tabloid. The small percentage who read the serious dailies comes largely from the continuing students. Newspaper reading may form most of the means of maintaining literacy after leaving school early when the teenager is likely to go into manual or factory work which does not require him to read instructions or documents of any kind, or an office job where sustained reading is not part of the day's work even for a typist. The level of reading ability may well decline after leaving school, so that some attention should be paid in school and college to newspaper reading.

Many teachers and librarians are unaware of what pupils are reading out of school. One English department head was heard to comment favourably upon a particular boy in his class of fifteen-year-old boys and girls as the 'only boy who reads a newspaper'. Subsequent enquiry by the hearer revealed that the boy was the only one who brought a newspaper into class but by no means the only member of the class to read a newspaper. His parents were in the fortunate position of being employed at a place where several daily papers were provided for the staff and did not themselves have a morning paper delivered. The boy therefore bought one for himself each day on the way to school. The rest of the class all 'looked at' their parents' paper at some time each day.

The phrase 'looked at' is more accurate than 'read' in most cases of newspaper reading amongst teenagers. When asked what they read in their papers many report turning to the 'funnies' first before, in the girls' case, looking at the horoscope and in the boys' case, at the sports news. Some, like a fifteen-year-old boy in an approved school, read 'whatever catches my eye', in his case in the *Daily Mirror*, provided along with the *Daily Express* by the school. A glance at the front page headlines seems to suffice unless it indicates a sensational human interest drama when the reader is likely to stay with that story.

Only amongst college students and sixth formers is there a likelihood of reading newspaper accounts from a sense of duty as well as interest in order to be informed in current events, world affairs, political, financial and social issues. Even so, many teenagers who choose to read thus in their daily papers at home and at school, choose their Sunday papers for their entertainment value.

The lack of provision of newspapers in schools and colleges is governed partly by expense and partly by fears of political bias but there is no doubt that where several newspapers are supplied daily in the school library, or the young adult library, not only is the library fulfilling its role as an information centre but is enabling the teenager to see several interpretations of the news from several angles, thus offering him an opportunity for critical thought and balance.

Easy availability is one of the basic reasons for such large reading figures and the majority of teenagers read for the entertainment value rather than the hard news value. Apart from availability the other factors making for wide readership are topicality, readability and drama packed human interest stories with pictorial emphasis requiring little sustained concentration. These are the magnets which attract so many teenagers and adults to a reading medium which makes little demand on reading ability yet gives a lot of interest in return.

The same magnets attract a similarly large proportion of teenagers to magazines and comic books.

MAGAZINES

Teenagers are avid readers of magazines varying in topics which can be divided into the following categories in popularity order:

1. For girls.
2. Pop.
3. Cars and motor bikes.
4. News, current affairs, etc.
5. Fashion and home.
6. Hobbies and sport.
7. Sex.
8. General magazines.
9. Underground or alternative press.

They can be further subdivided into so-called 'upper, commercial and conventional, [and] lower, sensational and full of kicks'.[96] There is, however, no clear-cut distinction between the able reader and the less able or between the early school leaver and the college student in the choice of upper or lower magazines, most teenagers reading frequently in both categories. It is difficult to draw a line of demarcation between what are termed teenage magazines and the magazines which cover interests held by other age groups also, and the directories of magazines such as Willing's in Britain and Bowker's in America use different terminology for the categories and include some classifications known to interest teenagers while ignoring others equally popular. Some are differentiated by sex which produces a long list of magazines for girls and a short list for boys. Whatever the definition there can be no doubt that the estimated eighty or so magazines produced for teenagers in the States and the twenty or so in Britain, have a large circulation, both official and later by exchange between readers.

The teenage population of America of which 24 million are in high school or college, gets through approximately 21 million copies of the teenage magazines and about 9 million teenagers in Britain of whom approximately 5 million are in school or college, achieve an estimated teenage magazine circulation of 1½ million copies. Such readership is uncoerced, largely self purchased and mostly loyal to that choice though many other magazines of similar type will be read according to availability from friends and other loan sources.

The most widely read and bought magazines are those for girls, catering for their interests in pop stars, boy/girl relationships, fashion and make-up by means of gossip columns, informational articles, strong pictorial content, short stories and strip stories of romantic interest, with readers' letters and agony columns; much of the content is presented in teenage argot, creating those feelings of identity and relevance which loom so large in adolescence, as detailed in Chapter 1.

In America the most popular magazines in this category are *Seventeen*, *Ingenue* and *Teen*, and the Sabre Teenage Group's many publications. In Britain *Trend*, *Jackie* and *Romeo* head the polls. The combination of interests is maintained in each issue and forms the pulling power for the thirteen to seventeen age group from all social backgrounds. Pop star photographs and signed columns, personal profiles of pop stars, information on pop records and occasionally the words of pop songs, these take up a large proportion of the content of girls' magazines, closely followed by articles, picture strip stories, short stories and advice, all on the topic of dating, love found, love lost. The notable feature of all these in all such magazines for girls is the highly moral treatment of these themes and the heavy moralizing put into the mouths of the lead girl in the short stories and picture strips. Rarely is the physical aspect of boy/girl relationships mentioned and a chaste kiss is the limit depicted pictorially or textually. Rarely does the story go beyond the 'I've got my man' stage after innumerable upsets and heartbreaks, and always there is the implication that the path of true love once found, runs smoothly for ever after.

The characters are usually evenly divided between the goodies and the baddies, the male characters portraying the rich, good-looking playboy type heart-throb versus the poor but honest, steady boy-next-door type, both involved with the pretty, slim girl with the tip-tilted nose and big eyes who wants the high life and does not mind who she tramples on to get it, and her friend, not so attractive but honest and good-hearted who attempts to restrain the implied excesses of her flatmate and who consoles the poor-but-honest lad who has been stood up. The morals drawn from these situations are often put into a 'thinks' balloon in which the girl bemoans her loss of the steady boyfriend in a welter of remorse for having treated him so badly, and of unselfish joy that he has found a nice girl else-where, or thanks her lucky stars that she saw the worth of her steady in time, after her foolish fling with the worthless playboy.

Such stories are avidly read and identified with by girls throughout the age range. This conforms very closely to the mental and emotional reactions of children before the con-ceptual ability has developed, when a happy ending is necessary to ensure security and comfort and where no grey areas cloud the issue. This is one of the important psychological reasons why teenage girls buy and read such large quantities of these magazines; when uncertainty over boys, romance and love is rife and when concern over physical appearance is common, it is a comfort and a sustainer to have the whole situation pre-sented in a black and white treatment of good and bad, right and wrong, infatuation and love, the search, the chase, the successful catch, the happy ending or occasionally the unhappy ending for the main character but with a clear moral explanation for such an end.

Exactly the same reasons apply in post-teenage years when women's magazines are enjoyed for the same wish-fulfilment and identification of interests, only the characters in the stories are young married couples or older people and the articles and gossip columns pertain to the interests of that age range.

It is a curious fact that a great many boys, particularly at thirteen and fourteen who are in early puberty and mature later than girls, are keen but perhaps secret readers of the girls' magazines, not from a prurient interest but because the boys too have problems of identity and uncertainty and ignorance and the girls' stories and agony columns fill the need for them also. In addition the pop music information tends to be treated differently in the girls' magazines, from a human interest angle rather than the news angle usual in pop magazines. Although boys rarely buy the girls' magazines they frequently read any available in the home or at school, usually with joking references to offset any embarrassment. However at the older end of the age range girls begin to externalize their feelings and can read these magazines with wish fulfilment and with willing suspension of disbelief, later recognizing that life is not so black and white, that frequently there is no happy ending and sometimes no just reward for either the good or the bad.

Again and again real life letters and problems revealed to the magazine editor show the teenager's need to cling to every tiny piece of evidence that the other sex is interested, often magnifying the casual look or word into signs of intense desire, and every time the advice given by the magazine is to see the situation in perspective and to look coolly at the problem. The absence of such detail in most of the stories and the apparently dispassionate and decisive way in which characters react to each other is again another reason for their popularity.

Adults criticize the girls' magazines for their stereotyped characters, the formula plots and the lack of realism in the stories, and for the excessive adulation given to pop stars and their personal lives but it is interesting that both girls and boys comment that it does not matter that this does not happen in real life, this is how they would like it to be. While applying that standard to the stories they pay attention to the details of fashion, make-up and diet in the same magazine in order to approximate more closely to the appearance they would like to have. Such magazines

1. offer the information about the teenage world which enables the teenage readers to feel in the know,
2. subscribe to the teenager's need for wish fulfilment,
3. provide an outlet for the expression of anxieties and queries,
4. present a visually and textually attractive and interesting medium of information and entertainment,
5. are easily available,

6. are of suitable format for carrying around, hoarding or swopping,
7. Enable the individual to indulge her personal and private dreams while providing her with a common and communal core of subject matter.

The pop magazines such as *Dig, In Magazine* and *Teen Screen* in America and *Popswop, Melody Maker* and *New Musical Express* in Britain, derive directly from the recognition of pop music as part of the sub-culture of the teenager, not simply the chart music but the whole range of types of music played and sung by pop groups and pop stars. A liking for pop music is not confined to any one type of social background or age range but the pop magazine is written and illustrated with the teenager in mind, as a reader of pop magazines, as a listener to radio and records at home and at discos, and as a buyer of records and cassettes. Where the girls' magazines contain general information and pleasant articles about the more popular stars, the pop magazines dig a little deeper into the minds of the musicians, apply more critical standards in descriptions of their music, reveal biographical information relevant to the music scene, provide specific information on new releases and concerts, and are written often by people who are closely connected with the world of which they write. Advertising too is heavily directed at the teenager with stars in his eyes, pop stars; but as a whole such magazines are informed and informative and tend to be bought, read and swopped amongst most teenagers who, with the music itself, the pictures and the text of the magazines, amass by these audio-visual means a formidable amount of detailed information about pop music.

The glamour of the pop star, his music, his way of life and his money are the attraction for the reader and most pop magazines, by the clever use of photography and vocabulary liberally sprinkled with emotive words and superlatives, create a visual and verbal excitement which gives pace and an extra dimension to what would otherwise be descriptive prose. Such treatment therefore adds to the attraction and, as with the girls' magazines, creates the 'into' feeling that is desired by so many teenagers.

However, pop magazines attract more males than females and more in the sixteen-plus range, possibly arising from the differences in attitude towards pop, the girls tending more towards the romantic/emotional hero worship and less towards the music while the boys are attracted by the music, the technical paraphernalia of the pop world and the animal attraction of the beat and volume. There is possibly a male competitive element and a certain amount of wishful thinking which also differentiates male from female attitudes towards the presentation of material in pop magazines.

While girls' magazines and pop music papers and their related interests seem to be an all consuming interest among the girls, statistics show that boys have in addition to the above, very varied and often wide interests, the most intense, numerically, that of cars and motor bikes.

Particularly in the States, the teenage male population is prepared to read and re-read the magazines connected with hot rod, custom, stock car, drag racing and driving, the more sober, wider age range journals with the adult automobile driver in mind and the many magazines and journals on motor cycle driving and mechanics. Magazines such as *Hot Rod Magazine* and *Rod and Custom* are eagerly read in America and Britain by a much larger number than the circulation figures indicate and by the teenage boys who, in school, appear unable to read or who read with difficulty. Amongst the disadvantaged youth cars and bikes are part of the wishful thinking and the escapism from their environment, and speed and power are part of the psychology of male adolescence in all social levels.

A very high proportion of teenagers in America have access to a car, unlike British teenagers, and a substantial number of boys in both countries own a motor bike but readership of motor magazines is not confined to those with ownership and access, particularly in the aspect concerned with stock car and drag racing where the noise, the excitement and the danger attract a following and the drivers build up a reputation amongst those who attend the race meetings. Although female teenagers attend car and motor bike races and follow the riders, and females are involved also in the Hell's Angels and Chopper gangs, the interest in cars and motor cycles is predominantly male and the readership of relevant magazines almost wholly so.

In a British survey of teenage reading interests[97] 46% of the teenagers questioned in schools and youth clubs read *Motor Cycle*, all male and all at secondary modern level. More recent estimates suggest that the interest has spread to a wider social and educational range and a higher percentage for motor cycle magazines in general.

Readers tend to look first at the photographs of machines, both in articles and advertisements, then at the small ads for possible buying and selling of items, at the pages answering readers' technical queries, then at the gossip and news items, before settling down to any more lengthy articles requiring more time and concentration. The 'upper' and 'lower' classification is applicable here in differences between the more technically informative magazines for the owner/driver/rider and the hot rod type with the brisk, personalized jargon and the use of rousing style and presentation, read mainly for kicks, though readership of these is not mutually exclusive.

Unlike the pop magazines and girls' magazine reading which fades or transfers to women's magazines, the motor readership tends to continue into adulthood. So too does the readership of news magazines.

The college and university bound students form the greater proportion of teenage readership of the news and current affairs magazines. Though few actually buy a copy, extensive use is made of those provided by school, college and public libraries, where particularly in schools, a chance and glance encounter by the non-academic student has been found to occur frequently in addition to the deliberate and intensive reading by the more academic.

In the absence of such journals specifically for teenagers they have adopted a number of adult journals such as *New Society*, *New Statesman* and *New Scientist* in Britain. These titles are in tabloid newsprint format with little colour or illustration and cover interesting developments and current affairs comment rather than strict news items.

The American teenager in the seventeen to nineteen age category puts *Time* and *Newsweek* at the top of the preference list for news magazines and these titles appear on such lists for the whole teenage range. The difference in format between such British and American magazines is striking, the latter containing a high proportion of photographic illustration, an international coverage of news though with an American slant, and a brisk yet informative style, between a glossy and usually eye-catching cover. No such news journal exists in Britain but there are British editions of *Time* and *Newsweek* which are provided in many school libraries and most public libraries. The visual attraction allied to the editorial treatment in the American examples are again in line with the features of all magazines found to be acceptable by teenagers. However, the current affairs conscious student in Britain while enjoying the major American news magazines is also prepared to read the less attractive British journals for information and interest, though this is a minority readership.

Confined largely to the older teenage girl, there is considerable interest in and enjoyment of the magazines concerned with fashion, marriage and home, most of which are bought by an adult member of the family and read by the younger members of the family. Fashion magazines such as *Petticoat* and *Miss Chatelaine* designed for teenage girls, are bought and the circulation is high, though few girls pay any more attention to following their fashion advice than the older reader does to those ideas depicted in *Vogue* or *Harper's Queen*.

Numerous surveys in America and Britain emphasize the fact that the majority of girls read women's magazines, mainly the popular weekly rather than the monthly magazines, and that often more than one such magazine is read regularly, apart from the casual reading of other titles from various sources. In most cases the women's magazine is subscribed to by the mother, and another is chosen from the newsagent's on the basis of a particular offer in the magazine or an eye-catching article. The teenage girl therefore reads her parents' newspaper and what her mother reads because it is there, and because it suits the attributes and ambitions of the family and conforms to the whole group's outlook on life.

As educational opportunity increases there is a greater likelihood that the children of a family will have the benefit of a lengthened education, thus increasing the possibility that the children in their teens will have reading requirements and interests different from and more demanding than their parents'. However the entertainment value of the women's magazine and its availability in the home make it acceptable reading matter for most levels of intellect, and most teenage girls reading women's magazines adjust their reactions according to their level of intellect and according to whether the magazine is a major part of the total reading experience of the reader. The range of magazine reading interests of boys is revealed in every survey. Though boys do not read in as much quantity as girls they cover a much wider range of subjects than girls.

The magazines of the uniformed organizations, such as *Scout* and *Guide* in Britain and *Girl Scout* and *Boy Scout* in America, with *American Girl* and *Boys Life*, have extensive circulation, as have the Braille editions *Trefoil* and *Fleur de Lys* for blind scouts and guides. The early and middle teens form the major readership for these and for the hobbies magazines connected with modelling and stamp collecting. In Britain and America the interest in fishing is curiously high amongst boys of all ages and environments, and magazines such as *Angling Times* and *Fishing* are bought by teenage boys, read in public libraries and provided in some establishments such as the approved school where boys deprived of their liberty, most of whom were from deprived homes, nevertheless continued their eager interest in their previous leisure time pursuit by pouncing on each new issue of the fishing papers.

A comparable hobby amongst the girls and similarly not confined only to those who have the opportunity to practise it, is riding and many girls from all walks of life read the relevant pony magazines. Many other magazines reflect interests such as model railways, photography, cage birds and radio and are mentioned by boys from differing environments, such interests often continuing into adult life.

The interest in sport which also continues, is especially high in early and middle teens when magazines ranging from strip picture to strictly technical on a particular sport are bought and swapped regularly and knowledgeably. Predominant amongst the sports is football and the weekly and monthly football magazines are read by an estimated 60% of male teenagers in Britain and America. Most of these magazines are bought directly by the interested teenager on a regular basis, starting at early teenage with the picture strip football comics and adding a glossier weekly around fourteen before dropping the comic strip, maintaining allegiance to the weekly and adding a monthly with more depth. In the late teens readership declines as hero-worship fades with maturity and the opportunities for personally playing the game are lessened.

The mixture of biographical information, technical tips,

critical comment, gossip, news and quantity of illustrative material in football magazines is closely allied to the same mixture in the pop and girls' magazines, and the formula produces a similar detailed knowledge in the readers, enabling them to discuss, display knowledge, compete with each other and bet on massive quantities of details of names, places and dates. Other sports have their devotees and their readers amongst teenagers, but none has the overwhelming support given to football.

Another area which is often considered a sport by less sensitive male teenagers is that of sex and a great many teenage boys buy and read sex magazines which are not normally on open bookstalls, and the 'men's' magazines which are considered legitimate publishing. In America it has been estimated that one-third of the readers of *Male* and *Stag* are boys aged ten to seventeen and that many more regularly read and swap other titles less easily available.[98]

A group of teenagers questioned in an English survey[99] showed a substantial preference for sex magazines at the thirteen to fifteen age, declining equally substantially over the next two or three years. The climate of opinion is such that most boys who read or look at sex magazines, do so surreptitiously and often teachers and parents are unaware of the extent of such reading.

As in adult reading, much of the reading is done while standing at bookstalls and news-stands, an apparently casual cursory look while flipping through, as if assessing before buying. In this way a great many magazines can be looked at regularly, without the embarrassment attendant on asking for a particular title, and with the advantage of being able to see more magazines than could be afforded. Newsagents and magazine sellers are well aware that the sex magazines 'disappear' very easily and many boys admit to the unauthorized and unpaid for removal of such magazines from a market stall or open display, at some time in their teens.

The really 'blue' magazines which circulate amongst the teenage boys have certainly been obtained illegally or at second hand, from an 'adult' book shop. From time to time these shops are raided by the police and material confiscated followed up by prosecution, sometimes on a charge of selling to an underage person. Many of these shops also carry on an exchange business, so that on returning a used magazine and exchanging it for another, the reader can get through a tremendous number of titles and issues. While many boys look physically older than their actual age and could therefore easily buy 'blue' magazines, few do, obtaining them instead from older members of the family and from friends.

Although the interest in sex magazines for the pictorial content is intense around fourteen to sixteen there is gradual transference of interest from illustration to text in the older boys, though visual titillation continues to attract throughout adulthood. Many of the older boys who were previously attracted by the forbidden fruits of the blue magazine lose interest in reading and looking at them when as one of them put it, 'we can get the real thing'. There is an interesting anomaly here in that whereas the older teenager loses interest in the photographic representation of sex, he does not lose interest in the fictional representation of sex in paperback novels and in series such as the Skinhead and Hell's Angels titles, although most of these have a compound content of sex, violence and adventure.

Very few girls ever see the 'blue' magazines and rarely show interest, openly or secretly, in the men's magazines available on most magazine stands. Both boys and girls occasionally look at the more general men's magazines such as *Esquire* and *Penthouse*, and are interested in the articles and illustrations on sexual matters in the magazines intended for women, such as *She*, *Nova* and *Cosmopolitan*, though in all these cases, the readership is amongst the minority of the better educated teenager and young adult.

The general adult magazines, particularly the picture magazines, are popular with many teenage boys and girls though they rarely buy them. *Life* and *Look*, *Reader's Digest* and the *National Geographic* are all looked at whenever encountered in schools, colleges, public libraries and newsstands. The colour supplements of newspapers can be put into the general magazine category in that they are often available in schools and colleges separately from the newspaper, and are well used there for browsing purposes. Other magazines such as *Punch*, *Which* and *TV Times*, though all with a basic emphasis are read by a cross-section of the teenage population.

Young college students in the seventeen to nineteen age range seem, on the basis of numerous surveys across the States, to prefer general picture magazines above all other reading matter including books, reporting *Life*, *Look*, *Saturday Evening Post* and *Time* as their chief preferences.

One more general type of magazine must be noted though it is relevant largely to American teenagers in school, the range of magazines intended for teenagers in school published by Scholastic Publications and sold through school agencies. *Scholastic Newstime* has a circulation in excess of a million; *Senior Scholastic* for the older teenager and *Scholastic Scope* aimed at the less able teenager in school, have a wide readership resulting from the acceptable content and the availability, in that the magazine is brought to the reader in the school in the same way as the paperbacks emanating from the same company. The total circulation of their range of magazines is estimated at fifteen million.

Reading in the general magazine field, though widely undertaken, is much more in the nature of a casual encounter than the regular purchase common to the other types of magazine outlined. Reading the underground or alternative press, is, conversely, a precise, deliberate and mental process, found almost exclusively in the college student and the teenager, with a cause in which he is personally, racially or religiously involved.

Examples such as *Private Eye*, *It*, *Friendz* and *Nasty Tales* are devoted to anti-Establishment satire and the promotion of information on subjects taboo to the ordinary press, providing a voice which is denied to those on the fringe of traditional society. Others are more specifically geared to the interests of the political, revolutionary, philanthropic or religious. Many appeal to the teenager who is likely to be sympathetic towards anything rebelling against the *status quo*, others are read because they are part of the student scene and some are read and contributed to by the older teenager and college student who has a specific interest rather than the general student interest. Rarely does the underground or alternative press appeal to the working teenager or the less able student, and rarely is it found in libraries except those which make it their business to preserve such literature for sociological reasons or for posterity. The readership is therefore almost wholly voluntary, undertaken with enthusiasm and often with promotional interest. The life expectancy of much alternative literature is very short and the outlets for its sale are few, so that usually some effort must be made to obtain it unless within the student body.

At the other extreme there is almost saturation in the promotion, sale and readership of the picture papers. It is necessary to include in this section on periodical publications, comics, comic books and the serial publication of war and romance stories in picture strip format, as these form the staple diet for many young people who get no further in their reading and who continue to buy these publications regularly in adulthood.

Brief mention of the 'funnies' comics suffices as these are popular in childhood up to around thirteen and then, though still read, decline in popularity as more mature interests emerge. Since the Comic Code was introduced the 'horror' and sick type of comic has been restricted and the fantastic adventures of super heroes have increased in popularity amongst a wider range of young people. Nevertheless the dedicated readers of super hero magazines are most often found amongst the college and university students who make a cult of the science fiction type heroes and who follow them over many years. The considerable casual readership is attracted by the fantasy, the pace, the action, the plot and the super heroes such as Metamorpho, Element Man, The Hulk, Superman and Batman, or the teamwork of the Teen Titans, the Fantastic Four or the Defenders, but the serious readers follow the fortunes of the characters with an eagle eye for consistency of detail in characterization and plot, with a keen interest in the art work and with such devotion that the readers' letters page in most of these comics is filled with knowledgeable comments and suggestions showing evidence of analytical coverage of each issue.

Although readers are mainly male, partly by self identification with the mighty super hero and partly that the subject content of space, adventure and scientific machines and plots covers the traditional interests of boys, girls are catered for by the introduction of super women like Wonder Girl, Aquachick, Element Girl and Super Girl, who have the traditional feminine attributes and features in abundance but with superhuman powers.

The comic strip format, available on average monthly, the escapist content in terms of hero, adventure, and triumph of right over wrong conform to the recognized liking for visual action and exciting suspenseful plot. The large numbers of comics produced in America by the Marvel Comics Group and the National Comics Group, and the multiplicity of 'funnies' emanating from the Charlton Group, the Archie Group, and in Britain the IPC and the Thomson Companies, are read by large numbers of teenagers. *Superman* and *Batman* have an estimated circulation of over two million each month and each copy is likely to be read by several other people after purchase. No similar comics are published in Britain covering the super and the horrific and British teenagers read the imported American titles in large quantities and with similar enjoyment and long standing loyalty, and with the same degree of knowledgeable interest.

By contrast a liking for war and romance picture strip books is evidenced in many young people's buying and reading habits, to such an extent that Matthew Arnold's term 'blotterature' is applicable. These pocket sized paper covered books of picture stories in black and white crude artwork contain a complete story in drawings with the minimum of balloon talk and story-line captions. The war stories glorify the British or American soldier and villify the enemy troops with a high degree of exaggerated caricature in both cases.

The Westerns similarly distinguish between the goodies and the baddies by gross emphasis on racial differences and anti-social behaviour. Such caricature and emphasis appear in all comics be they humorous or the super hero type, but blatant racialism and jingoism evident in war comic books is psychologically a different matter, the implication in each issue being that the war stories are based on factual battles.

Several publishing companies run series under compound titles such as IPC's *Air Ace Picture Library*, *War Picture Library* and *Battle Picture Library*, producing eight titles a month under each head; or Micron Publications *Combat Picture Library* and *Cowboy Adventure Library*, with four titles a month under each head. Thomson's *Commando*, war stories in pictures, also appears in four issues per month, all issues retailing at 6p per issue. The American companies produce similar series, for example the *G.I. Combat* series and the Charlton series *War and Attack*. The features are similar in every case. Bravery, heroism, cowardice, envy, greed, hate, dare devilry and old pals ribaldry appear in each story, upholding the traditional attributes of the 'he-man' and spotlighting the traditional deficiencies of men in conflict. Rarely is a woman encountered in these picture stories which centre on the battle scene. The terse utterances of men at war lend themselves to the balloon talk employed, thereby adding a touch of authenticity, pace and tension with the minimum of words.

The absence of first-hand experience of war is no deterrent to the growth of popular teenage interest in these picture stories. The content is read for the adventure, the fear-full thrill of the tight situation, the character testing and the relief and elation of victory. The psychological analysis of these stories would suggest that they relate to the animal kingdom where the male fights to protect his territory from marauders and displays aggression to assert his superiority and dominance over other males. Viewed as adventure stories with a wartime setting they are part of the general male interest in war films, war books, war anecdotes and war jokes, which starts around the age of twelve and continues throughout adulthood. In picture strip form the story becomes more immediately assimilable and is therefore more acceptable to the young teenager and the less able older teenager, both categories buying and borrowing the war picture books in great quantities.

Picture stories for girls are acceptable for similar psychological and presentation reasons, the romantic interest being equally a traditionally female preference and the presentation also assimilable in digestible and apparently satisfying portions. IPC's *Love Story Library*, *Miracle Library*, Top Sellers' *Pocket Romance Library* and D. C. Thomson's *Star Love Stories* are similar to the American picture romances such as *Falling in Love* and the Arleigh Group's *Young Romance* and *Girls' Love Stories*, in their publication monthly of several titles in each of the series.

Characters and plots seldom differ in outline, the stereotype and the formula being part of the attraction for female readers. In much the same way as children are happier with the familiar, so many teenage girls and the less mature women seem to need the security of the familiar style and formula which obtain also in the textual stories so popular in girls' and women's magazines. Although the terse and restricted vocabulary is suited to the restrictions depicted in the war picture stories, such brevity appears out of place in the romance stories and results in ideas and emotions compressed into shallow words and illustrations which lack the power to give any depth. The perpetuation of old enmities in the war stories can be compared with the perpetuation of social divisions in the romance stories, the physical features of the pretty girl and the good-looking boy who play the leading roles in every romantic story spring from the same origins as the clear eyed, clean cut, rugged jawed hero of every war story.

The need for a strongly defined and depicted hero has long been noted in teenagers' reading preferences and the picture stories without exception provide such a hero. Male and female share this preference though girls are happy with a heroine in addition.

The types of periodical publication outlined are all read by teenagers of their own volition and the notable features of this magazine reading can be summed up in the following points:

1. It appeals to the majority of teenagers, cutting across social and educational divides.
2. Teenagers who seem unable to cope with reading in school voluntarily and successfully tackle their chosen magazines.
3. The level of subject knowledge in many of the individually chosen magazines is very high, and complex information is assimilated because of the reader's motivation.
4. Girls read a greater quantity of the same type of magazine whereas boys read a greater variety of magazine.
5. The majority of teenagers read at a very shallow level in carefully packaged magazines, the content of which, textually and pictorially, has been designed to present information in brief, easily digested portions to tickle the palate rather than provide nourishment.
6. The majority of teenagers do read consistently in the medium of magazines, mostly in the range of picture magazines, a preference which may well be related not only to the known psychological attraction of the visual and the age-old recognition that man remembers what he sees better than what he hears or reads, but also to the fact that teenagers have been accustomed from birth to visual presentation via the television screen and therefore find the picture magazine a more familiar and more acceptable medium of information and entertainment.

PAPERBACKS

There is a large amount of evidence to show that teenagers read paperbacks and buy paperbacks in preference to or instead of hardbacks. Many who seem to be unable to read anything in school, regularly buy and devour paperbacks, with quite difficult sentence structure and vocabulary but on themes which interest the reader. Many who do not normally use a public library and who rarely patronize the school library unless for assigned work, buy paperbacks on themes not supplied by the libraries. Some buy for the particular subject that forms their hobby and some for a temporary purpose connected with school or interest. In addition to these, and perhaps amongst them also, there are those who buy for the joy of ownership even where they could borrow.

Book buying amongst teenagers is predominantly paperback rather than hardback, not only for the lower cost but also because of the now recognized preferences for the paperback format, arising from its cover attraction, its pocket size, its dissimilarity from the school book and its content, which is often available only in paperback. Despite the fact that the size of type and the page layout tend to be close packed and the quality of the paper decidedly inferior, both features which are offputting in a hardback, the popularity of the paperback seems to rest on its visually attractive exterior, its handleable nature and the readability of its content, determined by the motivation of the reader rather than the typeface.

The outlets for paperback sales have made unprecedented growth in the last few years. From bookshops and the large stationers sources have widened and now include stores, supermarkets, the neighbourhood newsagent, stalls at railway and bus terminals and in markets, and through the agencies supplying to school and college bookstalls.

The number of teenagers buying paperbacks is shown and substantiated in surveys in Britain and America. The figures reveal that there is little difference in quantity of paperbacks purchased between the educationally able and the educationally less able; the only significant difference between male and female teenage buying is that a higher proportion of able girls do *not* buy any paperbacks. Book borrowing figures indicate that such girls are regular library users and evidently find sufficient satisfaction in library stock to preclude the necessity or the desire for buying.

A survey undertaken amongst English secondary school students[100] on paperback buying in the preceding year, excluding magazines, comics and picture stories, revealed that 77·6% of girls and 81·8% of boys in the higher educational streams, and 79·5% of girls and 78·8% of boys in the lower streams, had bought paperbacks; the largest percentage of students who had not bought any was in the grammar school or higher stream girls. An emphatic 55·1% of all students questioned had bought more than ten paperbacks in the previous twelve months, 30·6% boys and 25·5% girls.

An American survey[101] produced similar figures, with 59·5% of American secondary school students averaging 2·6 paperbacks a month. What they choose to buy depends on the reading interests, the proximity of a bookselling retail outlet and the type of paperback offered from that outlet. An element of doubt as to whether teenagers decide what they want and go to the appropriate source for it, or buy what they see at the nearest or most frequented outlet, has been resolved on the basis of many surveys and much experiential evidence, that most teenagers who buy paperbacks for light entertainment get them from their local newsagent's shop or from the big stores, initially on a chance basis, later to get more of the same.

Teenagers who buy the better quality paperbacks for leisure reading or in connection with studies, tend to buy from a bookshop or large stationers such as W. H. Smith in Britain, and do so with a specific title in mind. The retail outlets and their contents could be divided into two categories:

1. Newsagents
   Stores
   Supermarkets
   Stalls, etc.
concentrating largely on paperback fiction dealing with sex, war, violence, adventure, love, horror and mystery.

2. Bookshops
   Large stationers
   School/college paperback clubs

concentrating largely on adult novels, teenage novels, film books, humour, biography and paperback non-fiction.

The patronage of the first category far exceeds that of the second, most of the population having many reasons to enter such establishments frequently, so that proximity and availability are important factors here. But the stock is not there by chance, publishers and stockists having taken note of the reading interests and preferences of the masses for themes in the first category, preferences already discussed in the field of magazines.

Many big stores and stationers have discovered an increase in the number of teenage boys, identified by their 'uniforms' and appearance as belonging to one or other of the groups or gangs, who make their way directly to the racks or shelves which house the paperbacks covering the fictionalized stories of skinheads, bootboys, Hell's Angels and bike boys, but who disdain to look at anything else on their way in or out of the book section. This particular interest is not confined to this category of teenage boy though it is significant to note such readership where there was previously little interest in reading.

An extensive, usually underground circulation of these paperbacks has been common for a few years amongst boys and girls in the thirteen to fifteen age range, the attraction in every instance being the title and front cover followed by the mixture of uninhibited sex and sexual deviation, physical violence, anti-social attitudes, motor bikes and cars, and a teenage hero or rather anti-hero.

Such titles as *Skinhead*, *Big Mama* and *Rogue Angels* published by the New English Library, can be bought at many neighbourhood newsagents' shops and most big stores and stationers and are swopped or loaned particularly amongst the younger teenagers who, because of the sex content, tend to try to do so in secret. An example is Richard Allen's *Skinhead* and its sequel *Suedehead*, where a fictional character in a highly probable realistic situation goes from one bed to another and tries to carve out status in the gang, with the girls and against authority. Joe Hawkins from a deprived background is bent on 'aggro'. Written in a mixture of short sentences and long words, though the concepts are not difficult, occasional comments are inserted, not as part of Joe's philosophy nor to explain it, but almost as editorial comment, the intrusion of the author's opinion.

Action packed with little or no description, the books are designed to appeal to readers who need excitement to carry them on from page to page. There is no indication that there are qualities of character less base than those depicted in Joe and his associates. Devoid of the finer feelings he is typified as concerned only for self, with an unthinking hate for authority and specific categories of people. There is deliberate use of titillation and glorification on the grounds that the Joes of this world live like this. The only evidence that this way of life has its snags is the ending of each book with Joe in trouble or in prison, but even this is with the implication that it was just bad luck rather than a realistic and very probable outcome of his way of life.

Some school teachers and parents discovering such books confiscate them thus encouraging further interest as with all banned material. Some have used the interest to further critical awareness, discussing the books with the readers, and at least one teacher has described his attempt to use these books in a structured English class to demonstrate the application of literary criticism and standards to the popular literature as well as the school type English literature.[102] Such an approach rather than a condemnation on moral grounds had the effect of making the class really look at what they were reading and assessing the books as exciting and escapist though with thin plots and crudely outlined characters.

Boys and girls, ranging from the inmates of detention schools, members of various gangs, working boys, fourteen-year-old boys and girls in school and seventeen-year-old sixth form boys have all stated to the writer that they like these books because they are exciting and 'real', with plenty of action, little description, and real life use of 'bad' language in conversation and sexual description. The usage by both male and female characters of the opposite sex for personal gratification and exploitation at whim and at will was also considered by many to be like real life; the absence of responsibility in this matter in most of the books is part of the wishful thinking of many young teenage boys and thus forms part of the escapism of the books.

Violence is given equal treatment, with graphic descriptions of the gang warfare and individual brutality, to such an extent that the glorification of violence becomes obscene. Such glorification is evident also in the many war books which are bought by teenage boys. Purporting to be fictionalized accounts of real wartime experiences, the emphasis is on the physical aspects of combat rather than the human. Some adults and a handful of teenagers take the view that gang warfare and war combat *is* obscene and therefore is being depicted as such. Others view this type of literature as pandering to the animal in man or encouraging a 'sick' interest in brutality. In both types a mature adult reader would consider the characterization crude and shallow, the plot a series of incidents loosely linked together and the style of writing lacking in structure, grammar and depth. But the eager teenage readers of these books are not looking for a literary experience, nor analysing as they read. They are concerned only with the fact that they find them exciting, titillating and frightening in that though many of the readers may not behave like the hero they know of boys who do, informative about sexual practices and supposed prowess which they had vaguely heard of, though the information may be grossly distorted in the cause of the plot and the titillation.

Whatever parents, teachers and librarians may feel about this keen interest in the sex and war paperbacks the fact is that a great many teenage boys and some girls, from all walks of life, do read them openly or surreptitiously. It may be some comfort that though a minority read nothing else, such paperbacks usually form only a part of the reading experience of the teenager, and are a passing phase.

The romantic interests of teenage girls are catered for by a variety of paperback novels including historical fiction, romantic fiction, the more lurid sex novels and the authors with a uni-sex readership such as Grace Metalious and Harold Robbins. Most popular are the light 'love' stories of the type found in many women's magazines. Those who buy these tend to be the working teenage girl and the girls in the middle and lower ability range. However, mystery and ghost stories also feature in the book-buying interests from all sources as do humorous works, novels and collections of cartoons rather than comic books.

Less often but encouragingly, teenagers will buy in their own interest fields and many highly technical works or books on obscure specialist subjects are part of the buying preferences, as are biographies of footballers and sporting stars.

Book buying through school clubs follows a similar pattern given the differences in what is available through normal retail channels and what is offered through school paperback clubs. Some schools make their own arrangements with a local book-seller but many take advantage of the nationwide facilities of Scholastic Book Services in the States and its subsidiary in Britain, Scholastic Publications Ltd. By a system of age graded club magazines and catalogues, children from nursery school to secondary school and college are encouraged and enabled to buy paperbacks through the agency of the interested teacher in the school; no fees or commission are involved so that no accusation of pressure on the children could be laid by any detractor of the system. Indeed the schools participating report intense interest and purchase of paperbacks by all age groups involved.

The sections applicable to teenage students are, in America *TAB* (Teenage Book Club) for grades 6 to 9 or ages eleven to fourteen and *Campus* for grades 10 to 12, ages fifteen to eighteen; in Britain the names are different and *Scoop Club* for twelve to fourteen year olds is the only section for teenagers though one for older teenagers is under consideration. A monthly selection of paperback fiction and non-fiction is described in the illus-trated monthly club news, which has annotated entries, the annotations designed to whet the appetite through their informative and interesting style. The books offered are all from those provided by reputable hardback and paperback publishers or commissioned for Scholastic Publications and are selected by editorial boards and advisers including teachers, librarians and educationalists. The standard therefore is high yet realistic in its range of interests and abilities covered.

Mary Bingley, the editorial director of the British company Scholastic Publications Ltd, has tested adult teachers' and librarians' opinions on what they think children choose to buy, using the club news sheet items, and has discovered a marked discrepancy between what librarians think would be popular purchases and what Scholastic Publication's sales records show is actually bought by the young people. In one test administered to forty school and children's librarians from different parts of Britain, only two achieved a two out of three result when asked to guess which were the three best sellers of those offered on a recent monthly club news sheet. The rest were completely wrong or guessed only one correctly. All the titles were well known to every librarian present.

The humorous books such as the Armada Lion *Book of Humorous Verse* which is annotated thus:

> A book crammed full of the daftest and silliest and stupidest and craziest and maddest and crankiest and screwiest and nuttiest poems that you ever could hope to read.[103]

the ghost and horror stories such as *Ghosts* and *Haunted Houses*, the sporting biographies and biographical works such as Arnothy's *I am Fifteen and I Do Not Want to Die*, the war stories such as Minney's *Carve Her Name With Pride*, are all top of the list of the most popular books in terms of purchase. It is a salutary experience to librarians to note that the standard works supplied for teenagers in libraries are bought in very small numbers through the book clubs by comparison with the examples given. It is also salutary to note that many of those who buy paperbacks through a school club have never previously read for pleasure and may never have bought a paperback of the kind offered through the club.

As all such sales are normally made on the basis of the catalogue's annotated entry without the student seeing the book in advance it follows that apart from teachers' and librarians' recommendations, the books are sold on the appeal of the cover illustration and its accompanying annotation on the news sheet.

There is strong evidence too that the adult titles offered are snapped up even by the younger teenagers, titles such as *Dr Jekyll and Mr Hyde*, Raymond Chandler's *The Long Goodbye*, Alistair MacLean's books, Baroness Orczy's *The Scarlet Pimpernel*, Hilton's *Lost Horizon* and Conan Doyle's *Sherlock Holmes*. These in addition to the popular titles already mentioned have the same things in common, regardless of whether they were written with children, teenagers or adults in mind: action, pace, suspense, excitement, strong characters, extraordinary situations and events dealt with simply and logically but with an emotional appeal which involves the teenage reader.

It seems that though teenagers will read a great variety of books available for borrowing, when it comes to buying for themselves the majority of those who buy do so for the qualities outlined above whether through the normal retail outlets or through school book clubs. There is a curious attitude towards school club buying which persists amongst many teenagers, particularly boys. Many who would not set foot inside a bookshop eagerly spend their money on books in the school paperback club. Many when told that their choice was available in the school library and they could borrow instead of buy preferred to buy, some on the paradoxical grounds that what was in the library was school-type literature and therefore presumably to be shunned as 'educational' reading, whereas what could be bought with pocket money must be more exciting, a child-like but nevertheless valid viewpoint akin to – what is given to you is someone else's choice, what you choose for yourself is your responsibility. The freedom to spend, in adults and children, has a palpable excitement not present in the freedom to borrow, but to many young people that freedom is cancelled out by the deterring atmosphere, arrangement and unspoken rules of the average bookshop. These differences account for the fact that left to themselves teenagers will buy the kind of paperbacks obtainable through supermarkets and local stores, but would not encounter the more demanding fare sometimes because it is in hardback, but largely because it must be obtained usually from a bookshop.

When books, which have been approved for quality, interest and entertainment by editorial boards, are offered through the informal channels of the paperback clubs and eagerly bought, the whole psychology of adolescence and the attitudes towards books and reading come into play.

However, what teenagers buy to read often differs from what teenagers borrow to read. Reading preferences of those who use libraries are frequently sampled by means of analysis of issues and request records and by questionnaires and observation.

Analysis of responses to the literature read by teenagers produces a list of responses which vary in priority according to the ability of the reader, the academic, the less academic, the teenager in school or the teenager at work. By collating information from many investigations it is possible to produce some basic positive responses which teenagers expect their reading to evoke. Older academic teenagers who read regularly like books which touch off new questions, deepen awareness, stimulate the intellect, stir the emotions, provide moral and social

6

insights and have an escapist quality which takes the reader
out of himself. Even the young bright teenager reveals a preference for reading matter which involves the intellect whereas
the less academic of any age tend to put the escapist aspect
first. A survey of reading interests of eighth grade students aged
thirteen and fourteen exemplifies this.[104] The results showed
that there were differences between the bright, the average and
the dull in priorities and in level of difficulty of the content
within the type chosen.

Bright boys	mystery	93·7	adventure	87·5	humour	81·2
Average boys	adventure	92·1	mystery	52·0	humour	40·2
Dull boys	mystery	64·2	adventure	46·1	love	39·2
Bright girls	humour	61·1	mystery	55·3	adventure	50·0
Average girls	love	59·2	adventure	50·0	humour	43·0
Dull girls	love	95·6	mystery	78·2	adventure	47·8

It is interesting to note that humour has a high priority place
with the bright boys and girls, humour in text as opposed to
pictorial humour in comics, requiring a bright mind which can
distinguish the verbal play or the incongruity.

The content therefore is acceptable according to the level of
response it evokes and the measure of that response against
the expectations of the reader.

In the Walsall Teenage Library a survey was undertaken to
see what use was made of the fiction stock in order to find out
what teenagers liked to read and to assess the reasons for the
popularity.[105] The resulting list of popular titles and reasons is
shown in Appendix B but a summary is relevant here. The
popular titles were those in the following categories:

Books specifically for teenagers.
Adventure stories.
Crime and mystery stories.
Science fiction.
Ghosts and horror stories.
Classics if in paperback format.
Adult historical stories.
Girls' stories normally found in the children's library.

Generally adult titles in these categories were well read. This
conforms to the findings of a recent survey of what children like

to read[106] in which 78% of the sample preferred to read about children older than themselves. The Walsall survey, however, was undertaken before there was a large body of teenage work available in Britain though later assessments suggest that in Walsall at least the growing number of such novels is well used.

When the whole field of literature is included, the non-fiction read by teenagers covers as broad a spectrum as adult reading but with emphasis on social themes even amongst the less academic, and on sport and biography. Required reading or assigned reading must be outside the scope of this study although the readability factors outlined at the end of this chapter are applicable as much in school-required as in voluntary reading.

The writer noted down the books requested by seventeen- and eighteen-year-old boys in a Borstal training establishment. Some were requests for specific books and included the following:

Susann	*Valley of the Dolls*
Greer	*Female Eunuch*
Williamson	*Tarka the Otter*
Guillot	*Kpo the Leopard*
Harris	*Fanny Hill*
MacLean	All titles

Subject requests included drugs, accident prevention, guitar instruction, motor bike workshop manuals, blues and soul, witchcraft and magic, first aid, languages, football, cookery and aircraft identification. Some requests had been disallowed by the governor of the institution on the grounds that they were detrimental to mental or physical well being or would reinforce undesirable features of the inmates. Such requests covered Hell's Angels type books, autobiographies of escaped convicts, technical works on locksmithing or firearms, and in one case, a book on antiques because the requester was serving time for stealing antiques.

However, the range of acceptable requests indicates some of the aspects that largely deprived teenagers wanted to read about. In addition to the 'sexy' books read by a large percentage of the teenage population at some time during adolescence, teenagers choose to read books on sex and marriage and those public, college and school libraries which include this aspect in their stock invariably find they are well used both in the library and in circulation. The analysis of book lists later, shows the recognition by many librarians of this teenage concern, and the attempts to supply the reading need, though numerically the number of titles available is small.

The Enoch Pratt Free Library's Young Adult Service is particularly noteworthy in this respect, its book lists combining the librarian's knowledge with the adman's psychology and the design artist's expertise.

A survey of young adult college students[107] produced the information that although fiction came first in the list of reading preferences, it was closely followed by socio-political commentary and then by religion, including the eastern religions. Tied in fourth place came philosophy, personal and developmental psychology, technical works, biography, poetry and the arts.

There is therefore a divide between the non-fiction reading of the academic and the less academic, but in terms of treatment of theme rather than the theme itself. Many of the themes suggested by the teenagers in the few library selection teams open to them, substantiate the evidence of interests in reading in social matters.

The Youth Advisory Committee, aged thirteen to twenty-one, at the Scott Free Library, Merrill, put forward suggestions on general stock building and maintenance and offer specific titles of paperbacks and cassettes for committee approval.[108] Arising from this, two non-fiction categories were suggested as necessary and likely to be popular: 'New Ideas' which covers new movements, counter culture and anything and everything new, turned out to be the most popular non-fiction section, followed by the other suggestion 'Current Issues'. Other sections for paperbacks such as 'Youth Scene', 'Law and Crime', 'Russia, China and Communism', give some idea of the interest in socio-political themes amongst the whole age range. What the Wisconsin teenagers choose on behalf of their peers for the library collections relates closely to most surveys of what teenagers choose to read.

What teenagers choose to buy or to borrow is usually discussed in terms of content but the physical content and style are equally significant in the teenager's choice of reading.

Summarized, the many surveys of these aspects indicate that the teenager chooses to read books, both fiction and non-fiction:

1. With an interesting cover.
2. Of a comfortable size in format.
3. With large clear, legible type.
4. With appropriate illustrations, preferably in colour and at least half page size, with recognizable content, providing satisfaction in proportion to how real and lifelike the illustrative content is.

Readability to the teenager also means in terms of style, vivid, colourful, lucid, clear, fluent, and entertaining in concrete language.

Add to these the teenager's choice of content as:

1. Intriguing title.
2. Narrative style.
3. With an omniscient author.
4. A realistic story.
5. Set in contemporary times.
6. High on physical action.
7. With one main character, usually a male of own age or older.
8. With an explicit moral for boys and an implicit moral for girls.

Readability for most teenagers is not the result of a graded vocabulary or sentence structure but the visual and emotional appeal of the books most easily accessible and available.

What most teenagers choose to read is not found in libraries nor is it borrowed but bought. Only a minority of teenagers borrow regularly and voluntarily from school or public libraries. The sociological and psychological reasons have already been explored; some indication of the attitudes towards books and libraries has been given; some stumbling blocks created by teachers and librarians have been outlined. After the brief description of what teenagers choose to read it is necessary to look at what librarians provide from the publishers' selection, and on what both base their selection, in order to determine how closely it relates to what teenagers want of their reading matter, how much it is a reflection of what librarians think teenagers ought to read, and how effective it is in creating or maintaining teenage use of the public library.

Chapter 5
Book provision for
the teenager

Public library provision of books for teenagers is a separate
issue from provision by schools, the schools having a statutory
duty to educate and the primary purpose of books in the school
being to aid the educative process through a common course
leading to a common standard. Selection of books for school
libraries has, therefore, a more direct and straightforward
purpose than selection for teenagers in the public library, where
the tradition of education, recreation and information for all
has been treated in varying order of priority with statutory
compulsion to maintain a service but no legal requirement that
special categories of people should receive special attention.

There is, therefore, in librarianship today a body of librarians
who firmly believe that the librarian is under no obligation to
provide books for those teenagers who show no inclination to
read them and that to attempt to do so would mean lowering
the library's standards. They consider that their duty lies in
selecting books which will encourage those who do use the
library to progress further and deeper into good reading and
which will provide them with a reading foundation on which a
lifetime's reading can be based. They believe that reading is
not everyone's passion and should not be foisted on those who
are indifferent.

There is also a body of librarians who equally firmly believe
that provision for teenagers is as much of a luxury and as
unnecessary as selection specifically for senior citizens or for
young marrieds, and who consider that selection for children
up to fifteen covers the younger end and selection in the adult
department covers the older end of the age range, refusing to
jump on what they consider to be the bandwagon of pandering
to the commercially created teenage market.

At the other extreme is a body of librarians who believe that
the librarian has a missionary role to spread the values and
joys of reading as widely as possible in order to bring others

into the stimulating and satisfying experience of the book world. This body of librarians tends to be outward looking both personally and professionally, selecting books to be taken to the community whereas the first two categories of librarian select for the community's teenagers who come into the library. Selection therefore depends to a high degree on the basic philosophy of the individual librarian as to the role of reading and the role of the librarian. No one has yet committed librarianship as a whole to any one of these bodies of opinion, but there are many good librarians who have committed themselves to provision of books on a passionate belief in one of these categories. Names that hit the headlines tend to be those in the third category such as Janet Hill in England and Margaret Edwards in America, who are noted not so much for their selection as for their promotion of that selection.

However, all librarians with any responsibility for provision of books to teenagers are anxious to identify books suitable for that age range. It is possible to turn for help to the publishers who produce and publicize books for teenagers and to look at what they decided to put into that category. Another source of identification is the review journal which classifies the works reviewed under the heading teenager, young adult or older reader, thus adding the reviewer's selectivity to the publisher's. Book awards may also indicate the outstanding works for young adults, creating the acme of selectivity. In addition to all these, panels of librarians and others produce lists of works considered suitable for teenage readers, to aid the librarian in need of guidance.

It is supposed that the publisher has researched the market and has selected those works which will appeal to that market, has then packaged the work to add to that appeal and has aimed the publicity at those anticipated readers and those who buy on behalf of the expected readership. The librarian is in the latter category and selects from what the publisher advertises as intended for the age group. It is useful therefore to look at what publishers offer as series for teenage readers.

Perhaps the earliest series are in the realm of the career novel which presents an indication of the nature of the job by following the main character through a series of situations in story form.

The Bodley Head's Career Books for Girls with titles such as

Air Hostess Ann, Kate in Advertising, Pauline Becomes a Hairdresser
and *Judith Teaches*, follow a pattern of entry into the job,
making friends, aspects of the work involved, romantic interest,
happy ending with successful completion of training or examination, possibility of promotion and/or hints of a permanent
relationship with the current boyfriend.

Shirley Darbyshire's *Sarah Joins the WRAF* typified the series
in a helpful and entertaining if rather rosy picture of recruit-
ment into the service, initial training and job possibilities within
the service, with the brochure type information given flesh and
blood by being set around Sarah and her family and friends
with a very slight and unrealistic romantic interest. Marred by
the inevitable inaccuracy of facts which have changed since
the book was written, it is nevertheless readable and informative and though the characters are slight, the book and its
fellow career novels are read as undemanding novels in their
own right as well as for the career theme.

A different kind of career novel series is that for older girls
where the character is followed through a sequels series. The
Bodley Head Sue Barton (nursing) series and the Carol (acting)
series are typical. Helen Dore Boylston's creation is seen in
progressive stages of a nursing career, usually one stage to each
book. In *Sue Barton, Rural Nurse*, Sue and her doctor fiancé are
in a backwoods area of the States and take second place to the
selfless concern for relations and patients. The text is high-
minded, very moral and easy to read and is akin to the major
women's magazine stories in style and content and in the
pleasantly flowing pace.

Similarly Chatto and Windus's Career Novels are an inno-
cuous introduction to a job, the types of problem that might
arise professionally and technically and an indication of the
need for moral and personal decisions relative to the job. The
jobs covered include social work, music, riding, librarianship,
hotel work, electrical and motor mechanics, estate agency and
the RAF. As the male counterpart to Sarah in the WRAF,
Duncan Taylor's Jim Bartholomew of the RAF is a rather
wooden character with little evidence of humanity to relieve
his dedication to being a good serviceman. In the Chatto titles
for boys there is much more information slotted into the plot
than in those for girls in the Bodley Head series.

Some of Cape's titles in the Jets series fall into the category of novels in a particular job situation with a large amount of glamorized adventure. Constance White's *Sally of St Patrick's* follows Sally as a student nurse in and out of one hospital event after another, each one a common event in hospitals but presented in such a way as to stereotype or caricature the event. The romantic interest involving medical students is little better than pulp literature romances but the large print, short sentences and black and white illustrations are designed to appeal to the reluctant or retarded reader and the known appeal of nursing to many girls assures the book of a consistently large readership.

Similarly James Stagg's *Sam Best; Reporter* has little description, much action, a forced plot and stereotyped characters. The unnatural dialogue may be the result of the short sentences but the reporter/newspaper relationship is inaccurate in factual terms. However, these titles are not offered as career novels and should be taken in the same context as novels with a job theme.

On the whole career series are a mixture of school story, light romance, career information and novel on a subject theme, and have a wide readership in school and public libraries despite the datedness of much of the information. While all novels should be evaluated on their literary merit, improbable situations are acceptable in the cause of the plot and currently impossible situations and characters are permissible in fantasy and science fiction, but in the interests of preventing distortion of the job, the improbable and impossible should have no place in career novels. The realism required here is the factual information and the unsentimentalized and unglamorized depiction of a job, but such a requirement tends to produce a stilted and dull character and book. In terms of readability the Sue Barton type novels and the Jets are successful with large numbers of teenagers because the degree of sentimentality is greater and the author is not bound by the amount of job information he ought to include.

Librarians select career novels for a variety of purposes including the provision of job information in a digestible and 'human interest' form thus taking note of the teenager's desire for the latter and of books on themes and characters relevant to teenagers, since the career novels are all based on teenage characters. Where the library has a career section, the librarian differentiates between the careers information novel which depicts the job accurately and complements the non-fiction stock and the careers theme novel which ought to be housed in the general stock.

A long-standing British series intended for the younger teenager is Penguin's Peacock series in which, often, the paperback edition of a previously published hardback work is chosen for 'older readers'. Many of these titles were not originally for children or teenagers but have the human interest, the romance, the adventure and the mystery in the right proportions; titles such as Broster's *Flight of the Heron*, Elizabeth Goudge's *Towers in the Mist*, Jack Schaefer's *Shane* and Margaret Kennedy's *The Constant Nymph*. Other titles have an appeal originally aimed at teenagers as in Beverley Cleary's *Fifteen* and L. M. Montgomery's *Anne of Green Gables*.

Sales and library use confirm that many of these titles are popular and most teachers and librarians know that *Fifteen* is read by every teenage girl who sees it and by many boys. In a youth club in a 'tough' area, the present writer found that every girl there had read the book and enjoyed it despite the facts that (a) Jane was a middle-class 'nice' girl, (b) the American background was foreign to them, and (c) Stan was considered to be a bit slow in his dating behaviour.

The teenage interest in books filmed or serialized on television can be seen in the popularity of *Walkabout* and *Anne of Green Gables*, available in the Peacock series.

Heinemann's hardback Pyramid series is designed to cater for the older teenager who needs a simpler form of fiction, in terms of vocabulary and concept, which in the short length books at the same time manages to retain a quality of style. Although there are differences in style, theme and message, the works in this series contain the qualities of readability required by teenagers and appeal to reluctant readers despite the absence of illustrations.

Michael Hardcastle's *Don't Tell Me What To Do* is a fast-moving story of Tom who, after hitching a lift gets involved in a diving adventure with dubious connections. Although the style is literate the adult relationships tend to be overplayed and the romantic interest shallow, but the overall effect of the story is pleasing to a non-bookish teenager. Similarly Irma Chilton's science fiction story, *Take Away the Flowers*, has pace and suspense and is equally attractive to girls and boys. Other titles in the twenty or so available cover the themes of young love, motor bikes, leaving home, death, desertion, football and finding an identity and two of the books, though undoubtedly suitable for teenagers, are not part of the contemporary setting common to the other titles, Steinbeck's *The Red Pony* and Swarthout's *Whichaway*.

In this series is one of the few British books for teenagers to depict West Indians in a sympathetic light. Joan Tate's *Out of the Sun* manages to catch the Caribbean flavour of the characters in a story which is an antidote to the racialism and prejudice usually shown in books with black leading characters, in that Jenny and her family are human beings rather than black human beings.

Where this series is provided in libraries, both keen and reluctant readers make their choice amongst the titles, the reluctant tending to go for the catchy titles like *Cycle Smash*, *Goals in the Air*, *For the Love of Mike* and *Whizz Kid*. Heinemann have two other series aimed at the teenager, the Lone Pine series where Simon Baines, created by Malcolm Saville, assists his father in solving crimes and mysteries, and which appeal to the young teenage reader, and the William Abbs Stories for Today series which is designed for the backward reader and which in short words and sentences on contemporary themes tries to cater for the interests of the less able. Although this series cannot be considered in any way literary, nor is it intended to be, it is very shallow in character and theme.

Intended as supplementary readers in addition to normal reading, the New Windmill Series under the general editorship of Anne and Ian Serraillier, is a collection of contemporary books in hardback form from young teenage books to adult titles, recognized as good in their own right and as suitable for critical purposes also. Heinemann also produce the Modern Novel series, outstanding modern novels with commentary and notes for study for students.

Perhaps the best-known British series for · teenagers is Macmillan's Topliner series, well known because of the indefatigable advisory editor Aidan Chambers, who champions the cause of the reluctant reader by writing books for, writing about, reviewing and advising on books which will speak to the adolescent in his present condition. Many of the titles in the series were commissioned specially on the evidence of the author's previous publications where 'theme, story, style, treatment and maturity'[109] had appealed to teenagers. The range of interest and reading ability required is equally deliberate, to satisfy the eleven to sixteen age range with Hildick's *Birdy Jones* and *Louie's Lot* at the younger end and Gunnel Beckman's *19 is Too Young to Die* (originally *Admission to the Feast*) at the other end. In between come the books which appeal to the whole range, *Ghosts*, *World Zero Minus*; an SF anthology, both compiled by Aidan and Nancy Chambers. The seven stories of SF are written by Asimov, Temple, Clarke, Wyndham, Sheare, Christopher and Bradbury, thereby ensuring well written work with thought-provoking punch lines, liked by good readers in their teens though not written specifically for them.

The romantic interest inherent in Dianne Doubtfire's *Escape on Monday* and John Foster's selection *That's Love*, also ensures wide readership. Joan Tate's translation of Gunnel Beckman's book provides English readers with the story of Annika, a Swedish girl who discovers by chance that she has leukaemia. She goes to her childhood holiday house to sort out her emotions and agonizing memories in the light of that knowledge. Particularly moving is her reasoning for and against suicide as a way out of her illness. The novel has great strength in its coverage of elemental matters which exercise the minds of thinking teenagers, and a higher standard of reading and conceptual ability is required for this work than for any of the other titles in the series.

An indication of the linkage with what teenagers do read can be seen in Vicky Martin's *September Song* which was originally serialized in the magazine *Honey* and has a similar holiday romance theme to, for instance, Betty Cavanna's *Scarlet Sail*.

Approximately forty titles are available in this series and Macmillan are at pains to stress that none is written to a formula nor are the authors limited by the publishers to a style or a theme. It is evident in the books themselves that their claim is accurate and the accusation most often levelled against the series, that the standard varies, is not valid when the publisher's aim was to provide a varied collection to suit the varying ages, abilities and interests of those who are not able to tackle fully demanding adult books or even fully demanding teenage and children's books. It is open to librarians to select from amongst the titles if an even level is required for a known readership.

Designed for the youngest teenager, Macmillan's Club 75 appeals also to reluctant readers in the middle teens who can identify with the young characters in contemporary working-class situations. These illustrated pocket-sized paperback short-length stories are attractively produced under the general editorship of Aidan Chambers. One of the six titles available is John Kitching's *Anyway*, five stories about Terry who lives in a high rise block with Jock his dog and Mum who is separated from Dad. Each story reveals schoolboy antics and anti-social tendencies: shoplifting, non-payment of bus fares, first love, teacher baiting. Each story has an unhappy ending but each shows the development of thought about aspects of life and people, the delights of going against authority or tradition or rules, and the consequent pains, whether the rebellion is going up the down escalator or shoplifting, the unfairness of life, when rescuing a boy from a fighting girl Terry is blamed, and the strangeness of adult attitudes as in the very moving story of the death of Terry's dog.

The setting, vocabulary, emotions, attitudes, conversations are all closely aligned, with no jarring or obvious patronizing of a working-class boy, and closely allied to a young teenage boy's real situation. Though the author clearly has sympathy with the situations that create a lawless and loveless child, he is able to show the human reactions in a very acceptable way, avoiding stereotypes, sentimentality or distortion. Because of the pace, action and length, the stories read aloud well and the present writer has used them with educationally subnormal teenagers to great effect, though the sad endings caused momentary distress.

In contemporary settings, the Tempo series provides very short stories in limited vocabulary with plenty of illustrations but capturing the atmosphere and the appearance necessary for slow learning teenage readers.

The Jets series, produced by Cape under the general editorship of Margaret Kamm, offers a dozen titles intended particularly for male teenage readers who need pace, action and a short length novel. Apart from the two titles mentioned in the careers context, the themes range from detective, war and space flight to motor bikes, farming and pop groups, all themes known to interest the teenager. Robert Bateman's *Skid Pan* interlinks the desire to own a motor bike with a small gang's plan to rob a warehouse and manages, as do all the authors in this series, to present the morally and legally 'right' way to behave as part of the plot. James Webster's *The Four Aces* traces the creation of a pop group of four boys who work hard to achieve their dream of playing in public. Stilted vocabulary and moral in outlook but a fast moving plot, the characters seem old-fashioned now and bent on redeeming each other, 'I reckon he's had to learn his lesson the hard way. When you stir up trouble for other people, you sometimes make a much bigger stink for yourself.'

However, the books are intended for the reluctant reader who likes to 'get into' the book immediately and prefers, as surveys have shown, to have an explicit moral. Several series intended for the less able teenager are produced by a growing number of publishers in Britain. Perhaps the best known is Benn's Inner Ring Books in several groups of fiction and non-fiction.

Alan Pullen's *Devil's Dump* involves three teenagers who need wood to build a bar in their youth club. They go to the rubbish tip, find a small girl trapped there and restore her to her family. The controlled vocabulary precludes any deep exploration of character or plot and the pace is slow, the story dull and the love interest forced. The same author's *River Cats* has much more substance and less tendency to preach through the characters of Sam and his girlfriend in a dockside episode at the Cat Club run by Father Green for the teenagers known as the River Cats.

The second series within the Inner Ring is less dated but equally variable in didacticism. Michael Hardcastle's *Smashing* has Tony and Jan witnessing a car smash, aiding the victims and acquiring their written-off Mini. The fairy godfather who provides spares and licence money for the re-building and subsequent use of the car introduces some 'sensible' thoughts on driving fast and old people's safety on the roads, which jars somewhat. Apart from this, the story flows though the characters never come alive.

All the books are designed to cater for the backward reader and are written in short words and sentences on simple ideas. Richard Kennedy's black and white illustrations on every page reinforce the story. Another series within the Inner Ring is the sports series with such titles as *Goalie, Run, Top Spin* and *Splash*. The latter, written by David Clarke, follows Ruth, a keen but lone swimmer, through her entry into a swimming club, coaching for swimming competition and preparation for future success in the sport. Set in a shallow story line, the characters are dull, though the swimming information is accurate and helpful.

The Inner Ring Books have been available for about seven years in normal and in Braille editions and readership has extended from schools to public libraries. Literary judgement is difficult when the works are tailored in vocabulary and sentence structure and are not intended to be literary works, but basic plots and characters are wooden and dull. Well used by backward readers in the absence of other provision, these books have not the substance achieved by an Australian series for teenage readers, the Trend series produced in Australia by Cheshire and in Britain by Ginn. Under the advisory editorship of J. A. Hart, a noted authority on and author of books for the backward reader, the series has a vigour and a more realistic outlook not found in the Inner Ring series.

Although the themes covered are similar to other series, bikes, dope smuggling, radios, dancing, moving to a new place, boy/girl relationships, the average impression is that the Trend teenager characters have flesh and blood and are part of the situations described rather than planted in them.

Laurie Seawell's *Some Trannie That* has a simple plot of a middle-class boy given a transistor radio for his birthday, on which he hears a police message about a stolen car. With the reward for finding the car he throws a party and some confusion in his girl interests causes a certain amount of distress but he ends up with a good party and the right girl. Portrayed as a thoughtful, well-behaved, somewhat reserved boy, part of a normal and sympathetic family, Tony is a good example of the fact that not all books for teenagers depict them as criminal, neurotic or dissolute.

Terry Nash's *Watcher on the Wharf* has a more restricted vocabulary content but covers a plot in which the short pithy sentences are suited to the suspense-full story. Marco, fishing on the wharf, uncovers a drug smuggling scheme in a frightening experience with rats, both animal and human.

For the romantically inclined Kurt Hogan's *It Happened on Saturday*, manages to combine humour, emotion and romance in a very restricted word and sentence structure. Lin has a dog called Fred and a boyfriend Ken. Fred, hit by a car is taken to the vet, sees a cat and recovers rapidly, 'Dog knows what he wants.' Evidence of emotion is seen in the reaction to the dog's 'death' and in Lin and Ken's relationship. This is one of the few books aimed at girls.

Rarely in this series is there an explicit moral or an emphasized message. Most of the works have a simple but interesting plot, a fast pace and a good grasp of human relations and reactions. The format, illustration and cover in each case is part of the series design. Pocket sized, each work has black and white illustrations and one other colour splashed in rich profusion on the cover and some of the page illustrations. *Some Trannie That* has bright yellow on some of its sixty-eight pages, Bettina Bird and Ian Falk's *Hey That's My Bike* has black and red illustrations on each of the fifty-three pages. The use of visually attractive colour, modern style illustration, large print, plenty of white, simple vocabulary and teenage interest themes makes this series unusual in the combination of controlled vocabulary and satisfying story.

Other series for teenage backward readers such as Methuen's Forward series, also available in Braille, and Dent's Manxman series, and Schofield and Sims' Data series, while catering for the less able reader are more school texts with teacher's notes and graded titles than fiction for teenagers. Cassell's Patchwork and Onward Paperbacks have simple sentence structure, large type, short lines and plenty of action, as have Heinemann's Booster Books, Joan Tate Books and Wide Horizon Reading Scheme.

With similar educational intent but covering fiction rather than 'readers' a number of publishers offer educational editions of works chosen for readability as in Blackie's Teenage Bookshelf series with titles such as Clifford Hanley's *The Taste of Too Much* and Bill Naughton's *A Roof Over Your Head*. With information notes and questions, this series is firmly in the educational category.

Hutchinson's Unicorn series under the general editorship of James Reeves, produces secondary school readers with starred difficulty grades, e.g.

1. J. R. Townsend   *Gumble's Yard.*
2. M. Baldwin   *Grandad with Snails.*
3. J. Wyndham   *The Day of the Triffids.*
4. J. le Carré   *The Spy Who Came in from the Cold.*
5. M. Duffy   *That's How It Was.*
6. E. O'Brien   *The Country Girls.*

The Oxford University Press Pictorial Classics is akin to the cadet editions produced by many publishers. Charlotte Brontë's *Jane Eyre*, re-told by Muriel Fyfe, retains the language flavour of the original and incorporates much of the actual text but most of the scene setting and descriptive passages are omitted or condensed into a sentence or two. The characters lose most by this condensing and the relationship between Jane and Mr Rochester and Jane and St John Rivers, which in the original is cleverly and delicately drawn, appears unlikely in the re-telling and would seem inexplicable to the teenage reader who had no knowledge of the original story. However, the book is ideal for the backward or reluctant reader who has seen the film as the two complement each other. The illustrations do justice to the period and the mood though the mad Mrs Rochester is drawn almost as the stereotyped caricature of a mad woman. Every page has an illustration which appeals to the reader put off by the slabs of text in the original.

The Pictorial Classics, therefore, enable the teenager who would not or could not read the original to achieve a measure, if not the full measure, of enjoyment and satisfaction. This is true also for many deaf young people who could not be introduced to the classics by the reading aloud method common to other teenagers.

At the top end of the reading ability range comes the Bodley Head New Adults series covering hardback fiction and non-fiction, the content and style of which are considered to appeal to the top end of the teen range who would be reading adult books. Some of the titles chosen by the Bodley Head for this series would be unlikely to have found their way into the children's library and would possibly be lost in the adult collection so the creation of such a series spotlights works which might otherwise have been passed over by the selectors in libraries.

There is no question of formula writing in this series; the

works are diverse in theme, origin and style and cover a variety of intellectual levels. Stephanie Plowman's *Three Lives for the Czar* is an English work on an historical theme; Gunnel Beckman's *A Room of His Own* is a Swedish work on a young man's growth to independence; Rex Warner's *Athens at War* is the re-telling of the history of the Peloponnesian War; American Paul Zindel's *The Pigman* looks at responsibility and Australian James Couper in *Looking for a Wave* covers the story of a young man's search for summer excitement and his involvement with the people he meets.

The reading adult and young adult whose mind and interests are verging on maturity or who has mature abilities is offered a novel such as *The Pigman* where varying levels of intellect will derive satisfaction and be provoked into useful trains of thought. The pen portraits by John and Lorraine who write alternate chapters, reveal that their actions are in keeping with the self-expressed desire to shock but graduate neatly into interest and concern in the Pigman as a person, drawn by the element of mystery about him.

The silliness of adolescent horseplay becomes involvement in a personal relationship with the elderly man, bringing with it a sense of responsibility. The breakdown of trust and the failure of responsibility cause death and the two young people realize that they are responsible for their own actions and for the effect on others. John, for all his bravado and his self-considered superior intellect, does things unthinkingly, 'I didn't realize,' and guilt and concern follow. Lorraine acts as a brake on John's behaviour and is a bewildered unsure girl seeking confidence in John's assuredness.

Identification with these two is not difficult for the teenage reader and the attraction of the mysterious Pigman is in keeping with teenagers' interest in the unusual. Eccentricity is writ large in the house, personality and language of the Pigman, who is lonely and finds purpose in life by visiting the ape at the zoo. The betrayal of his relationship with John and Lorraine shocks him, compounded by the death of his friend the ape.

The quirky adolescent humorous style alternately colloquial and poetic in a mixture of stream of consciousness and report style causes chuckles, despite the apparent solemnity of the theme, much of John's text reading like the off-hand, throw-away humour in adolescent talk. The outward bravado and the inward sensitivity are clearly revealed, both only too typical of the teenager and both likely to be seen and appreciated by the mature reader. Though many adult readers and librarians consider Zindel's books to be grim and concerned with the seamy side of life, many teenagers find them funny and have confessed to laughing aloud, not in sacrilegious manner, but in genuine amusement at some of the incidents, the use of words and the fellow feeling with the characters.

Conforming to the teenager's liking for ghost and mystery stories, Stephen Chance's *Septimus and the Minster Ghost* allows the reader to wallow in suspense. One sixteen-year-old reviewer, a highly intelligent and extraordinarily articulate boy, considered that this book was redeemed from a certain amount of 'square-ness' more suited, he thought, to adults, by the graphically phrased fact that 'bits of sin keep dropping in'.[110] Again the teenage interest in 'sin', manifested so extensively amongst non-library readers, is revealed in a book reader with a very high reading ability and experience and suggests that the Bodley Head has its finger on the pulse of teenage reading needs and interests.

Totally different in theme and style is another offering in the New Adults series, Rex Warner's re-telling of Athens at War. Taken from Thucydides' *The History of the Peloponnesian War*, the brilliance and tragedy of warring peoples is made memorable by the very clear and compelling style; in Pericles' words, '. . . the brilliance of the present is the glory of the future, stored up for ever in the memory of man.' This is a good example of the purpose behind this series, that of bringing to the attention of parents, librarians and teachers some of the books which young people with adult understanding would enjoy, but which would otherwise be lost between the adult library and the children's library. Never intended for teenagers only, the series has been noticed by older readers and teenagers, by reviewers and librarians. Unlike most other series, then, this is not a collection of a particular genre or within specified subject, vocabulary or content limits, but an extraction from the publisher's own output and titles published overseas, of books which have an appeal to the thinking mind of the eighteen-plus reader.

In a sense, therefore, the publisher has done what the librarian would otherwise have had to do, select titles suitable from the mass.

Current American series for teenagers can be identified in the Rosenbergs' Young Peoples Literature in Series,[111] but the large paperback series like Dell's Mayflower and Harcourt, Brace and World's Voyagers, Scholastic Book Services' Teenage Book Club and the Archway series tend to be similar to what in England are called books for older readers and have a vastly greater sale to libraries than any paperbacks series in Britain has proportionately at present.

What the publishers select for presentation in their catalogues and where they place the works for teenage readers may also influence the librarian's selection. Most publishers have a schools catalogue and a 'trade' catalogue, not always duplicating the material even where appropriate. Within each catalogue 'library' books are often divided into fiction for younger children and fiction for older children and it is the latter category which differs considerably from one publisher to another.

Few publishers take the opportunity to publicize appropriate adult stock in this section, often on the grounds that printing costs are high and the catalogue must be kept within tight limits. Of all the British publishers' catalogues, Gollancz's Books for School Libraries comes closest to the ideal in its section headed Fiction for Older Children and the following section, Science Fiction. Here Peter Dickinson, Erik Haugaard, Madeline L'Engle, Ruth Arthur and Jean Fritz rub shoulders with Kingsley Amis, A. J. Cronin, Giovanni Guareschi and John Le Carré. Ursula LeGuin and Andre Norton are linked with Asimov, Clarke, Heinlein to form a usefully co-ordinated list for the selector for teenage readers.

Other publishers who have series for teenagers tend to publicize these in individual catalogues. Foremost among these for attractive presentation of information is the Macmillan Education 1973 catalogue for Topliners with reproduction of the book covers, annotated descriptions of each title, review quotations and effective use of colour. If publishers were to include some of the teenage titles in their adult catalogues and publicity information, those many libraries in Britain without a section for, or a service to teenagers might be helped to include stock suitable for that age group.

The majority of teacher librarians in Britain select library stock from publishers' catalogues and information material and the school catalogue could therefore be a much more powerful influence on the inclusion of more suitable adult books in the school library. But as more and more library systems adopt the on-approval arrangement, publishers' catalogues become a checklist and a reference source rather than a selection aid for public library selectors and the *Bookseller* and *Publishers' Weekly* and/or BNB and Library of Congress lists are more often used. The opportunity for publishers to group books through those means is limited and it is possible that publishers would benefit from a re-arrangement of the 'trade' catalogue to differentiate between older children and the teenager or young adult by doing a lot more pre-selection themselves in order to create a list inclusive of teenage titles, adult titles known to be popular with young people (and every publisher has several such titles), and adult titles containing the ingredients known to be required by librarians selecting for the age group.

Pre-selection and evaluation in the review journals is better organized in the States than in Britain, there being only haphazard and intermittent reviewing of books for teenagers in British review media whereas several American journals devote a regular section to books for young adults.

The Hornbook Magazine entitles its relevant section Outlook Tower, with the aim of highlighting 'Current adult books of interest to high-school readers and occasionally books for younger teenagers'. Most of the works in this section are biographies, history or relate to social issues. The interest in things Chinese and Russian mentioned before is a notable indication of the relevance of the selection to known interests, as in the inclusion of Solzhenitsyn's novel *August 1914* and Mao Tse-Tung's Poems in one of the issues. Books for the younger teenager are covered in the section Stories for Older Readers.

Similarly *School Library Journal* has a section labelled Adult Books for Young Adults which is edited, somewhat controversially, by a panel called the San Francisco Bay Area Reviewers, controversial because some librarians in other areas of the States feel that the books are evaluated in a manner biased towards the particular problems of young people in the Bay area. Divided into fiction and non-fiction, the range of books covered tends to be wider than in Outlook Tower, by including romances, science fiction, counter culture, hobbies and careers. There is little difference in the style or length of annotation in the two journals though *School Library Journal* reviewers perhaps have the potential teenage reader more firmly in their sights in relating content to adolescent needs and interests. *The Hornbook Magazine*'s six issues a year means many fewer titles covered than the number possible in the *School Library Journal*'s monthly issues and its reproduction in *Library Journal*.

In Britain *Junior Bookshelf* in six issues a year covers a variety of books for teenagers in the ten to fourteen range, both fiction and non-fiction, but the treatment of books for over fourteens is haphazard, there being the occasional inclusion of a section labelled 'For the Intermediate Library' with one or two titles reviewed. From time to time articles appear on aspects of books for teenagers but the overall coverage is intermittent.

Growing Point has nine issues a year in which Margery Fisher groups reviews by theme with the likely inclusion of titles appropriate for teenagers within the theme group. Occasionally a group relates specifically to teenage readers as in, for example, Speaking for Youth, Life-work and Family Stories for Older Readers. Usually there is a very brief section labelled Adult Books, again on a particular theme but only one or two titles are reviewed and these may be adult books about literature rather than adult books for teenage readers. Were the librarian to read each section of Margery Fisher's admirable review journal, he would undoubtedly come across titles relevant to teenage readers but the arrangement does not facilitate quick access to these.

Children's Book Review makes no attempt to differentiate between books for teenagers and those for others in age groups though relevant titles are covered within the fiction section in each of the six issues a year.

Books For Your Children, a quarterly journal has a pattern of reviewing and the reviews and articles by parents, teachers, librarians and children may cover teenage books only once a year. When they do, as in the summer issues of 1972 and 1973, the information is down-to-earth, refreshingly worded and usually revealing.

The School Librarian separates its book reviews into those for Sixteen to Upper Sixth and Eleven to Fifteen, covering all subjects and fiction under those headings. Published quarterly, the coverage and the quantity of books relevant to teenage is greater than in the other British journals, and the reviews are alive to the fact that what teachers and librarians may consider good and informative, and moral about the books may not be so considered by teenage readers. This recognition is one of the strengths of the teenagers' reviews in some of the issues of *Books For Your Children* where the candid comments of teenage readers, admittedly the more intellectual reader, can surprise publishers, teachers and librarians.

Nationally produced lists are available in Britain and America for the librarian concerned with teenage book selection. The Library Associations' Books for Young People eleven to thirteen-plus compiled by the North Midlands Branch of the Library Association and reaching its third edition in 1960 was intended at the time of publication as a guide to the best books available. The list was arranged in classified groups to facilitate selection for chronological and reading age differences, and was a good solid coverage of fiction and non-fiction, helpful to teachers and librarians, but by present standards is now rather dull and dated both in appearance and content.

The School Library Association's *Eleven to Fifteen*, a basic booklist of non-fiction for secondary school libraries, compiled by Peggy Heeks and revised in 1963, did not set out to cover the best but to suggest information books which would be of value in the school library showing, where appropriate, differing treatments of a subject. Allied with two other SLA publications it is possible to consider that the basic books for teenagers in school are represented: *Fiction, Verse and Legend*, a guide to the selection of imaginative literature for the middle and secondary school years. Compiled by Dorothea Warren and Griselda Barton in 1972, it widens the fiction range to include books which may not be the best but which have been found acceptable by teenagers not considered to be good readers.

Grouped by theme, the titles are intended to provide a checklist of books not covered in standard or classics lists but offering an enjoyable and worthwhile imaginative experience. Taken in conjunction with the SLA's *Contemporary Adult Fiction 1945–1965* for school and college libraries, a list of books with a short list of critical works on the modern novel, chosen and annotated for the use of sixth form and other students, the reading and age abilities are covered. The latter work lists about 300 titles most of which librarians would think of if asked to produce a list and which many keen reading teenagers would substantiate as valid recommendations. The selection is graded by A for advanced reader, L for suggestion that the librarian or teacher should read the book before shelving in the library and x for books especially good of their kind. For example Iris Murdoch's *The Italian Girl* is A, Jack Kerouac's *On the Road* is L and Joyce Cary's *Prisoner of Grace* is x.

National Book League publications also cover a range of interest and ability amongst teenage readers.

Many books selected from the whole range of literature have been adjudged suitable for young adults by panels of librarians and educationalists. Chief among these is the Best Books for Young Adults Committee of the Young Adult Services Division of the American Library Association. Their annual list includes around thirty titles considered by the ten committee members to be the best works, published in the previous year, which could be promoted for young adult readers.

The criteria for selection are that the books have proven of potential interest for young adults and meet accepted standards of literary merit, the whole list to cover a variety of subjects for a range of tastes and reading levels. Announced in *American Libraries* each April, the list is then published in leaflet form with annotations to the fiction and non-fiction selection.

The Library Association County Libraries Group published in its Reader's Guide series a twenty-eight-page booklet called Attitudes and Adventure,[112] a list intended to help those who work with young people. Compiled by Sheila and Colin Ray, the annotated list suggests books for teenage readers, under theme headings, as in attitudes to the opposite sex, work, family, society, to social climate, to growing up, and, under adventure, historical, people, humour, science fiction, mystery, supernatural, high adventure and romance, short stories and true adventure. By combining teenage and adult books of quality on each theme this is a most useful list relevant to adolescent needs and interests and could form the basic collection for a service to young adults although the majority of books included are for the able readers and the older teenager. A new edition is in preparation.

The Young Adult Reviewers of Southern California, a panel of librarians, consider a range of books suitable for work with young people and produces an annual list of fiction and non-fiction, reviewed alphabetically, and with a section on books that are *not* recommended, a most useful aid for selectors when most reviewing media have already pre-selected the 'better' from the worse.

A useful British list is Reading for Enjoyment; for twelve year olds and up, chosen and introduced by Aidan Chambers and published by the Children's Book Centre, London, the children's bookshop with possibly the biggest range of books for children and young people in Britain. Approximately ninety titles are listed and annotated, descriptively and evaluatively and the coverage of children's, teenage and adult books makes this list almost a core collection which could be used as it stands as the basis for a teenage library collection.

Individual lists are produced by individual libraries on themes and types of book for young adults and some of these are analysed at the end of this book. It is sufficient to say here that such lists are compiled for teenager use, to publicize the local stock, whereas nationally produced lists are mainly used by librarians rather than teenagers. The locally produced list is also intended to fit the needs of the local community and to cater for subject information requests, perhaps for school work, to publicize the local stock and to provide guidance within it. In this sense, then, such lists are not relevant to this section which is concerned with the influence on the librarians' selection.

In both countries many books with a teenage readership are published outside a series, and are identified in the catalogues and lists only by a grading key symbol or the publisher's advertising descriptions. The numbers of books suitable for teenage readers is such that a list here would serve no useful purpose either of fiction or non-fiction, and the identification of adult titles in reviews and lists is such that many selections are personal and subjective. However, in both countries books with a teenage readership have won either juvenile or adult literary prizes but some prizes are offered specifically for works for teenage readers and are considered as an aid to selection processes and standards.

The American prizes specifically for the teenage group are headed by the Children's Spring Book Festival Award's section for twelve and up awarded to the most outstanding book from those published from January to May in America in any one year. Some of the winners exemplify trends and types of book, such as Nat Hentoff's *Jazz Country*, Erik Haugaard's *The Little Fishes*, Geoffrey Trease's *This is your Century*, Jill Paton-Walsh's *Fireweed* and Mary Rodger's *Freaky Friday*.

An award, now discontinued, for the best science book for youth aged thirteen to seventeen was the Thomas Alva Edison Foundation National Mass Media Award which went to Mather's *The Earth Beneath Us*, Gray's *Exploration in Chemistry* and Beadle's *The Language of Life*. The same Foundation also provided a prize for the work for ages twelve to sixteen, of special excellence in portraying America's past and Scheer's *Yankee Doodle Boy*, Meltzer's *In Their Own Words* and Abernethy's *Introduction to Tomorrow* received this before the award was discontinued in 1968.

The National Association of Independent Schools Awards offers an annual prize for the ten best adult books for pre-college readers grades 9 to 12, books which have 'literary merit and importance of content'. For example, the list for 1967 was:

Jan de Hartog	*The Captain*
Robert Ardney	*The Territorial Imperative*
Alan Moorehead	*The Fatal Impact*
Joseph McCoy	*The Hunt for the Whooping Crane*
Kamala Markandaya	*A Handful of Rice*
Charles Weltzner	*Southerner*
Justin Kaplan	*Mr Clemens and Mark Twain*
Horace Gregory and	
M. Zatwenska	*The Silver Swan*
Rob Coughlan	*The World of Michelangelo 1475–1546*

The *Seventeen* magazine short story contest encourages young people between thirteen and nineteen inclusive to submit previously unpublished short stories judged for 'literary worth and convincing characterization'. The award offers nine money prizes and publication of the top three stories in the January issue of *Seventeen*.

There are no British awards specifically for books for the adolescent age group though the 1972 *Times Educational Supplement* award for the best information book for children up to sixteen went to Magnus Magnussen's *Introducing Archaeology* (Bodley Head) which is certainly for the older end of the range. The Carnegie Medal has been awarded several times to books for teenage readers and there is some discussion as to the advisability of introducing a special section within the Carnegie award for books for teenagers or teenage readership.

The inclusion of adult books in many of the prize selections and the inclusion of books for teenagers which cover 'touchy' themes, is an important forward-looking element necessary if the adolescent reader is to grow into an adult reader, yet it is on just this point that many librarians and teachers fail to agree. Robbing children of their innocence, pushing them too soon into the adult world, exposing them to the corrupting language and behaviour depicted in these books, removing the protective covers of childhood and exposing the adult way of life, these are some of the thoughts and expressions of those who oppose, restrict or ban the selection of the adult books and outspoken books for teenagers in libraries for young people. Others are equally certain that these books can help young people by educating their feelings, showing them patterns of life, verbalizing emotions, introducing them to concepts and opinions which are thought-provoking, character building and stimulating to the imagination.

Recognizing that most young people read adult novels of one kind or another, many writers, librarians and publishers feel that they are responsible for ensuring that what little is read by teenagers should have a constructive and productive quality in addition to the escapist enjoyment.

> The best juvenile [i.e. teenage] novels ... allow a little liberating laughter. The ones that raise human questions without providing pat solutions and stock scapegoats. Those that recognize and salute youth as part of the continuum of life.[113]

Similarly Geoffrey Trease believes that biographies and teenage novels help the reader to 'learn more, gently, privately and without embarrassment about the complexities of adult life'. Thus the portrayal of adolescence as a maturing process rather than in a vacuum is suggested as a good guide to the validity and value of the content.

Recognizing too that teenage readers are interested, and always have been interested in their own physical and emotional development, many writers have set out to speak of those areas of life about which teenagers are concerned or in which they are involved.

Nat Hentoff in a perceptive and challenging article about writing fiction for teenagers says:

> There is no reason [for such writing to be self limiting] if the writer can free himself of his own strictures concerning what books for 12+ ought to leave out in terms of language and subject matter. The conflict then will not be inside the writer but between him and certain librarians and certain editors in the juvenile department of publishing houses – at this stage probably most librarians and most editors of books for the young. If they resist language and themes which the writer knows are essential if his book is to be read by the young, then he will find out if he has indeed written a novel, period.[114]

The language and themes of some books not specifically intended for young adults also speak to the teenager who, far from being unaware of or unprepared for the big issues of moral and social concern, spend a lot of time watching and listening to talk about them on television, discussing them in school and arguing about them amongst themselves, questioning long-held views and traditions. This leads them to find a few books which set the points at issue in manageable proportions which, if they do not answer, at least give an airing of the subject, and if they give an answer, it is not necessarily the answer that the average adult reader would accept.

Award winning books like the *Autobiography of Malcolm X*, Griffin's *Black Like Me* and Salinger's *Catcher in the Rye,* and others like Sillitoe's *The Loneliness of the Long Distance Runner* and Lynne Reid Banks's *The L-Shaped Room,* all written because the author had something to say, something passionately felt, have been read by large numbers of teenagers who do not often read.

Strong themes, strongly depicted characters, strong words, these are the books which many teenagers go for, teenagers brought up on television, not shielded from the adult themes on the screen whether fact or fiction.

John Rowe Townsend believes that the emphasis on quality and contemporary mores and values contains the risk of

1. writing, publishing and selecting books that children will not read,

2. expecting authors to write with one eye on the moral climate thus stultifying their creative impulse,
3. judging books by the wrong standards.

'It is not irrelevant that a book may contribute to moral perception or social adjustment or the advancement of a minority group or the Great Society in general; but in writing there is no substitute for the creative imagination, and in criticism there is no criterion except literary merit'[115]

Criticism of books for teenagers is well covered in several works which contribute opinion, research and information on the genre and form a basic body of analysis which has been read and pondered upon by most librarians dealing with the teenage range (see Appendix D). From this body of knowledge and with the regular information aids about new publications, the librarian embarks upon choosing books for his or her specific library, the actual and potential users.

The evidence of successful book selection is the usage of the library and the circulation of the stock. The librarian's errors of judgement are the permanent fixtures on the shelves, an accusatory reminder that they are not the right books for the readers. But all librarians make selection mistakes, often from the best of motives and all librarians are faced with the problem of providing books both for the known clientele and for the potential reader, the former determined by analysis of appropriate records and by observation. All librarians must provide for variations in reading ability, levels of knowledge and personal interests, and most librarians are unsure of their position in relation to the provision of what the reader wants as against what the librarian considers the reader ought to have.

This dilemma, or less strongly, problem, seems to reach a peak of intensity when the reading public served by the librarian is of teen age, an intensity compounded by the lack of standard practice as to just where the teenager should be served, children's, adult's or teenage library and by whom, the children's librarian, the lending librarian or the young adult librarian. Added to this is the question, a problem felt by many librarians serving teenage readers, of responsibility for what teenagers read, acting in *loco parentis* on moral issues in reading matter and in place of the teacher in the matter of good literature which will stretch, educate, develop the teenage mind.

The variations in practice between Britain and America pale into insignificance when compared with the variations between one town and another in provision for teenage readers. It is not surprising, therefore, that the question 'selecting for whom?' has no stock answer. Nevertheless, the question is, or should be asked by every librarian responsible for selecting for the teenage range and the answers each librarian gives produce an amalgam linked to the definition of a teenager given in Chapter 1.

The age range numerally is different now from the original obvious ages of thirteen to nineteen, as those who work with young people have discovered; 'teen' is now considered to cover the twelve to seventeen range but many librarians class the younger end as children and the older end as adult, leaving themselves with the fourteen to sixteen group which they consider truly teenage in every sense. Others classify the sixteen to twenty range as young adult. But within both labels the younger people will be

1. at school, college or work,
2. bright, average, dull, retarded,
3. real readers, reluctant readers, marginal readers, non-readers,

and their reading needs differ accordingly. Whether or not there is a separate physical location within the library for books for teenagers does not matter in basic selection terms. The librarian is selecting for the age and interest needs of the teenager as such, rather than the library section where the librarian has pigeon-holed him. It is up to the staff to devise means of promoting the literature wherever it is located.

However selection for such an amorphous mass is unworkable and many librarians provide their own limits, such as selection for the locally resident teenager's general and recreational needs, leaving his subject needs to the school library and the reference library, selection for the teenage student's informational and recreational needs, selection for the 'real' reader then for the 'light' reader, selection only for the teenagers who use the library rather than with an eye towards getting in those who do not. The public library in Merrill, Wisconsin, found that between six and seven of every ten persons using the adult department daily were between the ages of thirteen and twenty-one, and the library staff adjusted their selection and services accordingly.

Some librarians looking at their reasons for providing books find that, having decided why, the who and the what follow automatically. There is a certain amount of common ground on the 'why' select and provide. According to many accepted viewpoints in many countries, librarians are selecting books for teenagers in order

1. to enrich their lives by aiding personal growth through emotional appeal and the identification of problems of adolescence and of human behaviour,
2. to extend their boundaries of thought, knowledge and experience,
3. to redress the balance, outweighed by shallow doses of opinion, information and entertainment via television and the press,
4. to cater for the whole person, study, personal and leisure needs,
5. to provide educational, spiritual, social and moral upliftment,
6. to counteract uniformity and conformity,
7. to provide enjoyment also in each of the above,
8. to encourage the apathetic to read more,
9. to provide information needed for personal or school study.

While most of the reasons for selection spring from the *raison d'être* of librarianship as a whole and all are acceptable in principle to most librarians serving teenagers, the emphasis in the 'what' to select is often placed on just a few of the 'why' such as numbers 3, 5, and 8 to the detriment of the others, thus creating boundaries which are likely to spring from the limitations of the librarian rather than the needs and interests of the user.

In order to overcome this problem, national and local standards of book selection have been devised, mostly directed at quantity in terms of volumes and finance. The ALA standards incorporate a brief recommendation for selection for young adults, of the one-sixth volume *per capita* up to 500,000 population, one-third should be for children and 5% for young adults. Thus a library system serving 500,000 population should purchase annually 4,166 volumes for young adults.

The standards for England and Wales, suggested as basically

applicable annual additions of 250 volumes per 1,000 population up to 500,000 but made no recommendations for quantity of books for young adults, referring only to the importance of catering 'for the special needs of young adults' to stimulate a 'variety of skills and interests'. This is a reflection of the period in which the standards were compiled, there being little interest or literature for young adult or teenage readers in the early 1960s in Britain. However, were the American 5% to be applied to the British basic overall figure of 250 volumes per 1,000 population, an even higher total, 6,250 volumes, would be allocated to books for young adults. To duplicate these for distribution to appropriate service points would, of course, greatly increase the figure.

Consideration of quantity is followed by quality and other criteria, many relating to accepted selection criteria for any reader, some particularly applicable to selection for the teenage reader.

Scope, coverage at differing levels of vocabulary and intellect, readability, presentation, physical attraction, these are basic to any type of book, as are accuracy, bias, up-to-date information, plot, characterization, unity and expressive style. Criteria pertinent to books intended for teenagers are propounded by many librarians in policy statements, reports, publications and lectures and usually cover the following aspects.

The book must have something to say to an adolescent, some librarians add something of importance to say to an adolescent, their definition of importance being something which adults think it is important for teenagers to know. Taking into account the reading interests of teenagers, as already outlined, and their known psychological, intellectual and social pre-occupations in life, it is possible to determine whether the theme and purpose of the book is within the adolescent's interest or experience range. As shown in Chapter 1, one cause of teenagers' attitudes towards reading was the experience of books provided in public libraries. The necessity for books that attract and are enjoyable to read was related to the competition for the teenagers' interests and time, competition which offers attractive and enjoyable pursuits.

The book must be of high interest, those which reflect the teenager's physical and emotional situation, actual, potential, or desired, and though there are many adult novels which fulfil

6. A view of the Teenage Library, Walsall.

7. One of the Withers Rooms showing the Musicians' Gallery in the Teenage Library, Lincoln.

these conditions, the rise of the teenage or junior novel sprang
from the need for relevance. Many of the teenage novels have
gone from relevance in the total-self sense to relevance in the
realism sense. Both allow relevant concepts and emotions to be
displayed and explored, although some adults closely connected with the literature feel strongly about the proliferation
of teenage novels set in seamy context, exploring the miseries
of life.

Sheila Egoff, despairing of the emphasis on the dark side of
life said,

> They [the young] appear to be the unhappiest, most upset,
> distressed, suspicious, alienated, introspective generation the
> world has ever known.[116]

Sylvia Engdahl, on the other hand, saw the climate as one in
which

> . . . a writer can express what seems to be true to him when
> his opinions are not in accord with the cynical bias of our era.
> He is free not only of the old requirement that he ignore
> aspects of life, but of the adult market's demand that he view
> those aspects in a sordid and sensational way – and to me,
> both of these freedoms are vital.[117]

The evaluation of what the book has to say to the adolescent
lies not only in whether what it has to say is relevant, as this is
identifiable, but also in how it is presented. In this sense
whether the theme be dark, miserable and unpleasant, or light,
happy and attractive, it becomes unacceptable to librarians
only when treated in a sordid or sensational way. It has been
said that one man's realism is another man's science fiction so
that what appears to be distortion of experience may be only a
manifestation of the saying that truth is stranger than fiction.
The distortion of superficiality, caricature characterization,
glamorized experiences, leading to false expectancies, didacticism, and an author's ulterior motives are some of the features
which evaluators find unacceptable rather than the theme of
a book.

It may be unfair to use specific books as examples here in
that there is a danger that the reader may consider them as all
good or all bad, but an interesting comparison can be drawn
between S. E. Hinton's *The Outsiders* and Richard Allen's

7

Skinhead, both on the theme of gang and inter-gang warfare, both with a deprived teenage boy as the main character, both with anti-authority and pro-violence content, both with the boy depicted on the paperback cover as a gang member, identifiable by clothes and posture. There the similarities end, the treatment of the theme taking differing lines.

Ponyboy, one of the outsiders, is drawn with depth and sympathy, the development of the character is related to the plot, the events live through the power of identification with Ponyboy. Joe Hawkins, the skinhead, is superficially sketched as a character and though his insensitivity is realistic in the context, the character does not develop with the plot but seems to be translated from one situation to another. The glamorizing of experiences in *Skinhead* ignores those aspects of similar experiences in *The Outsiders*, which involve the human emotions of fear, pain, cowardice, pride, friendship, creating a distortion of experience in *Skinhead* but adding depth of experience in *The Outsiders*.

Didacticism in trying to get across a message or a moral has disappeared in most adult and children's books but appears in many books for teenagers, obtrusively in *Skinhead*, whereas the conclusions to be drawn from the content are subtly built into the plot and characterization in *The Outsiders*.

Richard Allen interjects a sociological comment from time to time which interrupts the flow of action and which jars in the evaluation of style, while Ponyboy and his friends make similar comments upon society but in their conversations and their projected actions. The former intrudes upon his story, the latter is an integral part of the story.

A group of boys and girls who had read *Skinhead* were told that there was another on the same theme but set in America, of the same length (40,000 words) and in paperback, *The Outsiders*. They all read it and when asked for their comments said that *Skinhead* was more exciting but *The Outsiders* was more satisfying. Hall Ellison's *Tomboy*, with a fifteen-year-old girl as the leading character, came midway between the two in popularity with both boys and girls and was voted as 'real'. All three books have realism, relevance and high interest rating but *The Outsiders* achieves these without sacrificing coherent plot, powerful characterization and expressive style.

The book, therefore, must have something to say to the

teenager, be of high interest and be said at a conceptual level understandable by the teenager. As indicated in the section on literature in schools, many books are studied which are conceptually beyond the teenager required to study them, producing apathy or antagonism in all but the mature teenager.

Psychologists, controllers of mass media, politicians and admen have long realized that even in adulthood the majority of people cannot identify with abstract characters or situations. One study of reading deduced that although 70% of secondary school students in America go on to college only 20% of those graduate from college, largely because most of the works in the college library are at university level, encouraging lack of comprehension and plagiarism and discouraging growth in reading skills.[118] Many college librarians in Britain can also substantiate that situation.

Books must, therefore, be selected to cater for the varying conceptual needs and levels. Some books of relevance and high interest to teenagers are deplored by some librarians, teachers and parents, though it is more often parents and community officials who deplore the actions of teachers and librarians in selecting and making available works which are considered unsuitable. There are a number of schools of thought:

1. that which selects on literary value without regard for whether it teaches the traditionally correct attitudes, believing that the book is a literary product not a moral text,
2. the pedagogical viewpoint that books should be selected for their influence on inculcating knowledge, advancing thought and enriching the mind,
3. the moral school which selects for moral, spiritual and social uplift and which wants to protect the teenager from the works which might offend, sully, corrupt the adolescent mind or incite prurient curiosity,
4. the 'open' viewpoint which considers that selection must cover all textual matter available within the law,
5. the school of thought which believes selection should take account of all these aspects and steer a middle course.

Whichever the viewpoint there are many occasions, many more in the States than in Britain, when the librarian is called to account for the presence of a book which has offended someone other than the teenage reader for whom the selection was made.

All embracing standards on inclusion or rejection have been stated in the American recommendation, applicable to books and information for teenagers and through the absence of any clause excluding them, the implicit recommendation that library collections must contain material with 'various views on important, complicated, or controversial questions, including unpopular or unorthodox positions' and that 'selection must resist efforts of groups to deny access to other segments of the community'.[119]

The English standards do not cover these points at all, perhaps because the incidence of complaints is so small as to obviate the necessity for statements on impartiality and censorship. Janet Hill condemns the too-careful approach to selection which limits the reader to 'watery versions and to excessively well balanced opinions, particularly in politics and religion'.[120] She suggests that a little prejudice is healthy to counteract the teenage reader's feeling that the works chosen to offend no one are dull and uninteresting.

The ALA policy on Free Access to Minors which allows parents to restrict their own children's reading but not to limit the librarian or other readers, does not have 100% backing even amongst librarians, to say nothing of library administrators and local watchdogs.

To cope with this problem many American libraries have a section of their book selection policy devoted to selection in 'touchy' areas. LeRoy Charles Merritt in *Book Selection and Intellectual Freedom*[121] outlines the touchy areas as profanity, frankness in sex, sex information, and religion, and suggests that profanity and frankness in sex are all right if they contribute towards understanding and provide a clearer vision of life, that sex information should be on the open shelves and that books on religion should not be selected if they are obviously denominational or belittling, but general religious works are acceptable.

Others are more liberal, suggesting that

1. the 'offensive' passages must be related to their context in the whole work,
2. the author's norms and values should be considered,
3. crime and violence are enjoyed and coped with by most

teenagers in films, books and magazines and there is no evidence of any co-relation between reading supposedly dubious books and juvenile delinquency. The crime rate is high amongst comics/sub-literature/crime book readers, not because of their reading but because of their poor environment, the lack of education and intelligence amongst such young people. Therefore, given the basic criteria of book selection, this category is acceptable,

4. horror stories and ghost stories, like the horror films, are enjoyed for the thrill and fearful excitement, and are known to interest a very wide range of ability and intellect. Selection should be undertaken with that range in mind,

5. sexual references in books should be considered in the context of the whole book, the selector distinguishing between the pornographic or lewd treatment, the adolescent ribald vulgarities rather than obscenities and the treatment of sexual matters and relationships as an integral part of the story.

All subjects under restriction are usually talked and written about in terms of protecting the adolescent.

Although we do not want to give young people pallid, untruthful, sugar-coated pictures of life, neither do we want to give them too large a dose of ugliness, frustration, immorality and vice, even though these may be portrayed for us with understanding in novels of fine craftsmanship. It is not that we wish to keep the facts of life from young people but that, again, their lack of experience makes it difficult for them to evaluate properly the characters and their problems and actions in many novels.[122]

It is interesting that most magazines for teenage girls maintain taboos on the mention of drunkenness, deformity, illegitimacy, colour and religion, politics and sex, and only a few novels for teenagers mention these, however responsibly, whereas many of the great classics and works studied in school, which are offered to teenagers, or are required reading, are heavily concerned with the powerful presentation of these forbidden or 'touchy' areas. As W. H. Auden wrote in his letter to Lord Byron,

> The pious fable and the dirty story
> Share in the total literary glory.

Although traditionally school teachers have acted in *loco parentis* on many matters concerning the children they teach, legally in matters such as physical care but without legal requirement in others such as reading censorship, librarians have no such legal obligation to train, educate or protect their readers nor to act as the arbiters of public taste. However, some library authorities have required a code of practice or have drawn up a list of banned books, or decreed that in case of doubt the committee shall deliberate and pronounce judgement. This is common in America but rare in Britain, indeed the majority of public library systems in Britain lack a written selection policy and many lack even a generally accepted outline. In far too many, the selection policy is non-existent and each book is assessed on its individual merits in a haphazard way without regard to the overall collection or the needs of the actual and potential readers, using the librarian's subjective reaction to the books as a rule of thumb.

Much restriction is negative, is imposed by people other than the librarian, particularly in the States, people who are concerned about sexual references in books and counter-issues in magazines, who in order to maintain the innocence of the teenage reader usurp the role of the librarian who ought to be above religion, politics and morals in making the public library the place for the availability of all views and facts. As one librarian put it in the title of an article on getting young people to read, 'Innocent Children or Innocent Librarians?'[123]

The more positive restrictions some apply are on:

1. the books which are purposely designed to promote the titillation of the senses in sex and violence,
2. books of physically poor quality in terms of binding, paper and print (with the possible exception of the paperback format),
3. books of poor literary quality in terms of shallow characters, thin plots, poor construction,
4. works with factual inaccuracies in subject information,
5. books with a level of conceptual difficulty above that of the known or potential readership,
6. dull books,
7. out of date books.

In these the criteria, apart from the first, are based on the literary, factual or physical aspects of the book, aspects which librarians are trained to assess, rather than indictment of the content which is a personal and individual rather than a professional assessment.

Books that have something to say to an adolescent, books of high interest and conceptually understandable from the simple to the mature, are not confined to the genre known as teenage novels, and selection takes note of books for children and for adults which contain the readability factors outlined and which contribute to the enjoyment and to growing up in every sense.

Mature books for children are selected for the younger end of the teenage range, most of whom are reading children's books as well as teenage and adult works, especially the girls. Teenage or junior novels fill the middle stage along with a selection of adult books. Preparing for adult reading or moving into adult reading requires the extraction from the range of adult novels and non-fiction of those which contain the previously stated qualities found to be popular with teenagers and assessed as desirable by librarians.

Apart from the popular works, many librarians consider that a core collection of titles and subjects is necessary, books which may not be popular in terms of extensive usage but which are likely to be of value to some who use the library. Such a collection is likely to include representatives of the best contemporary writers of 'good' novels and short stories, a complete set of each of the series written for teenagers' recreational reading, attractive copies of the classics, good coverage of books concerned with education, sex education, careers, health, beauty and personality, survival, social issues. For example, Walsall Teenage Library stock is selected with particular categories in mind.

1. Paperbacks – suitable adult titles and teenage series.
2. Remedial stock mainly for immigrant readers.
3. Normal hardback stock, adult and junior titles as suitable.
4. Non-fiction geared to school work/leisure interests/known needs.
5. Careers stock.

Some librarians believe that curriculum subjects should also form part of the core collection. In this category non-fiction geared to the local schools' curriculum is often selected as a reference collection and added to when there is a change of syllabus or when a more up to date book is published. Much depends upon the self-sufficiency of the local school libraries, the proximity of the public library to the bulk of teenage readers, the provision of a separate library or section for teen-agers and the existence, or not, of a public library service to schools. There is no doubt that where a special consideration is given to gearing selection to the curriculum the stock is well used, even where school libraries are good and a service to schools exists.

The selection of paperbacks rather than hardbacks has been considered by many librarians, who appreciate that the former are known to be attractive but may feel that the greater number of issues obtained from the hardback edition outweighs attraction when budgets are limited. The American Library Association study[124] suggested that most libraries get eleven to twenty circulations per paperback title and that where offered paper-backs circulate better and amongst more readers than hard-backs. Other librarians point out that in schools there is no fuss over replacing a hundred baseballs that have had the covers worn off but replacing a hundred worn paperbacks would be strongly commented upon and in public libraries more opposi-tion is made to the purchase of what are considered short-lived paperback books than to the short-lived electric light bulbs that illuminate them in the library.

Undoubtedly the most telling reasons for selecting titles in paperback lies in the knowledge that they will be read by more people. A secondary but vital point is that more titles and/or duplicate titles can be bought for one hardback outlay. Some librarians avoid paperbacks on the grounds that they can barely cope with existing readers and hardback stock, and would be overwhelmed if by adding paperbacks they also added more readers. Sympathy for understaffed and understocked libraries adds validity to such a viewpoint but the most usual reason for not selecting is that of durability, which produces a possible situation where lack of durability must be balanced against lack of readers. In Britain particularly, where few libraries extend a service specifically to teenagers, this may even produce the equation – lack of paperbacks = lack of teenage readers.

Where relevant the needs of particular sections of the teenage community are considered, as in the case of immigrants, although there is a diversity of opinion and practice as to whether maintaining the national cultures and customs retards integration. Practice in Britain and America ranges from lack of provision because of inertia or apathy; a policy of not selecting specifically for immigrants in order to aid assimilation; to the careful assessment of immigrant communities' wants and needs and subsequent provision of reading materials and services.

For instance, some British librarians have found that there is compulsive reading of native material because of homesickness, deliberate reading to maintain language facility and a desire on the part of parents to acquaint the second and third generation children with the vernaculars and background, be it Asian or European, West Indian or Latin American.

Selection for immigrant teenage readers takes account of

1. the availability of books about the culture and customs in the language and in English,
2. the importance of current affairs information via newspapers and periodicals in the vernacular and in English,
3. the provision of recreational and informational books in the vernacular,
4. the necessity for materials for learning English,
5. the usefulness of easy reading books for teenagers to facilitate the transition from reading in the vernacular to reading in English.

There are several selection aids to books in English for multi-ethnic readers[125] and many publishers produce books for those whose second language is English.

Special consideration is given also to the disadvantaged youth in book selection, some librarians subscribing to Daniel Fader's belief that 'now children read now books'. He stated that ephemeral children understand ephemera and that it was necessary to start with ephemera and 'now' books before moving on to the traditional book world. Thus a selection of newspapers and magazines and paperbacks ought to be maintained in the public library for teenagers if the disadvantaged young people are ever to think that the public library is for them. Only when they are in is there a possibility of leading them on to more demanding reading.

The Minimum Standards for Public Library Systems, 1966, supports this in the recommendation that 'selection must go beyond the requests of particular groups who have come to use the library regularly, and must appeal to segments in the population which do not as readily turn to it'.[126] Statistics show that the teenage segment and the less academic members of the population have least interest in library use and show also that libraries pay least attention to these groups.

The selection of newspapers and magazines for teenage reading is a problem which exercises the minds and taxes the budgets of many librarians. The popularity of certain newspapers and magazines has already been discussed in terms of what teenagers choose to read, but there are discrepancies between their choice and the librarian's choice or lack of it, discrepancies largely arising from lack of space and money. The mature teenager is usually catered for in the selection for adults as is the teenager with an adult specialist interest.

Standards for public libraries in Britain recommend a minimum of fifty representative periodicals and the American standards recommend at least one current periodical to every 250 people served in the area. How closely practice relates to this can be seen in the official expenditure on newspapers and periodicals by British public library systems recorded in the annual Public Library Statistics, produced by the Institute of Municipal Treasurers and Accountants.[127] The variation in expenditure per 1,000 population can be demonstrated by comparing, for instance, the figures for:

County boroughs – £16·71
London boroughs – £16·14
Counties   – £7·42

and within these the 1971–2 statistics for expenditure on newspapers and periodicals show, for instance, that the following variations occur.

County Boroughs		London Boroughs	
Liverpool	£38·96	Westminster	£44·56
Newcastle	£32·00	Waltham Forest	£6·44
Solihull	£4·65		

Non-County Boroughs		Counties	
Llanelli	£26·96	Radnorshire	£19·98
Accrington	£20·38	Buckinghamshire	£14·07
Stretford	£2·43	Pembrokeshire	£0·18

Urban District Councils
Llandudno   £34·85
Windermere   £25·55
Wombwell   £3·06

A study of the whole table from which this is taken reveals that there appears to be no significant feature which would link the low spending authorities nor the high spenders, an indication that the discrepancies are likely to be a result of the librarians' views and their influence on the apportionment of the book-fund rather than an indication of the population's needs.

A survey of reference services in American public libraries[128] found that small public libraries held on average 61 titles, medium sized libraries 153 titles and large libraries 458 titles in periodical holdings. Compared with the figures recommended for school libraries, 100 to 125 for junior high schools, 125 to 175 for senior schools in America,[129] and a select number 'of newspapers and periodicals, preferably those indexed', for secondary schools in Britain,[130] it would be unrealistic to expect the public library to provide anywhere near that quantity for teenagers. Where separate provision is made, some titles, relevant to more than one section, are duplicated, thus providing the periodical for the potentially interested reader in proximity to his other reading matter.

In Britain many public libraries neglect the periodical reading of children and teenagers, some through lack of recognition of the part such reading plays amongst young people, some through shortage of funds and some because the librarians believe that the selection for adults will serve all, ignoring the fact that the periodicals are usually housed in the central library with few, if any, titles at the branches, effectually debarring thousands of readers except those who use the central library. In this respect the downtown teenager is better off, theoretically, than the suburban and rural teenager in the availability of magazines and newspapers, but in fact is unlikely to take advantage of this facility because of his attitude towards libraries and libraries' attitudes towards him.

Surveys of periodical use in public libraries indicate that librarians and their readers want more newspapers and periodicals than are provided for them, particularly in the suburban and rural areas served by county libraries, in both Britain and America.

A survey undertaken in Leicestershire[131] reviewed the provision of periodicals in county service points in the light of the standards' recommended figure of a minimum of fifty, and indicated that of the area groups all but two provided less than twenty between their constituent libraries and some less than ten, many of the service points having no newspapers or periodicals. As a result of the survey and of subsequent team management, the situation has improved but most county libraries in Britain and many rural and suburban libraries in America do not provide newspapers and periodicals except at headquarters and at the large branches.

Recent surveys[132] have indicated a concern over the physical siting of periodicals and newspapers and have found that use increases with proximity to books or to the place where the bulk of readers are, as much of periodical reading in libraries is done while in the library for the primary purpose of book borrowing. Much is chance reading, some is glance reading and there is a growing feeling that a much greater proportion of periodicals is required in the general category rather than the specialist field, apart from major reference libraries. Undoubtedly the use made of periodicals is linked to proximity and there is every reason to suppose that periodical and newspaper reading of all kinds would increase were the materials to be supplied at the service points and in the various age sections of the library systems.

Of the periodicals offered by the libraries in Luckham's survey,[133] the percentages of fifteen to nineteen year olds' interest in, and library use of, various types of periodical is shown as

1. *Professional and Industrial*	2. *Domestic*	3. *Practical interest/hobby*
4%	26%	20%
4. *International/political/ religious/aesthetic*	5. *General Interest*	6. *Story, etc.*
7%	6%	2%

with largely female readership in category 2 and largely male in category 3.

The selection of periodicals and newspapers for teenage readers involves a number of factors:

1. Recognition that the physical format, the pictorial content, the short articles, the colour, the familiarity are attractive to teenagers.
2. The need for a policy decision on
   (a) the provision of periodicals normally bought by teenagers
   (b) the principles of newspaper provision, e.g. that the newspaper under evaluation contributes to the information service or to literacy
   (c) the question of liaison with local schools to duplicate, avoid overlap, complement and supplement holdings, form union lists, etc.
3. Identification of the periodical needs and interests of the teenagers in the community served by the individual library.
4. Analysis of needs and interests to determine the overlap of subject and title with adult readers' needs and interests.
5. Assessment of quantity required for such titles to be duplicated.
6. Selection of subject titles geared to the age and ability of the local teenage community.
7. Relating list of selected titles to available budget to determine priorities.
8. Decision on quantities and siting of selected titles in the public library service points.

The listing of actual titles here is of little use as the periodical world is notorious for the frequency with which papers and journals 'fold' or change title, but from evidence gleaned from many libraries and publications it is safe to list the categories of periodical publications, representatives of which can usefully be supplied for teenage library users:

General
News
Pictorial
Sport
Automobile/bike
Music – popular, jazz and folk
Girls/women's
Alternative press
Newspapers.

When these are sited within the section set aside for teenage readers or in close proximity, substantial usage is noted, and when publicity is given in the teenage section to the names of publications sited elsewhere, interest and usage is shown. Where neither provision nor promotion is made specifically for teenage use, little effort is made by the teenager to go to where the periodicals are.

Although book selection is the subject of this section, it must be stated that selection of non-book materials is part of the librarian's responsibility towards teenage readers but this, even more than periodicals, tends to be outside the scope of the average children's or young adult librarian, being confined usually to the music or record librarian or the media specialist. For this reason consideration of the place and selection of records, cassettes and film materials will be made in the section on public library service to teenagers.

After the why and the what to select, there follows the how, and practice varies considerably from one library system to another, ranging from the individual librarian's selection to team to committee selection.

A director of the Bodley Head, writing on the New Adult series,[134] pointed out the problem of getting it to the right readers, as children's book selection meetings are often separate from adult book selection meetings and, unless there is a separate young adult library, the books for young adults tend to fall between two stools. The reviewing journals and publishers' information material on teenage or young adult literature, particularly in Britain, is usually directed at the children's librarian, despite the fact that many children's libraries do not cater for older teenagers and the adult lending library either takes responsibility for teenage selection or expects the teenage reader to extract what he wants from the adult stock.

Whatever form the selection process takes, it involves a systematic reading of reviews in review journals, listings in the professional and national press, publishers' information cards and publicity announcements and bibliographies. For many librarians these are the only means of informing themselves of publications and the selection must be made on the strength of the reviews or information, with an occasional visit to a bookshop, exhibition or to a library supply agency.

Other librarians are able to see the latest publications

through an approval service which delivers the books to the library for a weekly or monthly book selection meeting. The length of time allowed for this varies, some library systems allotting a day for viewing the books, others two or three days and some retaining all the books after perusal on the practical grounds that what is not selected for branch or central use will go into the exhibition or 'in print' collection.

Under many selection arrangements it is possible for selection for young adults to be neglected where the library system has no young adult service and where the children's librarians and the adult library librarians have not worked out which is responsible for this section of their community. Where the children's selection meetings are separate from the adults' selection meetings, the opportunity to select from the adult books or to discuss adult stock is denied and as young adult provision is most often linked with children's services, if there is any provision at all, a stumbling block is put in the way of efficient selection for the transition stage.

It is common in small library systems, particularly in Britain, for the sole children's librarian to have individual responsibility for selection but local government re-organization in Britain, by creating larger authorities with more specialists, will enable the children and teenage specialists to share the responsibility. Although some counties and cities do not permit the branch staff to participate in selection meetings, though they may encourage suggestions which will be discussed at the meeting, most large systems have adopted a weekly or monthly meeting attended by the area staff responsible for work with young people, the headquarters co-ordinators and, where applicable, the bibliographical services head. Here the evaluation of new titles is made on the basis of reviews or visual appraisal, followed by selection based on stated criteria, known needs, anticipated interest, reading preferences, reading abilities, core stock requirements and finance.

Such a meeting is also used for the co-ordination of stock replacement needs and for the identification of stock which can be circulated or re-allocated in the system. Occasionally such a meeting makes a comparison of titles before purchase and for maintenance and considers questions of re-evaluation of stock.

Some meetings allocate sections of Dewey to members of

staff who undertake to identify and evaluate new titles in their sections and to advise at the meeting; some share out amongst participating selectors the types of fiction, thus not only sharing the burden where quantities of material make the task difficult for each person to find time to cover everything, but also allowing individual knowledge and interest to be used more effectively. Where the book selection for teenagers is but a part of the children's or adults' selection meeting, some systems delegate appraisal and an advisory role in selection to one of the participating members prior to group selection. Some library systems consider it as just one of the categories in the many under consideration at the children's book selection meeting. The majority of public library systems in both Britain and America have no young adult specialist staff and therefore no young adult selection team, and teenage selection forms a small part of the total selection business.

In some systems all new books are read and reviewed by one or more librarians and critical assessment made, the review being filed with the book or duplicated and sent out to service points, from which orders for titles are sent back to head-quarters, for co-ordination of orders and estimation of quantities. Where quantity is determined by finance, the selection meetings gear their choice also to the necessity to apportion funds to the peak publishing periods of spring and autumn, and, when the 5% standard is taken into account, to ensure that quantity approximates to the recommended standard.

Books are also selected on the basis of readers' suggestions and in at least one instance, on provision by the actual readers themselves, who add to a 'Put 'n' take' rack whatever they have bought and finished with, and take from the rack in exchange whatever catches the eye, without recourse to library procedures or records.[135]

Some librarians involve teenagers in selection by asking for suggestions or by inviting them to participate in selection meetings, usually informally and whenever available rather than officially and regularly, such as the Youth Advisory Committee at the T. B. Scott Free Library in Merrill and the Brown County Teen Advisory Board, both in Wisconsin.

Few authorities have a special audio-visual materials selection committee but those few have representatives from

the various sections of the system, including a young adult
library representative, to assess records and film material for
young adult use.

The evidence of the effectiveness of selection lies in the use
made of the library and the stock, deduced from circulation
figures and records, from readers' comments and suggestions,
from the stock untouched on the shelves and from the necessity
for frequent replacement of popular works.

A great deal has been written in professional literature on the
importance of providing the books that will stretch the
imagination and the intellect of those who use libraries and not
enough on the books that will encourage non-library users to
read and to use the public library. Most libraries contain books
for teenage readers which appeal to the born reader and to the
plodder and to the keen seeker after knowledge and most
libraries are conspicuously deficient in books which are anywhere near the level of the majority of teenagers. Librarians
serving teenagers are often known to feel that to cater for the
non-library user means lowering their standards and the
standards of the public library. Librarians who are concerned
to encourage use of books for a variety of reasons consider that
the appropriate term is adjust, not lower, in that levels are
relative and relevant to the community served rather than to
the traditional image or accepted standard devised by
librarians and educationalists.

This does not mean an adjustment which would limit the
provision of books which are 'above' the existing level as every
reader should have works to grow with and enjoyment of
reading does not require an understanding of every word. It
means an adjustment which will widen the field of operation
and provision to include the less able, the currently disinterested
and the hostile.

Publishers are increasing their stock of books for teenagers,
particularly in Britain which lags far behind the States in
quantity and range and, indeed, in acceptance of the idea that
there is such a thing as fiction for teenagers. The identification
of such works by the publisher for the readers of his catalogue
or his advertisement, by means of grouping under a heading or
indicating the age range, is increasing in both countries and,
while not obviating the necessity for librarians to look at all
advertisements and the various sections of the catalogues in the

interests of keeping informed on books in general, such identification by the publisher is time-saving and helpful.

More writers are turning their talents towards the interests and problems of the adolescent stage of life and an increasing number of books of good quality in the literary sense, is arising from the quantity.

More booksellers and library suppliers are becoming aware of the need to stock this category and more librarians are able to pick out from the mass of children's and adult books those works which have an appeal to the adolescent mind, though not written for, nor promoted as for that age range.

The success of a publisher's production, the book, is dependent upon the initial judgement involved at the manuscript stage, upon the appeal of the book, the right amount of publicity and promotion and its availability through the retail outlets.

The success of the librarian's work depends upon his initial judgement in selecting books for the reader, the right amount of display and promotion, and the availability of the book to the reader. These factors are the basis on which is built the public library service to teenage readers.

Chapter 6
An analysis of selected booklists compiled by public libraries for teenagers

The examples selected for analysis were chosen because they represent types of booklist covering general reading and subject themes, indicate the varying purposes of booklists and the differing sizes of public library and the variety of format. They also exemplify styles of annotation and they allow analysis of the frequency of inclusion of certain titles.

1. Purposes:
   (a) London Borough of Barnet Library Services. *Branching Out*: a list of books for twelve to fourteen year olds.
   No aim stated but the title suggests that the list was intended to introduce the young teenager to a wide range of young adult fiction beyond the children's book stage.
   (b) Camden Public Libraries. *15 to 19.*
   The list was compiled to give the teenager guidance when faced with the mass of books in the library, guidance to the 'good' and 'enjoyable' adult books.
   (c) Chester Public Library and Cheshire County Libraries. *Time Past*: historical fiction for young people.
   The listing of over 500 titles in print is intended to provide useful background to the various periods, for teachers and for young people aged ten to fifteen years.
   (d) Dudley Public Libraries. *In New Directions*: novels for young adults.
   The suggestions listed are intended to aid the teenage reader who finds himself in a reading rut.
   (e) Hertfordshire County Library. *Teenread*.
   No aim stated but the apparent intention was to identify paperbacks mainly for teenagers.
   (f) Islington Libraries. Youth Booklist. *Historical novels*.
   No intention stated but it appears to aim at introducing young people to adult historical novels.

(g) Islington Libraries. *Twelve to Eighteen.*
This list is 'offered as an introduction to the adult library' and to some lively books and their authors.

(h) Oldham Public Libraries; Junior Library Service. *Teenagers.*
No aim stated but the list appears to be designed to inform teenage readers of some books about teenagers.

(i) Walsall Public Libraries. *New Teenage Fiction.*
No aim stated but the title indicates the intention to inform readers of some new books.

(j) Enoch Pratt Free Library, Baltimore, Maryland. *Speaking of Books*: an index to book talks for high school students.
No aim stated but the title suggests that the 300 titles are intended to give the teenage student an idea of what to read in preparation for a book talk or book report.

(k) Enoch Pratt Free Library. *Love, Love, Love.*
No aim given, the assumption being that the list was designed to identify fiction on the theme.

(l) Boston Public Library. *Some Things Can Never Be Explained*: a selected list of books on the occult and the supernatural for young adults.
No intention stated but it appears that the list was compiled to enable the young adult to extract this widely popular theme from the general stock.

(m) District of Columbia Public Library. *Read On*: a book bag for young adults.
No aim stated. The suggestions may be intended to introduce the teenage readers to a wide range of fiction and non-fiction of all types and levels.

(n) New York Public Library. *Books for the Teen Age.*
The aim is implicit rather than explicit in the introduction, as a dual-purpose list intended as the guide to the central permanent exhibition of books on the list, and as a guide for the teenager to use in his local library.

Purposes:
1. Introducing the teenager to a wide range of teenage and adult books: a.d.m.n.

2. Guiding the teenage reader through the mass of books in the adult library: b.g.n.
3. Identifying books on a specific theme: c.f.h.k.l.
4. Informing on new books or new acquisitions: e.i.
5. Guiding for specific use of books: j.n.
6. Identifying specific formats: e.

Types of booklists:
1. General reading in fiction and non-fiction: e.g.j.m.n.
2. General fiction lists: a.b.d.h.i.
3. Subject lists: c.f.k.l.
4. New books: i.

Size of library system:
Large: a.b.c.e.f.j.l.m.n.
Small: d.h.i.

Formats of lists:
Leaflet: d.e.f.g.h.i.j.k.m.
Pamphlet: a.b.c.l.n.

Titles in order of frequency of mention: top ten. Adult titles receiving four or more mentions in the 13 lists:

1.	Alistair MacLean	All titles	8	mentions
2.	William Golding	*Lord of the Flies*	6	,,
3.	Ernest Hemingway	*The Old Man and the Sea*	6	,,
4.	Ray Bradbury	*Fahrenheit 451*	6	,,
5.	Charlotte Brontë	*Jane Eyre*	5	,,
6.	George Orwell	*Animal Farm*	5	,,
7.	J. D. Salinger	*Catcher in the Rye*	5	,,
8.	John Steinbeck	*Of Mice and Men*	5	,,
9.	John Wyndham	*The Day of the Triffids*	5	,,
10.	Harper Lee	*To Kill a Mocking Bird*	4	,,

Many other titles were mentioned three times and a wide range of adult books was covered. Less extensive was the coverage of teenage fiction.

Teenage titles in order of frequency of mention: top ten receiving four or more mentions.

1. Paul Zindel	All titles	6	mentions
2. Ruth Arthur	*A Candle in Her Room*	5	,,
3. Susan Hinton	*The Outsiders*	5	,,
4. K. Hunter	*The Soul Brothers and Sister Lou*	5	,,
5. Mary Stolz	*Pray Love Remember*	5	,,
6. Joan Tate	All titles	5	,,
7. Honor Arundel	All titles	4	,,
8. Betty Cavanna	*Time for Tenderness*	4	,,
9. Leon Garfield	*Black Jack*	4	,,
10. Alan Garner	*Owl Service*	4	,,

Annotations

Barnet. *Branching Out.* In one or two sentences the scene is set, the major characters indicated and a suggestion given that interesting and exciting developments will occur. Written in the present tense the annotations are accurate and informative if not gripping.

Camden. *15 to 19.* The annotations are eight to ten lines long, enough to provide vignettes of the books by including brief plot description, thumb-nail character sketches, apt quotation and qualitative or evaluative judgement. Phrases such as 'beautifully told', 'very entertaining indeed', 'high-powered study', 'frighteningly probable', 'strikingly modern', 'depressing, honest and exciting to read', are applied to the books and a brief literary comment on the author or the book puts the work in the sociological and literary context. These review-type annotations are the most informative and helpful of all those in the selected lists, but also require the highest reading and conceptual level of the teenager.

Chester and Cheshire. *Time Past.* One-line annotations serve merely to set the book in its appropriate period and to indicate the character; e.g. for Rosemary Sutcliff's *The Lantern Bearers*, 'Britain after the departure of the Romans', and for Jean Fritz's *Brady*, 'Slavery and the American Civil War'.

The annotations are adequate if the list is used for teachers as a checklist but inadequate for whetting teenage appetite. The sheer quantity of titles listed may also be overwhelming to the teenage user of the list.

Dudley. *In New Directions*. The informal arrangement in broad subject groups with light-hearted headings such as For Laughs, Trouble, and Suspense, facilitates the narrative style of annotation which discusses say, the comic novel through specified titles, and makes a readable introduction to particular types of fiction. The style of annotation, though informal, is evaluative and informative without getting bogged down in plot description, and is well suited to the teenage reader, a masterpiece of economy in achieving so much readable information about so many books in such a small amount of space.

Hertfordshire. *Teenread*. In about fifty words each annotation contrives to present a snappy, descriptive, evaluative and appetite-whetting account of the book. Emotive words like 'tense', 'macabre', 'romantic', 'sad', 'romp' and 'nightmare' are used to good effect and evaluative words like 'gripping', 'sane', 'funny' and 'disturbing' are helpful in pinpointing the mood of the book and the potential effect on the reader. The annotations would lead most teenagers to try out the recommended titles.

Islington. *Historical novels*. In one or two sentences the content is described in straightforward style. There is no attempt to evaluate and no suspenseful suggestion as a lure to the reader.

Islington. *Twelve to Eighteen*. No annotations are given for the fiction but a one-line description is appended to most of the non-fiction titles. There seems to be no logic in the choice of titles annotated and those presumed to speak for themselves. There is no pattern of style either, some annotations being comment on the subject field as a whole, as in Patricia Cooke's *English Costume*, 'Of growing interest as modern fashions take up and diversify the old', a comment which gives no aid as to how this book treats the subject. Some of the annotations are indicative of the content as in Jack Cox's *Modern Camping*, 'How to plan and enjoy a camping holiday'. The content seems to have been arbitrarily selected and haphazardly annotated.

Oldham. *Teenagers.* The style of writing and the planned content of the annotations are in keeping with the subject matter. The teenagers in the books are used as the focus of the annotation, e.g. each annotation begins with the name of the chief character, Nibs and Clee, Meg, Beverley, Robert, Sally, Jo, Dave, Louretta, Ponyboy and Katie. The psychological advantage of such a beginning links with the teenager's need for identification. In two or three sentences the emotional set up is indicated and the ending is left open, often by means of '. . .'. The style and content are well suited to the theme and to the potential reader.

Walsall. *New Teenage Fiction.* The annotations are in a compressed, clipped style which packs the plot into a sentence or two and which manages to suggest to the reader that he *must* find out what happened. There is no attempt to evaluate or comment, but simply to describe simply, except for the last item, Paul Zindel's *I Never Loved Your Mind*, where the annotator apparently found it necessary to indicate that 'this is an extremely funny novel', no doubt because a straightforward plot account might suggest the opposite.

Baltimore. *Speaking of Books.* Not annotated.

Baltimore. *Love, Love, Love.* The one sentence description of the content of each book manages to indicate the plot and to identify the type of love covered in the story, whether physical, inter-racial, infatuation, young married love, love under test or love everlasting.

Boston. *Some Things Can Never Be Explained.* In a mixture of description, comment, quotation and mysterious questions the annotations contrive to present emotive, compelling one-sentence introductions to books on an emotive and compelling theme. Even the annotations send a chill down the spine.

District of Columbia. *Read On.* Not annotated.

New York. *Books For the Teen Age.* Many of the works listed are not annotated though there seems to be no logical reason for the omission. Others have annotations of five or six words which are indicative of the content level, e.g. 'a general survey', or descriptive of the content as in 'America's early Indians', or questioning, 'Intelligent life on other worlds?' or interpretative as in Lipsyte's *The Contender*, 'Using boxing to escape the ghetto', succinct as in *Mr and Mrs Bo Jo Jones*

TABLE 10 *Chart showing the content and make-up of the selected lists.*

Libraries	Title of list	Fiction	Non-fiction	No. of books	Intro.	Annotations	Illus. cover	No. of pages	Printed	Duplicated	Illus. text	Colour
Barnet	Branching Out	+	-	41	-	+	+	6	+	-	-	+
Camden	15–19	+	-	60	+	+	+	16	+	-	-	-
Chester/Cheshire	Time Past	+	-	530	+	+	+	43	+	-	+	-
Dudley	In New Directions	+	-	55	+	+	+	4 folded sheet	+	-	+	+
Herts.	Teenread	+	-	10	-	+	+	folded sheet	+	-	-	+
Islington	Twelve to Eighteen	+	+	82	+	some	+	folded sheet	+	-	-	-
Islington	Historical Novels	+	-	17	-	+	+	folded sheet	+	-	-	-
Oldham	Teenagers	+	-	10	-	+	+	folded sheet	-	+	-	-
Walsall	New Teenage Fiction	+	-	26	-	+	+	6	-	-	-	-
Baltimore	Speaking of Books	+	+	296	-	+	+	4	+	+	+	+
Baltimore	Love, Love, Love	+	-	66	-	-	+	6	+	-	-	+
Boston	Some Things	+	-	56	-	+	+	8	+	-	-	+
D.C.	Read On	+	+	120	-	-	+	folded sheet	+	-	-	+
New York	Books for the Teen Age	+	+	1,256	+	some	+	48	+	-	-	+

+ signifies presence   – signifies absence

'who had to get married', or discursive as in the entries where a lengthy quotation forms the annotation.

Such diverse methods are suited to the diverse subjects listed though the absence of annotation for some and the uninformative comment for others, mar the effectiveness of the list as a whole.

In general the lists which are aimed at a known clientele, such as at Dudley, Oldham and Walsall or which cover well-defined areas as in the Boston subject list or Hertfordshire's paperback list, manage to achieve an informative and readable list which teenagers will enjoy reading and which will create interest. Most of the other lists are lacking in pace and interest, with minimal information to indicate the nature of the book or the level of subject content and could be used mainly as checklists in which case the annotation could be dispensed with, as in Baltimore's *Speaking of Books*.

Many librarians produce reading lists, booklists and bibliographies but few have worked out what they hope to achieve with their lists and few therefore design the list with any degree of forethought as to its expected use. The analysed lists are better than many library lists in all respects but there is ample evidence from many countries that libraries, with the best of intentions, generate a large amount of what turns out to be wasted paper.

Chapter 7
Public library service to teenagers

Having looked at the causes and the reasons for teenagers' attitudes towards reading, at the publishers' promotion of books for teenagers and at the librarian's selection processes it would seem logical that librarians organize the stock, services and staff in such a way as to facilitate teenage use, by enabling the teenage reader to obtain the materials he needs or in which he is interested.

However, logic does not prevail and there is much evidence that far from enabling the teenager to use the library many librarians positively hinder such use. Given that librarians are aware of the lapse in usage that occurs at about fifteen and concerned about the drop in library membership, how far do librarians go in trying to bridge the gap, to ensure continuity, or simply to try to understand the changed needs and interests of the teenage section of their community?

The provision of a library service to cater for those interests and needs is still largely an undifferentiated part of the basic library service to the public and the majority of public library systems in Britain and America apportion only a small area of space or service to the teenage reader; a minority make no distinction between readers except for children and adults, but a growing number of librarians are set apart to concentrate effort and knowledge on the teenage group and, in Britain where there is only one young adult librarian so nominated or set apart, the Youth Librarian in Lambeth, an increasing number of librarians are paying attention to library service to teenagers, providing books if not separate service and stock.

It is useful to note the actual usage by teenagers of the normal public library system, usage which can determine how often and for what purpose teenagers use the library and with what degree of success and satisfaction. Bryan Luckham's survey[136] of members and non-members of the public library found that 12% of the teenagers interviewed were members, that these formed 45% of the membership rate and were mostly students in full-time education, that 24% of them visited the library weekly and 41% monthly.

It ascertained also that the crucial ages of lapsing membership are fourteen (18%) and twenty (20%). A study of the use of libraries in Hillingdon as part of a community survey, was carried out in 1973[137] revealing that young people aged up to nineteen, in the community though not necessarily library members, had some strong views on various aspects of the public library service. They were not too busy to read or to make regular visits to the library, but they did not on the whole consider that it would be a great loss to the community if there were no public library. The majority of teenagers interviewed definitely rejected the idea that they were not interested in libraries though books were not considered to be particularly important in their lives.

Those who did use the library accepted the rules and regulations but there were adverse comments on the staffing and arrangement of the library. Many of the reasons were also expressed ten years previously in an enquiry which surveyed teenagers of fourteen to twenty in schools and youth clubs.[138] The enquiry and the Hillingdon project between them revealed that

1. public libraries did not have the right sort of books. 20% in the enquiry gave this as the prime reason for not using the library and 75% in the Hillingdon survey,
2. librarians are definitely unapproachable and are like schoolteachers,
3. it is easier to borrow from friends than to negotiate the public library hurdles of borrowing,
4. libraries are too quiet,
5. many teenagers blamed lack of time to travel the distance to the library,
6. many thought they had enough books at home.

The general feeling in the enquiry was that school subjects were underprovided in the public library.

Some American surveys have assessed usage as largely student orientated for school or college purposes.[139] Boston assessed teenage use as high school assignment orientated at central and branch libraries with some socializing also at the branches. The young adults were quite prepared to travel to the central library for study material if necessary.

Even where good school libraries exist great use is made of branch and central libraries for school work; reasons given ranging from the school bus limitations on staying after school, school activities precluding the use of the school library, part-time jobs after school putting off homework time and the final condemnation on the school, no opportunity to use the school library during school hours. The public library is likely to be closer to home and can be used in the evening.

Observation of the use of study rooms and subject materials and analysis of issues also substantiate the impression that there is heavy use of the public library in urban areas by young people for school work. Where a separate circulation record is kept of teenage borrowing this too evidences non-fiction supportive reading for school work. Walsall Teenage Library in Stafford-shire had loan figures in 1971 of 10,000 non-fiction and 6,500 fiction and extensive use of the study facilities was noted.

Recent research into public library use[140] looked at the fifteen to nineteen age group as part of the total library user survey of two widely separated library systems, and confirmed the knowledge borne out by experience, that those still in full-time education make more use, more often, than the working teenager and that more boys than girls in the student category frequent the public library.

Research therefore substantiates

1. experiential evidence that the majority of teenage library users are male and still in full-time education,
2. draws attention to the fact that a small number of working teenagers in the seventeen to nineteen group use the library but there is a dearth of fifteen- to sixteen-year-old working teenagers,
3. that this proportion is what is left after the drop-out at about fourteen and that many of those who have maintained their use will drop out at twenty when college and university fulfil their library needs,
4. that only half the users are satisfied with the general stock and the subject stock, and this applies to the working teenager as well as to the student user,
5. that if the user is unable to find subject stock he usually asks

the staff, only about one-third of teenage users surveyed attempted to use the catalogue.

Such use of the library is not unexpected in the light of the information given on the background to teenagers' attitudes towards libraries and literature. When the effects of social and educational background on reading are recognized as being productive of a middle class, able and encouraged to read, reared in an educational and social milieu which sets store by reading, culture and extended education, then the public library is catering fairly adequately for the study needs of the largely middle-class full-time student, but appears to offer very little to the teenager who is not in that category.

This situation is common to those library systems, the majority, where there is no policy decision to serve the teenage community and no separate staff or service. The situation alters considerably when responsibility is laid upon a librarian or a department for attention to be paid to young adults. In these cases the non-student, the working teenager, the deprived and depraved teenager, the teenager *outside* the library, receives attention also.

Generally in America, but less accepted in Britain, the value of a service to young adults is not in question, only the organizational placing of it. But the organizational placing in theory should depend upon the aims and objectives of a library service to teenagers, the purpose of the service.

A 1964 statement indicated major purposes of libraries for teenagers in such a way as to suggest that they were objectives also:

1. to stimulate and direct their reading interests,
2. to assist them in development of research skills,
3. to broaden knowledge and understanding of themselves,
4. to develop ability to evaluate and to enrich their appreciation of the good in all of the media of communications,
5. to create an ability to share with others the ideas and information gained from reading, viewing and listening,
6. to develop life-long reading habits and use of the library.[141]

Exception could be taken to these on the grounds that they are not purposes but aims, the purpose of the public library being to make available the materials in such a way as to facilitate the achievement of those aims. Few librarians ever attempt to assess whether they have achieved the aims or fulfilled the purposes.

A 1970 statement pointed out the library as an agency of education, information and culture but with the necessity for community involvement by the librarian. 'You must get your feet wet and work for your community in more ways than just getting books to them.'[142]

Applying this questioning of purpose to probing into the problem of to what extent the library is committed to the purpose of aiding upward mobility has led some young adult librarians to come out strongly in favour of the abandonment of the direct educative purpose of the teenage library service and to see the teenage library as a community agency whose purpose is to cater for expressed needs and wishes rather than a middle-class institution geared to improving by the imposition of middle-class culture and atmosphere.

In practice public library administrators may specify their purposes and objectives but they do not usually particularize them in relation to categories of people within their communities, thus the placing of a service to teenagers is rarely spelled out and often depends upon a subjective response by the director of the system.

The variety of placings would astound one who had not studied library history which reveals that the presence or absence of provision for children, science and technology, local history and periodicals were all at one time matters of great concern, hostility, outrage and despair, eventually accepted as desirable and presently considered the norm.

The organization of library work with teenagers has been equally chequered and is certainly not yet resolved, the issue currently being clouded in the States by the necessity for financial cutbacks.

In Britain only two systems have a separate library for teenagers, 28% of public libraries have books for teenagers in the children's room and 15% have them in a section in the adult library. The rest make no separate provision at all.

The most obvious organizational placing is as a separate department. The Walsall Teenage Library is situated between the adult and children's libraries in the Central Library, in such a way as facilitates entrance from either the main hall opposite the adult library or through the children's library. The accommodation is small but allows space for display and shelving of about 2,000 books, a browsing area and four study rooms which are situated next to the information bookstock in the Teenage Library and which are extensively used. Children's library staff supervise the room. West Norwood had an informal teenage area with a constantly changing stock but no separate librarian. The other separate room in Britain is in the Lincoln Public Library where the Teenage Library has a completely different purpose and type of user which will be looked at later in this chapter. Again the room can be reached by a short corridor from the adult lending library or through the children's library, or direct from outside via a door into the corridor, the means of entry used on club nights.

The physical location of separate rooms in American libraries varies considerably but generally teenage libraries tend to be adjacent to the children's department. Where there is no separate room the practice of allocation is divided between allotting an area of space or shelving for teenagers and teenage stock in the children's department or allotting an area in the adult library. Opinions vary and many believe that placing in the adult library is psychologically better for teenage use. In the branches a site near to the reference collection is often chosen to enable the school work to be done with the minimum of movement around the library.

Whichever physical arrangement is selected or imposed, the problem of a name for it arises. Librarians have tackled that problem, rarely to their satisfaction, in a welter of invention, as the following real examples show:

Young Adults Library	Older Children
Teenage Library	In-Between
Young Moderns	Youth Library
Teen-Time	Intermediate Library
Tween-Time	Young People's Library
Transition Library	Young People's Centre
The Bridge	Senior Section
Adolescents	The Room
New Adults	

The teenagers' reactions to separate provision and to the titles of the libraries or collections vary; some are relieved to find their

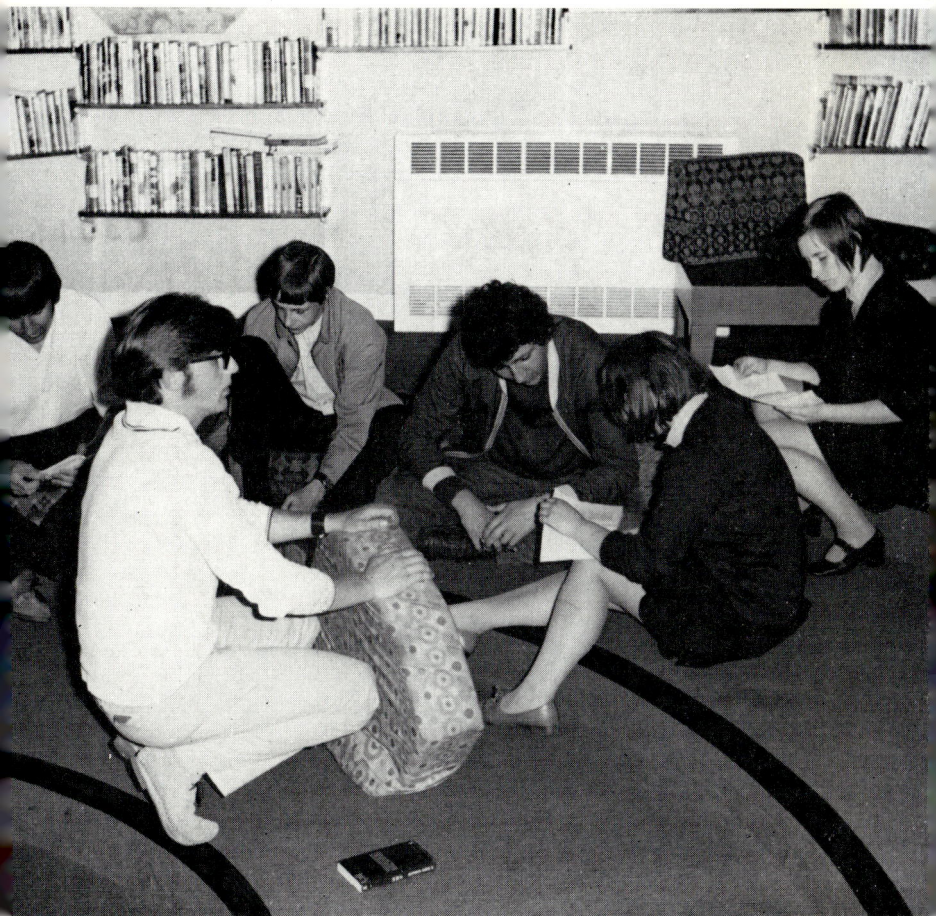

8. An informal group in the Teenage Library, Lincoln.

9. Record and paperback racks in the Teenage Library, Lincoln.

selection done for them, after feeling lost in the adult library and prefer to be able to make straight for a library or section which is identifiable as being for their needs; others feel that a captioned stack in the adult library draws attention to the users rather than the stock and this embarrasses the user; some find the names patronizing or unattractive, particularly Teen-Time, Tween-Time, Adolescents and In-between; some like the less obvious names but do not know to what they refer at first sight without explanation, e.g. Young Moderns, Transition, The Bridge, The Room and Intermediate.

Separate rooms and separate collections have given way in some areas to integrated stock but with specialist staff, allowing all users an opportunity to see the full range of stock and allowing the specialist staff to use the full range for guidance and information.

There are examples in Britain and America of such integration of lending stocks. A Californian branch library in 1971 found that it was later necessary to segregate the fiction because children found it difficult to select from so large a choice, but left the non-fiction integrated to the delight of the adults and young adults who found many children's non-fiction books suitable for their own purposes. The Stevenage branch library in Hertfordshire similarly integrated the stock and in the trial period the arrangement appears to be proving popular.

Other systems are moving away from a separate library towards an adult library book location for the teenage stock but with meeting rooms for teenage use, thus initiating into adult use of stock while catering for the social and cultural meetings arranged for the teenagers who would have used a separate teenage library for social and cultural purposes.

In many American cities and in a handful in Britain, libraries have ceased to expect teenagers to use the traditional library and, lacking space within the library to create a new look to attract them, have taken to heart the message that the library should take a service out to those who will not or cannot come into the library.

New York Queen's Borough Public Library sends a Library-in-Action mobile, stocked with paperbacks and magazines, round the district to the drug rehabilitation centre, detention centres and clubs. In California, Young Adult Project Centres (community clubs) are staffed and stocked and youth centres, parks and halls have manned and unmanned spinner racks of paperbacks serviced by the library.

In Lambeth, one of London's boroughs, a team of librarians and helpers, originally led by Janet Hill, take books and stories out to parks and youth clubs with increasing success at interesting the bored and anti-social teenagers.

Taking books and the benefits of library service out to teenagers in schools via mobile libraries, regular visits and loan collections is also practised extensively in Britain by the majority of library systems, although they are also in the minority in the matter of provision for teenagers in static service points. Many of these outward looking services to Borstals, remand homes, hospital schools and special schools are described in Chapter 3.

Those teenagers who use libraries therefore may have separate provision made for them by one or more of the following:

1. A separate room.
2. A collection of books, usually fiction, identified by a collective name, situated in the children's library.
3. A collectively named selection of books, usually fiction, situated in the adult library.
4. A selection of fiction and non-fiction in a mobile library.
5. No separate stock but a young adult librarian to guide in the adult library.
6. Integrated stock with specialist staff.

The common situation, particularly in Britain, is that unless the teenager comes to the library he is unlikely to benefit from a library service. Just a few systems provide books, magazines and guidance in the teenager's locality, where he spends his time and directed at his interests and abilities.

Where separate provision exists its content varies from library to library. Usually, whether or not the collection is housed separately, the content is recreationally orientated as the student teenagers who predominate use the adult library for books for their school work and the central reference library for information. The content of the basic recreational collection in practice includes mainly fiction in the following categories:

High interest books.
Low vocabulary books.

Adult novels in duplicate or multiple copies and represented also in the adult collection.

Teenage novels in duplicate or multiple copies and represented also in the adult collection.

Teenage series in duplicate and multiple copies and also represented in the children's library.

Older children's novels also represented in the children's library.

Many adults are known to use these collections when they are situated in the adult library, on the grounds that the books tend to be uncomplicated and digestible, with a beginning, a middle and an end, unlike contemporary modern novels, lacking so they say, a flowing plot and a satisfying ending. While this is true of much of the fiction selected by the librarian for such a collection it is reflective also of the 'play-safe' attitude adopted by many librarians.

In America many libraries stock as much as possible of the teenage collection in paperback, including the original paperback titles and the paperback editions of original hardbacks, in multiple copies where known to be popular. In Britain it is rare to find paperbacks in public libraries in any quantity and most teenage shelf collections are fiction in hardback.

Where there is a separate room and one of the objectives is that the teenager's basic reading needs and interests will be met, non-fiction for recreational purposes is included and some information books for school work. For these purposes books of biography, sociology, hobbies, personal matters in the sense of psychology, health, grooming, sex and dating, sport and travel are commonly provided and curriculum orientated information books and career literature, local school magazines and some periodicals are supplied and well used.

When asked for suggestions for stock in the teenage library young teenagers immediately volunteered their wants as books on dancing, jobs, sport; and other media such as magazines, newspapers, tape recorders, records, films and posters.[143]

Anne Osborn, a young adult librarian, wrote in an impassioned article entitled 'How to annihilate library service to teenagers',

The least a library can do for a teenager is to provide some of what he wants as well as what the library decides he needs.

He would like posters and art prints, records and tapes and cassette players, some material free to keep (perhaps discarded paperbacks). He would like circulating film and a film room to try them out. He would like TV. He would like headphones and tape recorders at each table because a huge proportion of 1972 teenagers can't study in the quiet. He would like some plain old junk like comic books, sex novels, hot rod magazines and scroungy underground newspapers.[144]

The Lincoln Teenage Library in England and The Room at Mount Vernon Public Library, N.Y., have made an approach to these in their respective rooms, available for socializing and book browsing, with music and magazines if required, rather than book provision for study in a restrictive atmosphere with an eye on the issue statistics. Both libraries have attracted teenagers who would not enter a public library for the traditionally offered services.

The inclusion of non-book materials for public use is on the increase in public libraries and vocal demand for the availability of audio-visual materials is frequently made by young people who either have access to hardware or who expect the library to make available on or off the premises, the equipment necessary for the information and enjoyment contained in the non-book media.

Television sets in the public library are still a rare occurrence and even more unusual in the teenage library despite the lip service paid to the library as a medium of communication and its place in the network of communication. As indicated earlier many young people spend a large proportion of their time watching television even if for no better reason than having nothing else to do. A study of youth's attitude to television[145] revealed that teenagers watch as much comedy as adults but fewer documentaries and news programmes, and that in America where there are a number of programmes specifically designed for teenagers, such programmes are not viewed in significant numbers.

Many of the teenagers interviewed indicated that television viewing was an anti-depressant and tests showed that the young people were more visibly excited than adults by much of the television screen content. A third of those surveyed said that television was helpful to school work and was much better at explaining current events than were teachers.

Those libraries with television sets have problems such as which channel, sound volume, seating accommodation for viewing and technical maintenance, but find the set well used both for recreational and informational purposes.

Visual material in the form of illustrations and posters have managed to make the acceptability grading of some librarians and are kept in bins or racks, for loan in the same way as books or picture lending schemes. Some are laminated before circulating, others are offered for exchange and are swapped eagerly by teenagers who like to decorate their walls with posters on pop art, pop stars, folk heroes or cars. As with the invitation to exchange personally discarded paperbacks, teenagers' own bought posters may require vetting and some librarians have found that the poster bin requires careful attention at first until a standard is commonly accepted by users and librarian.

The kind of stock held in the majority of teenage collections is the 'good' stock, carefully selected from adult, children's and teenage books; where there is a separate room this is extended to cover good non-fiction, magazines and records. Just a handful of librarians have opened their minds and their shelves to cater for some of the other recreational and informational media.

How is the stock identified as being for teenage readers? Methods vary from one library to another, not necessarily depending upon the siting of the collection. For example in Walsall's Teenage Library the book card in each book has a T to indicate teenage stock; in Kirby, a new town, the Lancashire County branch uses YM on the spine and the book card to indicate the Young Moderns collection, for the purposes of shelving and issue statistics. In Massachusetts libraries a white dot on book spines indicates the young adult collection and in Detroit a hyphen is used before the class number or letter on the spine so that the book can be transferred more readily from and to the adult or junior stock as required. Y seems to be the symbol most frequently used wherever the collection is situated, and the symbol is most often placed on the spine, on the book card and on the catalogue card, its purpose being

1. to enable the reader to find out at a glance, books for his age range and presumed interests,

2. to enable the library staff to shelve the books correctly,
3. to identify the type of readership in the issue records in order to calculate both readership and popularity,
4. to pinpoint in the catalogue the location of the book,
5. to show the young adult holdings in the catalogue.

Some librarians do not consider such identification necessary on the grounds that adding to and removing from the collection is better facilitated, though it is not possible to calculate the quantity of loans unless charging is done separately. Many librarians who make no special provision for teenagers attempt to overcome this by the compilation of lists of suggested reading which can be extracted from the normal adult shelf sequences, thus aiding the teenager who needs some guidance. Some have advocated coloured tickets for teenagers to enable a record to be kept of loans to teenagers from whichever section of stock they select.

Identification of material through arrangement on the shelves and in the catalogue presents problems for many librarians who have devised various means of overcoming them according to their own knowledge of their teenage readers' needs, dependent upon the availability of space, cataloguing help and readers' advisory staff, and unfortunately upon the degree of latitude allowed them by their superiors.

The purpose of the library collection for teenagers again influences the decision on whether a reader-interest category arrangement, which would suit the browsers, or a classified arrangement which would facilitate easy location of specific books, is better for the users.

Opinions and practices vary from that which believes that the teenage library should be less rigid in organizing its materials, on the grounds that self development is thus encouraged, and that which views the prospect of rigid treatment of multi-media resources as a tragedy, in that materials then become 'centralized, classified, catalogued and marginal to learning'.[146] Such viewpoints have lent themselves to the practice of grouping books under broad subject headings, not necessarily Dewey or LC divisions, but user-orientated headings such as Current Issues, History and Civilization, Law and Crime, Ecology and Environment, Youth Scene and New Ideas.

Other librarians have seen the purpose and use made of the teenage library as requiring close order on the shelf and in the catalogue and have shelved by classification number and provided a classified or dictionary catalogue. Walsall is changing to a dictionary catalogue after six years of a classified catalogue, and though cataloguing for the whole system is centralized the librarian advises on entries and headings for the Teenage catalogue. At Lincoln only the hardback stock is classified and catalogued, the paperbacks being shelved separately and uncatalogued.

Some young adult libraries have no catalogue, a policy sometimes arrived at on the grounds that the material is well used, short lived as much of it is in paperback and non-book format, and that it is selected at random so that the only identification required is a checklist for staff use rather than reader use.

Where there is no separate room the collection may appear in the general catalogue as a collection, or be identified within the catalogue by a symbol. Computer cataloguing has enabled some libraries to note the young adult stock and to produce a print-out of the collection or of appropriate sections of the total stock, for specific use with teenage readers. Many libraries in Britain offer no indication in their catalogues of which stock is for teenagers, even where a shelf or stack is maintained.

Guiding in the library by means of stock and shelf labels, by some form of classification and cataloguing, and most importantly, by the knowledgeable librarian, enables the teenage reader to go directly to what he knows he wants, or to browse among broad areas of book content or to ask the librarian to locate what is not immediately apparent. Few libraries offer a dual purpose service, which would suggest that a decision on arrangement and cataloguing ought to be easy – no rigid organizing for the recreational library, close order for the informational library. In practice the varying needs and interests of teenagers complicate such a decision, the traditional middle-class student type user finding little difficulty with a traditionally organized library for specific location of books and information whereas the non-library user, who is the object of much effort by young adult librarians, is averse to the outward regimentation of books in libraries, as he is to regimentation of any sort.

A few libraries have compromised satisfactorily with broad shelf arrangement for fiction and light non-fiction, plus a check-list, and classified arrangement and a catalogue for most non-fiction, backed up by personal guidance from the librarian where needed and/or requested. The main principle for most librarians working with young people is that the books and materials must be easily found or the potential reader will give up the search very quickly. This is shown to be the point at which adequate and sympathetic staffing plays a vital part.

In Britain only one post is specified as for library service to young adults, though many children's librarians posts encompass that age range, either laid down in the job specification or assumed by the individual. The one post is that of Youth Librarian at Lambeth with the flexible job description of 'to set up a more positive pattern of service to young adults throughout the system', and is occupied by Alex McIntosh. Some library authorities give to the senior post for work with young people a title which is all embracing, such as Esmé Green's post of Librarian, Education and Youth Department in the Nottinghamshire County Library system, or the several co-ordinators of work with young people which embrace children, teenagers and schools liaison, in other systems. The two teenage libraries, at Walsall and Lincoln, are staffed by Kate Massey and Christine Knight respectively, as part of their posts in charge of children's services. There is therefore little experience in Britain of the kinds of specialist service that are possible where there is a full-time application of planning, liaison, service and follow-up for teenagers.

Full-time young adult librarians are numerous in the States. In a survey[147] in which thirty-two library systems were questioned, twenty-seven had a supervisor of work with young adults, usually co-ordinators, half of whom reported direct to the director or deputy of the system, and half to a lower level such as the circulation librarian. More than half had a separate young adult budget averaging 3% of the total materials budget. Within each such system there were a number of young adult librarians assigned to the branches, as in Los Angeles Public Library where the central library and sixty-one branches, divided into seven regions, were staffed with a young adult librarian at all but the smallest branches, under the Co-ordinator of Young Adult Services.

Californian libraries on the other hand had a core of young adult librarians who worked at each branch on a peripatetic basis to up-date the collections from time to time and to follow this up by in-service training for the librarians at each branch, in the form of seminars on young adult work, so that all the staff at the branch are knowledgeable on the subject.

Many words have been uttered and written on the attributes necessary for librarians who work with young adults and the elements common to all the views expressed can be crystallized as follows:

1. Knowledge of adolescent psychology.
2. Informed and knowledgeable mind.
3. Pleasant manner, firm but not repressive.
4. A liking for teenagers.
5. Reading knowledge of the stock.
6. Extensive library experience in several aspects.
7. Young in heart and mind rather than body.
8. A good listener.
9. A good mixer to liaise with other departments and organizations.
10. Helpful attitude.

The duties of the young adult librarian vary according to her place in the hierarchy, the physical location of stock and the local requirements of the community but taking a concensus from many libraries' examples a list could be compiled which would include some or all of the following duties:

Planning the young adult programme in the library system.
Co-ordinating the work of the young adult staff in the system.
Managing the young adult work in a given library.
Liaison with children's, adults', reference libraries and cataloguing department within the system.
Book selection.
Organization of services to young adults.
Outreach to young adults in the community.
Service to young adults at their schools and colleges.
Readers advisory work.
Extension activities to promote library use and library materials.
Compilation of book lists and guide notes.
Liaison with youth organizations in the community.
Fieldwork in the community.

Attending book selection meetings, planning and staff meetings.
Up-dating knowledge by attendance at professional courses and
meetings, by reading professional press.
Devising and directing in-service training for staff.
Unofficial counselling.

The duties and functions of the young adult librarian are
laid down in the Young Adult Services Division Task Force
recommendations (see Appendix E) and in general works on
public library administration but it is apparent from a study of
library systems staffing and from the comments of many young
people that the qualities and duties outlined are not found in
many librarians serving young people, comments which are
accusatory, puzzled, frustrated and occasionally distressed that
staff treatment and attitudes towards teenagers are different
from their treatment of adult readers; that staff are strict and
repressive, fussy about matters of routine, too dedicated to the
belief that noise and movement are injurious to library use,
dictatorial about rules and regulations, hostile when asked for
information and discourteous in communication. An amalgam
of teenagers' ideas of what the librarian could do for them
centres on *help* and radiates from this to provision and activity,
help in homework assignments for those who are 'slow at
picking things up', help in finding information, help in choosing from a mass of books, help in finding more of the same, in
being shown something different, help in easy access to knowledge, even help in filling in time.

Some of these are further explored in this chapter but the
net effect of help specifically and generally given by librarians
set apart for the purpose is increased use and increased successful use of the library by teenagers, inside it or out.

The expansion of staff at a New York public library to promote existing stock and services in the 1960s, resulted in a sharp
rise in library use, the implication being that what is needed is
a more effective job with what is available rather than,
necessarily, more books.

However the financial obstacles to more specialist staff in the
early 1970s led to a need for re-thinking the effective deploy-
ment of existing staff. Too many library systems reacted to the
cutbacks in young adult posts with insufficient attempts to
ensure that the work was incorporated into either the children's

or the adult library's staffing arrangements, by means of re-arrangement of duties and in-service training, and found that teenage use diminished substantially. Although the Young Adult Services Department of the American Library Association is protesting strongly that the financial stringencies applied to education, libraries and youth expenditure will severely harm current and long-term services and damage relationships with the future adult readership, the trend continues towards the axing of the young adult librarian's post as being the most easily expendable. As in many library matters the personal attitude of the chief librarian is often the deciding factor rather than a rationalized approach to priorities and generally those library systems with flourishing young adult services have chief librarians who are sympathetic to the professional urgencies propounded by keen and knowledgeable librarians in their systems, or who have themselves personally subscribed to the viewpoint that such a service is valid.

There is a growing trend also in Britain for the specialist post to decline apart from the co-ordinator's post. The introduction of team management in some systems has led to the spreading of responsibility for work with children and young people amongst many staff and in a wide geographical area rather than at a single service point, thus enabling all staff to have contact with all readers within the authority's area. While lessening the personal knowledge of local readers it enables professional expertise to be spread wider and in greater depth than is possible when the librarian is hampered by non-professional duties at a single service point. However even with such an arrangement there is a danger that the teenager's needs will be inadequately dealt with unless training is available for all staff. The form the service takes differs according to the location and arrangement of stock, the job specification laid down, the personality strengths of the individual young adult librarian and the stated purposes of the service.

The lending service is basic to all libraries serving young people although the handful with a socializing function in an informal library place circulation figures very low in the priority order, preferring to encourage browsing and use on the premises by young people who would not and do not take books home.

Circulation figures for the Boston Public Library system were analysed[148] and the median percentage of books circulated on young adult cards by the stationary branches were compared with the adult and children's book circulation. The seasonal variations were:

	Adult %	Y.A. %	Children %	Total
July	43·7	15·2	41·1	100·0
January	36·3	13·8	50·0	100·1
April	36·5	13·1	50·1	99·7

The young adult book loans showed the least fluctuation over the year with a summer peak which indicates the leisure time recreational reading increase which followed school closure for the vacation.

A comparison of the annual figures for Walsall Teenage Library between Junior and Teenage Library loans reveals that the 1971 teenage loans were 16,500 as against children's library loans of 90,000. In both Boston and Walsall more than half the loans were non-fiction. The Walsall figures take no account of the considerable number of teenage loans from the adult department which are not credited to teenagers in the statistical records, nor do any of these figures record the use of the library for purposes other than borrowing books. Where records, films, cassettes and posters are offered for loan extensive use is made of the facility. Many young adult librarians believe that teenagers would make more use of their public libraries if the libraries would circulate material that is not at present considered suitable for circulation.

The use of reference services by teenagers is clearly indicated in all the reports, articles and statistics compiled by librarians and is most revealing in the analysis of questions of a reference and reading guidance nature, asked by readers within the teenage range. These are well exemplified in the Boston Public Library survey.[149]

75·3% of children asked such questions
43·3% of adults asked such questions
67·5% of teenagers asked such questions.

Other types of question were asked by
140% of children (median)
37·2% of adults
48·0% of teenagers.

Of the questions asked
  49·1% were asked at the children's desk
  19·2% at the adults' desk
  31·6% at the young adults' desk.

An analysis of the questions thought to require professional assistance produced the following results:
  75·3% of children's questions
  43·4% of adults' questions
  67·5% of teenagers' questions.

Such figures validate the call for specialist professional staff for young adults at all branches or at least the services of knowledgeable reference and advisory staff to cope with the large numbers of queries. Although many of the reference and reading guidance queries may stem from school work, a substantial number are of an informational nature for the genuine 'wanting to know' reason, rather than to be put to use in a school essay.

Use is made of any reference facility provided; many central library reference departments are overcrowded by school and college students, some of whom actually use the library materials and some of whom are simply using the library tables and chairs and the reference room quiet. When quick reference collections are provided in branch libraries and in young adult departments, consultation is frequent, though sometimes it is fruitless if there is no librarian at hand to guide.

Study facilities are well used in whatever form provided, plenty of well spaced seating at large tables near the reference collection or the non-fiction stock in the branch or young adult library, study carrels situated as part of the young adult area or made available in reference libraries and study centres in deprived areas where space and freedom from excessive noise are utilized by teenagers. These are the facilities found to be of use but all too often denied the teenage library user who is expected to use a library not designed or organized for the multi-purpose use made of it, with resulting conflict between librarian and teenager.

Some librarians believe that the reference service offers an opportunity to teach the teenager to find out and use the catalogue, the bibliographies and the reference works; others are convinced that an obsession with teaching the use of the catalogue has limited the personal guidance and promotion of books which the young adult librarian ought to be practising. Some librarians say that only the researcher will need such library skills in adult life and the majority of people who continue to use libraries in adulthood rarely want to look up information, therefore it is the librarian's job to provide the information and to promote reading actively.

Information provision is increasingly receiving attention as young adult librarians recognize the changing needs of teenagers in the community, but raises problems of who should provide it, the school librarian, the reference librarian or the young people's librarian. Generally the pattern seems to be that if there is a young adult librarian she co-ordinates the information requests and passes them on to appropriate departments or individuals or outside contacts. If there is not a young adult librarian the pattern is that the reference library takes the responsibility but usually not with any enthusiasm as far as serving the teenager is concerned. At branches the branch staff cope according to their respective abilities and in theory can utilize the telephone to central reference and information services for queries not immediately answerable at the branch.

Apart from the reference type queries already mentioned there are many other items of information required by teenagers. In Chapter 3 it was shown that there is a difference between the reference query needing research type answers and the questions to which an answer is required out of sheer interest or personal need. In few libraries is this type of information query catered for. Many librarians who serve teenagers know of the casual questions which are presented during the normal business of library use and of the diffidence with which many teenagers seek advice because of the personal nature of their query.

One librarian has called for the setting up of information centres or services in libraries to deal with what she calls the 'survival needs' of youth,[150] the needs for information on drugs, sex, legal rights, racial problems, politics and human relations counselling. Many young adult librarians already play a social role, a welfare role to the teenagers in their communities and many have had to liaise with medical services, counselling agencies and social welfare organizations in specific cases of young people who need immediate help. Elizabeth Bowen, when she was librarian of Kirby new town branch, was noted for her relationship with the violent and dissolute youths who came into the library, a social welfare and counselling relationship which bore fruit in that she was there long enough for the same youths to bring their wives and babies into the library for her to meet, years after the friendly truce was made between librarian and hostile youth. In that community where the average number of children per family was an unbelievable fifteen, a community uprooted from the Liverpool slums and placed in a new town without the old social cohesion and, more importantly without clubs and cinemas and coffee bars and meeting places the only facility was a library, and a library which, given the composition of the community, was a well-used service.

Alex McIntosh in Lambeth liaises continually with the social and community organizations in his area in order to take his library services to where they are needed, to the housing estates and the swimming pools, the sports centres and the youth clubs.

But neither of these examples fits the bill in the matter of a co-ordinated information service such as the Crisis Information Unit, which gives survival needs information discreetly, both informationally and geographically in the sense that the building is open for teenagers congregating for other purposes and there is therefore no embarrassment at having to walk off the street into an openly advertised and obvious office.

The advantage of the public library young adult section or librarian as a dispenser of information or a co-ordinator of sources of information lies in its acceptability as a 'neutral' agency. As seen in the outline of adolescent psychology in Chapter 1, the teenager is unsure and unwilling to draw attention to his uncertainty, easily embarrassed and loathe to depart from conformity to his peers. Some draw attention to themselves in ways which hide their insecurity, others withdraw into themselves as a defence; both types of young people, needing information which they consider to be personal, will use the sources of information which they find acceptable to the peer group, and the public library teenage service *at its best*, is in many localities respected, accepted and used as a result of good promotion.

Some view the concept as encroaching on the social agencies' territory and adding an unnecessary welfare aspect to the role of the librarian. For some, such an information service is seen to be in keeping with the concept of the public library as part of the communication network, as a provider of information within and without the physical bounds of the library or the books, an agency for the free flow of knowledge within a community.

Many young adult librarians and reference and information services do maintain files of contacts and organizations to which the teenager can be directed. They also attempt to keep up to date holdings of the brochures, pamphlets and publicity material compiled by these organizations and publicize their presence in stock by notices, displays and personal guidance.

It may be that for some communities a central agency for information for young people would be the best place to house the teenage library, as an outreach centre, rather than to retain it in its traditional location within the library.

The co-ordination of information for and about youth is being attempted in Britain by the Youth Service Information Centre in Leicester, which collects and disseminates information nationally, covering youth work, organizations and units dealing with drug addiction, drop-outs, immigrants, family planning, counselling, social welfare, youth activities and holiday centres, youth courses and conferences. Films and documents, periodicals, books and information are accumulated and made available by enquiry and loan services to anyone interested. It was hoped that the service might also attract use by young people and library facilities for them were considered. There was a suggestion that the youth library services of the Leicestershire County Library system and Leicester Public Library might be co-ordinated with the Youth Service Information Centre, but nothing further came of it. The YSIC is thus a body with a government grant providing a service to youth workers and through its annual *Information Digest* and newsletters, a source of information to which many public libraries subscribe.

It comes close to what some librarians feel should operate at local level for the teenagers themselves.

Advisory services form part of the work of librarians, incorporating advice in print and in person and a common means of presenting information to promote the use of books and materials is through booklists, compiled by young adult staff or those to whom work with young people has been allotted.

The purpose and usage of such lists vary from library to library but taken as a whole fall into a general pattern summarized as follows:

1. Those produced at regular intervals featuring new additions to stock; for use by young adult readers.
2. Subject lists on themes requested by readers, whether adult teacher or teenager; for use by readers.
3. Subject lists on themes suggested by staff and known to interest teenagers; for use by readers.
4. Lists to publicize particular sections of stock or forms of material; for use by readers.
5. Lists compiled at headquarters and sent out to branches; for use by staff and readers.
6. Lists which act as a catalogue to a core collection or an exhibition collection of books for teenagers; for presentation to, or use, or purchase by anyone interested as a reference tool.
7. Lists used as ordering devices for area staff, school teachers and selection aids.

In Britain the dearth of young adult librarians at local level and the absence of a national or centralized body catering specifically for young adults, has caused individual children's librarians in many public libraries to devise lists, periodic or spasmodic, which suggest titles thought to be of interest to the teenage reader and which are typed and duplicated for distribution over the counter to readers and to local schools and youth clubs.

It seems that only one public library system regularly produces a printed annotated list of a range of books recommended for teenage readers, Hertfordshire County Library's *Teenread*, an attractively produced monthly publication in which a dozen or so paperback titles are described in informal yet accurate annotations designed to catch the teenager's attention. At least one other large library system makes use of *Teenread* by obtaining copies in quantity from Hertfordshire on the premise that when a good list already exists there is no need to spend time and money trying to produce another. Nearest to *Teenread* in regularity and attraction is Islington's *Youth List*, but not every issue is devoted to books for teenagers as such, some cater for younger children.

Walsall's *New Teenage Fiction* appears as a duplicated pamphlet covering about a dozen titles annotated to whet the appetite of teenage readers. Many other British library systems produce general and subject lists of books for teenage readers from time to time, rarely printed because of the cost, and varying considerably in the degree of visual appeal, clarity of typewriter typeface, design layout, content, bibliographical information and quality of annotation, although many have no annotation.

By contrast the American booklist practice is both more widespread proportionately and more professional in physical format and appearance in that it is more usual to have publicity material properly printed either through the library system's own printing office or commercially, though there are still many libraries where material is typed and duplicated by the librarian as in Britain.

The Office of Work With Young Adults at the Enoch Pratt Free Library, Baltimore and the Boston Regional Services Division and the New York Public Library, all produce imaginative, attractive and relevant lists, using varied eye-catching designs in format and layout, matching the style of the annotation to the theme of the list, and using colour and illustration to create an all-round appeal.

Some annotated lists form the catalogue to a permanent exhibition of books for young adults, as in the New York Public Library's *Books for the Teen Age*, at the same time providing the public library teenage reader with a list of recommendations of fiction and non-fiction from which he can select, and then identify in the stock at his service point. This work is also used extensively by library systems throughout the States and overseas, as a selection aid.

Given the purposes of booklists as already outlined it appears that the aim and usage falls into two categories, those designed to introduce and describe holdings or potential holdings and those designed for publicity and promotion purposes. Few librarians who compile booklists have thought through to the purpose and intended use of their lists, as the evidence of countless lists shows.

Teenage collections are included in the exhibition collections maintained at central service points by some library systems, up-dated regularly as in Nottinghamshire County Library and West Riding County Library, and the new Birmingham central library stack, all open for viewing and advice to teachers and youth workers in the locality. The constant change of stock as new works are added and older ones removed, prohibits the production of a catalogue or even a publicly available list, a checklist for the staff being the usual means of identification.

However, booklists alone are generally considered insufficient forms of advising on reading and some libraries extend their publicity by instruction in library use, book talks on radio and television and to groups of young people within the library and elsewhere.

Such activities play a large part in library service to young adults in the States but are rare in Britain where the majority of extension programmes in the library are devoted to children up to about twelve.

It would seem from available evidence in many States, that between them all, young adult librarians in specialist posts, many of whom have separate budgets and space for a young adult programme, have done everything any young adult librarian thinks of and the range and the success or failure rates depends on how well the librarian has assessed the teenage community, how much enthusiasm and patience is expended and most importantly, the degree of staff continuity for programmes on library premises in tough areas.

Some librarians feel that many of the activities promoted for young adults conflict with the traditional view that the library's purpose is to provide books and related materials for loan or reference for the public's use in education, information and recreation. Others point out that the young adult library programmes are simply carrying out the library objectives and adding more means of achieving them by widening the traditional library – limited connotation of education, information and recreation, so that activities which seem to have very tenuous links with libraries, such as chess clubs, drama groups and discussion sessions, take on library connotations when the objectives of the public library are to encourage personal development, to enrich the mind and to facilitate recreation.

Some of the means by which young adult librarians attempt

to achieve these in the library, for the teenage library user, can be described in outline here:

1. Participation in selection. Several library systems invite teenagers to sit on selection panels either regularly or occasionally, as already indicated in the section on book selection. However formal or informal the arrangement may be, those who practise it report on the value to the librarian of such help.

2. Reviewing for library magazines. Many libraries produce a magazine with literary offerings by readers, news items by staff and reviews of books by both. In Westchester (NY) *Consciousness Three* is the title of the young adult magazine in which records, films and books are reviewed by young adult readers.

    Similarly Buffalo and Erie County's *Pulser*: a magazine of self expression for young adults, provides the space for such reviews. Both magazines are eight-page tabloids. In England many of the children's library magazines include reviews by young teenagers but there are no young adult magazines as such.

3. Library clubs. These are common in most areas of the States although there are a few for teenagers in England. Some are formally organized with badges, young adult members committees and specified rules, others are simply a name given to the occasion on which a young adult activity takes place. Some are active mid-week, others are a Saturday morning club.

    In most a varied programme of talks, films, discussions, music and occasionally handwork is offered either in the young adult library or a meeting room, or a suitable section of the library building. Drama clubs, poetry clubs, chess clubs are also to be found but are by no means common.

    At Mount Vernon, New York, the style adopted was a chat session, informal, sometimes unplanned in the sense of not having a pre-arranged topic, but planned in the sense of sparking discussion by book, magazine or topical event stimulation.

    The Room at Mount Vernon was set up for community purposes in co-operation with a community project, the library agreeing to provide a recreational and cultural programme for about fifty young adults in the area.[151] The progress of this library club project can be summed up as follows:

On the plus side: an attractive room with background music.

provision of paperbacks, periodicals, chess sets.

weekly film shows.

chat sessions.

informal chatting and lounging.

On the minus side: frequent changes of personnel as the staff were appointed as project leaders rather than library staff.

very little teenage participation in the organization of The Room.

no programme of activities apart from the films.

almost all black membership after an all white start, instead of the hoped for mixture.

Result: a decision to concentrate on the segment which decided it needs the library most, that is, those young people who continue to use the facilities offered, rather than to expend time, money and effort attempting to encourage those who have patently turned their backs on all previous attempts at outreach.

The library club at Lincoln Teenage Library was held on Friday nights, initially to provide something to do and somewhere to go for the youth of the area in the absence of coffee bars, discos, cinemas and sporting facilities. A large stepped room was built, with a gallery, stocked with about 400 hardbacks on wall shelves, 200 paperbacks on spinner racks, and some pop records. Floor cushions were provided for sitting on in the broad stepped area, pop records were played on request, films were shown occasionally and the young librarian from the children's library who had helped to plan the teenage library, moved amongst the young people, chatting. There was never any intention to push up the book circulation or to provide specifically for school work needs. The Teenage Library was conceived as offering book-shy teenagers a social meeting place in which books were around and could be browsed amongst, borrowed or ignored at will. Breaking down the 'stuffy' image of libraries, the club did bring in the non-bookish teenagers as well as the readers. After four years of operating in this way, growing hooliganism in the district advanced also into the library club, causing physical damage, frightening off the regular teenage readers and distressing many of the staff.

It was decided that the club should cease to meet until the situation improved but the library facilities remain. A year later the club has not yet re-opened.

4. Discussion sessions. These form part of the programme in many libraries either as a weekly session or occasional happening.

There is division of opinion, with one faction believing that readings must be set and projects undertaken in preparation for the discussion session in order to start from a common basis, while another faction believes that most young people have enough to do for school without giving them yet more required reading.

Success with discussion groups has been found to be variable, in attendance and in terms of knowledge or development derived from the discussion. Much has depended upon the kind of young people in the area, the able high school or college teenager being far more used to formal debate and discussion, and more interested in it as an academic exercise than the anti-social teenager who can or will only discuss informally on what is personally relevant to him. Thus the type of library user determines whether or not discussions are in the programme and if in, determines the organization and content.

5. Read-aloud sessions or storytelling. The latter term has been found to present a childish impression in some libraries and the euphemism or synonym is thought to be necessary. Teenagers are known to listen to stories on radio and tele-

vision with engrossed attention, even to stories for young children. They are also known to hover on the fringe of open-air sessions in parks and community centres, at first to scoff but eventually to listen as Janet Hill has found in her housing estate and parks projects in the tough borough of Lambeth. Elsewhere read-aloud sessions in the library appear as part of young adult programmes, incorporating serial reading, excerpts from old and new books, short stories and poems.

6. Film and record sessions. These are organized either as part of the general programme or in a film club or record club. The Young Adult Services Division's booklet on mixed-means programming with young adults, *Read, Look, Listen in Your Library*, suggests films and recordings with related books and periodical titles, for use with teenagers in the library, substantiating that school of thought which believes that the extension of the library's activities into the non-book media use and promotion is valid.

However, in practice, librarians' experiences reveal that those qualities and qualifications outlined as necessary for the young adult librarian are indeed vital and that knowledge of the local community is essential when planning programmes. Some time ago Richard B. Moses organized a fortnightly film show in his Rochester (NY) library for what he called the Upstairs Group, a bunch of unruly youngsters many of whom were semi-literate. His reasons, initially, were that the film sessions would attract teenagers and eventually lead them to reading; films would help the discipline problem by providing something to do that the kids liked.

After a suspenseful start when for the first few sessions nobody turned up, and then a trickle, which was followed by constant coming and going, eventually a steady audience of vocal but interested tough boys and girls was achieved. But Richard Moses changed his mind about one of his purposes and he believes it was this that turned the trickle into a flow, because he decided that showing films should not be a bribe to get the teenagers reading, that films were legitimate library fare and led the viewer into 'new experiences, new ideas, new ways of thinking'[152] as surely as reading, and in the case of his Upstairs Group more surely, given the low reading ability level of most of his viewers. He then based his service on the premise that as the library purveyed the world's thought it should not and did not matter in what form it was offered. He therefore exhorted young adult librarians to 'just show the movies, never mind the books'.

At the other end of the scale, film clubs are to be found in which the world of film making is explored, for connoisseurs of the art and for practitioners. Here cameras and projection equipment, the hardware and the software from the library's stock, are made available to the film club members, some of whom show their own home-made films.

Most young adult libraries' use of film, however, comes between these two aspects in that the showing of a documentary or entertainment film is part of what is thought to be a balanced programme.

7. Book fairs. These are often held to mark National Book Week or National Library Week or some topical or commemorative occasion. Less often the book fair is held to introduce the teenage school population in the locality to the range of books available for their age and needs.

Book stalls or booths devoted to subject areas present the stock in attractive, visible, tangible arrangements, more easily comprehended than in their normal stock sequences. The less formal, commercially familiar layout breaks the psychological barrier raised by the years of social, educational and library conditioning described in the first two chapters, and is therefore a useful ploy for young adult librarians. The Enoch Pratt Free Library, Baltimore, is well known for its frequent book fairs to which classes of school and college students are invited, with plenty of pre-publicity, free handouts of publicity material for library activities and booklists to hand during the visit.

Extraction of stock for similar purposes is practised on a continuous, rather than occasional basis, by the New York Public Library which grasped at the realization that a bus terminal on its doorstep was a gathering point for large numbers of young people who were not habitual readers or library users. A specially selected collection of paperbacks,

periodicals and audio-visual material, and the staff to supervise it, was extracted from stock and displayed in the library
in a spot conveniently accessible for use by these teenagers.

The idea of a bookshop agency within the public library
is gaining ground in Britain and the States. The arguments
for and against are numerous, but the recognition that
teenagers regularly buy books, indicated in Chapter 4, has
persuaded some librarians that as with the success of paperback clubs in schools, book sales are not necessarily a threat
to book loans, and that where there are no bookshops and
book buying is done by mail order or not at all, the public
library could provide a range of recommended books for
sale. This links up with the call for the public library young
adult librarians to use their knowledge and premises for the
promotion of literacy.

8. Literacy programme. The deep concern of government,
educationalists and librarians over the growing illiteracy
rate has led some librarians, particularly those who work in
disadvantaged communities, to suggest that public library
space should be made available for the tutoring of illiterates
and a programme devised which would require the library
to stock the reading materials used and to co-operate in the
compilation of lists of books vetted for reading level and
maximum interest level.

Where classes for illiterate adults and youth are organized
by colleges only a few attend; private tuition is offered on a
small scale for lack of tutors and is used only by those who
are desperately anxious to learn.

Many illiterates were turned off school, resulting in their
illiteracy, and are turned off still in their late teens and
adulthood by the thought of returning to school; it is thought
that the public library would be less of a barrier and more
closely linked with the end product of the exercise. Some
young adults have therefore called upon librarians for the
inclusion of a literacy programme in the young adult
extension activities in those districts with a severe literacy
problem.

9. Meeting rooms for activities. The changes in concepts of the
best way of tackling young adult library service are occa-
sioned by changes in social needs, professional growth,

influenced by financial and architectural considerations and by the suggestions of users. The current trend is towards integration of the stock but with specialist staff and the provision of special accommodation for the activities rather than for the stock.

In this sense, then, meeting rooms are necessary for the extension activities programme, for use either by the library for promotion of books and library use, by outside organizations or by young people themselves, on a pre-planned basis. Many recently built libraries have a suite of rooms plus a conference hall and perhaps a theatre-cum-lecture theatre, which are used by internal and external bodies, and the young adult programme is timetabled to take account of the necessity for booking these communally available rooms.

The St Martin's branch library was closed as a library when Lambeth borough re-organized its structure to create zone and neighbourhood libraries but has been retained as a centre for community use, including library activities and is housing the Centre 73 project of community care.

However the majority of library systems have no such facilities at either central or branch libraries; some use school or other premises for special occasions, and some turn this disability into a constructive attitude towards the idea of taking the young adult library's activities and services out to where the teenagers are.

OUTREACH

So far the extension activities described have taken place in the library and, with basic book provision and guidance, form the basic work of the young adult librarian for those who use the library.

To reach those who do not, the young adult librarians use many means. For example:

1. Library magazines and newsletters are sent out to wherever teenagers congregate.

2. Television and radio spots, regular and occasional, are used by some libraries, e.g. Detroit's educational television series for teenagers, New York's Radio Book Discussion, Boston's Teenage Book Talk, a monthly radio session.

In Britain individual librarians take part in children's programmes from time to time on radio and television and are able to cover a few teenage books or mention library activities. Local radio is often grateful for offers of programmes, either news or talks, and the writer has taken part in both types on Radio Leeds. The coming of commercial radio in Britain may force librarians to consider either commercial sponsorship or the necessity for setting aside funds for publicity.

3. Newspaper publicity in the local press is promoted by many librarians, in book column, news items and in advertisements of activities.

4. Talks by young adult librarians are very common, often in the librarian's own time in the evenings, to parents and teachers' meetings, talks to school classes of teenagers about books, and as with any outside speaker brought into school, the impact tends to be greater than when the same subject is offered by the familiar teacher or even the familiar librarian of the school. In many city and country areas in both Britain and the States, books and library talks are given to the able and the less able through the full range of classes in the secondary school.

No general list of books or methods used has been recommended for these occasions; regional differences, age and ability differences, the librarian's personality and ability, these all require each talk to be tailored for each occasion. Certainly a wide range of books on show is necessary and the writer has found on every occasion that a story told or read rivets attention and leads to questions about content, purchase or loan.

Visits to uniformed organizations to talk or display books are also common, particularly to guide and scout meetings in conjunction with the Reader's Badge work. Visits to youth clubs on an informal basis, rather than to deposit collections, produce useful contacts and provide something to do other than sit around, dance or fight.

The writer took a carefully representative collection of fiction (a) read by teenagers, (b) recommended for teenagers, (c) written for teenagers, (d) written for teenage backward readers. Within these categories were (a) books for girls, (b) books for boys, (c) 'neutral' books, (d) paperbacks, (e) hardbacks, (f) picture strip fiction, (g) comic books. The inclusion of comics, picture strips and 'dubious' paperbacks was deliberate in that these are read by the tough teenagers in the very tough district of the city and some of those teenagers attended the club. The inclusion was deliberate also in order to provide that element of familiarity with those materials which would bridge the gap between them and the other types of fiction displayed.

The collection was laid out haphazardly on low tables in the main hall where dancing, table tennis, chatting, fighting and courting was taking place, all to the accompaniment of pop music at deafening volume. One or two sixteen-year-old boys, attracted by a Hell's Angel paperback and a Batman comic came to look, asked what all this was for and settled down to read, having pulled up a chair from another corner of the room. Soon others came and they rushed around the room waving copies of paperbacks they had read, the dubious ones. When these titles were exhausted and they could not get to the comics which were being passed around on an 'after you' basis, they turned their attention to the other paperbacks, attracted initially by the titles and the cover.

The girls had all read Beverley Cleary's *Fifteen* and many of the boys freely and cheerfully admitted to having read it. Other titles were passed around, thrown down in disgust, read in snippets in less-than-five-minute sessions after which concentration expired. In between this they danced, smoked, chased each other round the building and talked to the writer. They talked of life and love and sex and crime, in all of which they were heavily engaged; they spoke of the thrill of the 'dubious' books and the sex magazines they steal from the news-stands, of their disinterest in anything that requires a mental effort, and school and library books were in this category.

Never at any time did those teenagers, aged fourteen to twenty, even touch any of the hardbacks on the table. But they would have listened to a reading from one of them if the noise had permitted.

Other librarians in many places make informal contact by taking books to where the teenagers congregate, some with books for loan, some for display, some for read-aloud sessions and all too few for sale. Margaret Edwards arranged a programme called VISTA in which portable paperback libraries, accompanied by staff, were taken to outposts in the community at Baltimore, and staff talked about, lent and gave away the stock as seemed appropriate.[153]

The range of internal and external young adult library contacts is extensive and can best be exemplified in Boston Public Library's programme shown in Appendix C.

5. On a more formal outreach basis circulation of stock is achieved by deposit collections and staffed collections organized through the circulation department with co-operation with the young adult staff or, largely in Britain, through the schools and children's services department to be found in most library systems.

Book collections to community centres, church halls, youth clubs, boutiques and youth organizations are taken to the location and left for subsequent use under the care of a volunteer or on a rota basis by library staff, or are kept fluid by using a mobile library specially fitted, stocked and staffed for teenage use.

6. Service to schools is in a different category from all the rest and is highly developed in Britain, so much so that in county library systems particularly, which, historically, have close organizational links with education, there has grown up a body of knowledge and service unrivalled anywhere in the world.

Based on the provision of (a) a loan collection of fiction and non-fiction, exchanged termly to supplement and complement the school library's own stock, (b) temporary loan of subject material book and non-book for comprehensive coverage of a topic for intensive short-term study, (c) temporary loan of individual titles for specific short-term use, some systems have highly organized arrangements such as the county library authorities of Wiltshire, Nottinghamshire, West Riding, Hertfordshire and Aberdeenshire; others such as Leicestershire have devised schemes which enable the school libraries within the library authority area to purchase their own stock through the library system thereby enabling school stock to be classified, catalogued and processed by the library system before arrival

254 Libraries and Literature for Teenagers

at the school. The Inner London Education Authority has a
different scheme whereby schools in the Inner London boroughs
are serviced and staffed by ILEA from a central unit with a
central library and resources unit to aid teachers and librarians.

Such organized service to schools is rare in the States.
Although many large schools have virtually self sufficient
resources and full-time staff, most schools rely on the public
library service to children and young adults and on the reference
services of the local public library. Some have a particular
arrangement with the local library for loan of material when
required.

When pre-planned programmed budgeting (PPBS) was mooted
there was a call for the complete handing over of responsibility
for library service to children and young people to the schools,
to avoid the apparent duplication of stock and service. Little
has been done because of the outcry from librarians and
educationalists, but many school and public librarians have
come to some agreement about complementing each other's
provision, and increasingly school libraries are relying on the
public library for the wider ranging material which no school
library could hope to afford and which is increasingly needed
with changed patterns of learning and teaching.

An arrangement found by some to be the answer to this
problem is that of the dual purpose library, where the school
library and the local branch library are one, the branch being
situated in the school and giving a joint service to school and
community. There are several in Britain and America and, as
indicated in Chapter 3, the potential is great.

The practice of taking library services to the teenager in the
community is growing, arising from social concern, professional
knowledge, internal library space limitations and a greater
awareness of teenage needs and interests on the part of recent
generations of librarian, through library school courses, professional and social publicity and personal experience.

The problem arising from this outreach to attract teenagers
is that those who come into the library situation do not always
stay attracted. How do the teenage libraries look to the teenager
unused to libraries?

The physical appearance of the room and its layout are
largely effective, deliberately, unintentionally or by default,
in determining behaviour in the library.

Tables and chairs encourage spreading out materials for study, dumping a pile of books to browse through, sitting on, sleeping on, writing on, encourage readers to linger, to spend some time in the library. Many libraries supply these and then object when they are used for those purposes. Lounge furniture encourages lounging, sitting about, relaxing, reading for long periods, informal behaviour and libraries which provide it have not always thought of the effect. Behaviour is determined by the presence of noisy areas and quiet areas and when these are not provided noise usually takes precedence in the mind and behaviour of the teenager whereas quiet is usually the librarian's priority. Conversation areas are occasionally found in teenage libraries and music is common; these librarians have presumably sat down and worked out what sort of atmosphere and behaviour is required and have designed the library accordingly.

Some librarians believe that there are enough clubs at which the teenagers can indulge their passion for noise and the library should not join the noisy brigade; others suggest that if the teenagers are made welcome they find no need to demonstrate their presence.

No tables and chairs requires standing only with the implication that the reader is not expected to stay long, nor is he expected to need to compare or browse amongst a selection taken off the shelves but will stand at the shelves for an on-the-spot decision and then depart.

A carpeted floor is intended by the librarian to provide quiet and comfortable walking but may be seen by the teenage users as ideal for sitting on. All these physical aspects and many more, are rarely thought through by librarians or architects although there are many cases where they have been suggested to the architect only to be sacrificed for space, economy or architectural convenience. But they are vital parts of the whole behaviour determining and attitude testing use of the library, and when most librarians' views on teenage users revolve round their behaviour it is essential that librarians pay more attention to the physical appearance and equipment in their libraries.

Another determinant starts with staff-reader interface. Some young people giving their views on the public library said that it was dismal, with dusty books, talking was not allowed and the staff were strict and frightful and fussy about torn pages 'when people have been reading in bed'.[154] What they wanted was a library with carpets and armchairs, bright paint and modern decor, where they could talk to their friends about the books and other things in a social centre atmosphere with a coffee bar and pop music; they also wanted study facilities, quiet cubicles adjacent to the social area rather than distant in the reference library, and someone who could help with homework.

However, the first adverse effect of the library hits the teenage reader the moment he wants to join. The official rules and regulations vary in the degree of freedom they allow the teenage reader and the age limit is a sore point in many libraries when a specific lower age limit is the rule. Some libraries stipulate that at the age of fifteen membership of the children's library shall be transferred to the adult library automatically; others transfer on request or at age eighteen; some do not allow borrowing from the adult library until fifteen or sixteen though reference use is sanctioned.

Dudley Public Library is an example of the use of cadet tickets which enable the young teenager to use the adult library and for an eye to be kept on his use. Boston Public Library (Mass.) exemplifies the custom of coloured tickets to identify young adults. Many public libraries, though they may use means of identifying teenage users, make no restrictions on use of any public department of the library system.

Certainly the registration procedures are enough to put off the reader unaccustomed to library matters. Regulations concerning opening hours are often restrictive and unsuitable for young adult use. In Britain as long ago as 1960 the Albemarle Report on youth services suggested that the later opening of public libraries would be useful for young people, but many libraries still close their children's department in which the young adult collection is sited, at 7.00 pm though other departments stay open till 9.00 pm. Many small town libraries and county library branches close at 7.00 pm thereby depriving the whole age range in the population. Only in the large towns and cities is the teenager likely to be able to get into his library up to 9.00 pm.

The situation is similar in the States and only in those libraries with a separate teenage library is the young adult likely to have full professional service until 9.00 pm or 9.30 pm. It has been suggested that later opening would increase hooliganism and violence and that staff would not agree to work late. This may well be and is not to be brushed aside lightly when planning opening hours but a 7.00 pm closure is not likely to attract or keep many teenage readers and is a cause of disenchantment in many areas.

Rules of behaviour are often inflexible for teenage users and frequently applied to teenagers far more prohibitively than to adults and children and with greater hostility on the part of the librarian. The Young Adult Librarian at the Maude Shunk Public Library in Menomonee Falls, Wisconsin, found that by selecting the right, relevant stock, involving the readers in activities both on the programme and by help in the library, being helpful when information was needed and friendly but firm at all times, behaviour problems were lessened. She suggested that the hard core troublemakers could be dealt with by learning their names in order to address them personally, speaking in a friendly manner but warning them as the occasion arose that they were being watched, kicking out the really persistent troublemaker or breaking up groups to avoid trouble, maintaining always a friendly but firm attitude, never showing shocked surprise at the attempts to shock but asking for opinions, ideas and help.[155]

Thus the staff-young adult interface is of vital importance to the behaviour in and use of the library, the attitude, knowledge, warmth of personality and strength of character of the librarian working with teenagers, counting for more than fine bindings, large numbers of staff and a vast array of books.

The library service to teenagers, then, encompasses the young adult who uses the library and the young adult who does not, either from ignorance or antipathy. At worst the library service to young adults is simply a collection of books. At best it involves intensive and extensive work within the library building and out into the community. It incorporates service for study and self education and service for recreation. The young adult librarians are using knowledge of adolescent psychology, the local teenage population, professional book knowledge and professional library techniques and a belief that young adults need sympathetic special attention by one library means or another.

All these practices, though varying in degree, are to be found amongst British and American libraries, but there are guidelines from local and national bodies which, by creating standards and recommending practices, may, it is hoped, give

9

credence to some of the ideas put forward at local level by young adult librarians but dismissed by directors of library systems, give authority to some of the services, impart information to all who work with young adults and set a standard to be worked towards. The consideration of these in planning a local service ought to be normal practice.

No one and no organization has yet put forward a set of standards, recommendations or even basic suggestions for library service to teenagers in Britain, so that the examples here are wholly American; the New York Library Association's Children and Young Adult Services Section produced in 1966 its Criteria and guidelines in planning for young adult services in public library building programmes.[156] The Young Adults Services Department of the American Library Association in its Task Force 1973 Standards covers amongst many things the following:

1. The entitlement of the young adult to non-judgemental attitudes, respect and participation in the decision-making process of libraries.
2. The creation of information tools and directories of community resources.
3. Liaison with other agencies providing information.
4. Indirect seeking out through clubs, community groups, etc.
5. The spectrum of information and materials and recreational materials.

The YASD is also considering the production of national guidelines on reviewing sources, social responsibilities and drug information, surveying community needs, and outreach programmes. These, with the various statements on selection, censorship and quantity mentioned in the previous chapter, form a body of informed and thought-through knowledge which is available to all who work with young adults. But librarians still speak out against the inequalities, the petty attitudes, the downright obstructions put in the way of adequate library service to teenagers.

Anne Osborn believes that

... a teenager deserves a library that recognizes reality. He needs an information source and study area that does not impose arbitrary, crippling rules on him. His library should recognize that dignity and silence are not prior requisites to learning.[157]

And Margaret Edwards deplored the passive rather than active service given to teenagers who are deprived by staff attitudes, too much concern with informational services to the neglect of other needs, insufficient promotion of reading and readers, by the apparent inability of librarians to meet the new challenges with new ideas.[158]

This chapter has shown that many library systems and individuals are effectively doing what Daniel Fader pleaded for. He said that teenagers' behaviour today is shouting out that 'attention must be paid', a cry for help which many librarians in America are answering but which has not been heard or which has been ignored in Britain. Throughout this study the enormous problems which militate against reading and library use have been discussed and explored, problems which stem from the society within which libraries operate, from the organization of education which is so closely linked with libraries and from within the libraries themselves.

It is evident that the profession is split into at least two major camps, the 'serve the teenagers who use the library' camp and the 'go out and get them' camp, and while the split remains there will be uneven and unequal service. The profession is also split into those who do not consider teenagers as a category needing a differential service and those who do. There are those who would like to do more and will when they have more staff, more money, more books, more time, and those who *are* doing more, despite these very lacks. And it is the growing number of these librarians who may well win the day, if with patience, perseverance, professional expertise, banding together to bring local and national pressure to bear, they continue to pay attention to the libraries and literature for teenagers.

Appendix A
Home background

Degree of importance teachers attach to the following:

1. That parents are interested in their children's activities.
2. That parents are prepared to spend time with their children, playing, talking, reading.
3. That parents answer and explain their children's questions.
4. That parents can stimulate and help their children to carry out ideas, etc.
5. That parents are intelligent, educated people.
6. That parents help the child with his school work.
7. That parents show an interest in the child's progress.
8. That parents are interested in education for its own sake.
9. That there is good conversation and correct speech in the home.
10. That there are good manners and social habits.
11. That the home is culturally rich, with the right amusements, sensible toys, etc.
12. That there is travel and holidays.
13. Visits to interesting places.
14. Familiarity with books and appreciation of reading.
15. Firm but kindly discipline.
16. A sense of moral and spiritual values.
17. A religious faith.
18. That meals, sleep, habits are regular.
19. That television watching is planned.
20. That there is cleanliness.
21. That the family is united and they are mutually considerate.
22. That the child is loved for its own sake.
23. That home life is stable.
24. That the home is not overcrowded.
25. That there is space to play.
26. That the family is financially secure.
27. That the parents enjoy good health.
28. That the mother is not working.
29. That if the mother is working she makes provision for children after school hours.
30. That there is good, sensible food.

31. That there is good, sensible clothing.
32. That the children are adequately fed.
33. That the children are sent to bed early.
34. That the children have adequate sleep.
35. That the parents were born in this country.
36. That there is a good home background.

E. J. Goodacre. *Teachers and their pupils' home background.* NFER 1968.
Adapted from the questionnaire on pages 94–97.

Appendix B
Walsall Teenage Library

Fiction suitable for teenagers

Author	Title	Suggested reasons for popularity
Aldiss, B.	Science fiction particularly p.b. editions	Any SF is popular
Allingham, M.	*Tiger in the Smoke*	Good, exciting story
Allan, M. E.	*Catrin in Wales*, etc.	Written for teenagers
Allum, M.	*Monica Takes a Commission*	Girls like career stories
Amis, K.	*Lucky Jim*	p.b. edition may account for some of popularity
Avallone, M.	*The Man from U.N.C.L.E.*	Spy, exciting, p.b. TV
Avery, G.	*Call of the Valley*	Attractive cover. Like Welsh stories
Banks, L.	*L-Shaped Room*	Problem theme, p.b.
Baxter, V.	Any of her career novels	
Baxter, G.	*Knightsbridge Players*	Written for and about teenagers
Blish, J.	Any SF titles	
Boyleston, H.	Sue Barton titles	Career books and girls like nursing themes
Bradbury, R.	*Fahrenheit 451*	SF
Brontë, E.	*Wuthering Heights*	Collier Macmillan ed. does not look like a textbook
Buchan, J.	All titles	Adventure stories with hero identification
Bull, R.	*Great Tales of Mystery*	Horror and the supernatural fascinate
Byers, I.	Career stories for girls	
Charteris, L.	The Saint stories	Adventure, mystery, TV
Chesterton, G. K.	Father Brown stories	Mystery, humour
Christie, A.	All titles	Mystery
Cleary, B.	*Fifteen*	American teenager, p.b.
Cookson, C.	Mary Anne books, etc.	Family, romantic
Crispin, E.	SF titles	
Cross, J. K.	*Best Horror Stories*	
Darbyshire, S.	*Sarah Joins the WRAF*	

Author	Title	Suggested reasons for popularity
Innes, H.	Any titles	Very popular with boys
Jenkins, A.	*Thin Air*	Ghost stories
Jerome, J. K.	*Three Men in a Boat*	Humorous
Kamm, J.	All teenage titles	
Keyes, F. P.	Any titles	Romantic, historical
Lee, A.	Miss Hogg stories	Mysteries
Le Carré, J.	*The Spy Who Came In From the Cold*	Thriller, adventure
Leslie, D.	Historical romances	
Lindgren, A.	Kati stories	Teenage romances
Mackenzie, K.	*The Starkey Sisters*, etc.	Teenage stories
MacLean, A.	Any titles	Exciting adventure
Mason, A. E.	*Four Feathers*	Exciting adventure
Mason, R.	*The Wind Cannot Read*	Romantic story
Monsarrat, N.	*The Cruel Sea*	War, adventure
Montgomery, L. M.	*Anne of Avonlea*, etc.	Family, romantic
Norton, A.	All titles	SF
O'Hara, M.	All titles	Horse stories
Orczy, Baroness	*Scarlet Pimpernel*	Adventure
Owens, J.	Career stories	
Packer, J.	Most titles	Family, romantic
Pilgrim, A.	Any titles	Light romantic
Poe, E. A.	*Tales of Mystery and Imagination*	
Porter, E.	Miss Billy stories	Old-fashioned but romantic
Read, Miss	Any titles	Family stories
Riddell, M.	Career stories	
Rohmer, S.	Dr Fu Manchu stories	Mystery
Saville, M.	Titles written specially for teenagers	
Seth-Smith, J.	Titles for teenagers	
Seton, A.	Any titles	Adult historical
Shute, N.	All titles	Adventure
Speare, E. G.	*Calico Capture*	Teenage, American, historical
Stacpoole, H.	*Blue Lagoon*	Romantic, desert island
Stevenson, D. E.	Any title	Romantic, family

Author	Title	Suggested reasons for popularity
Stewart, M.	Any title	Mystery stories
Stoker, B.	*Dracula*	Horror
Swinburne, D.	*Kit at Kerminster*	Career
Syme, R.	Any title	Exciting adventure
Tey, J.	Any title	Mysteries
Tickell, J.	*Appointment with Venus*	War, humour
Townsend, J. R.	*Hallersage Sound*, etc.	Teenage stories
Treece, H.	*Bang You're Dead*, etc.	Mystery stories
Unsworth, W.	*The Devil's Mill*	Teenage, historical, exciting
Verne, J.	*20,000 Leagues Under the Sea*	
Vipont, E.	*Lark on the Wing*, etc.	Teenage romantic
Vickers, R.	Crime writers choice	
Walters, H.	Any titles	SF
Welch, R.	*The Woolacombe Bird*	Historical
Wells, H. G.	SF titles	
Westheimer, D.	*Von Ryan's Express*	War story, p.b.
Whipple, D.	Any	Family stories
White, M.	*Girls in Flight*, etc.	Teenage stories
White, R.	*Up Periscope*	Sea adventure
Willard, B.	Any teenage titles	
Wilson, B. K.	*Path Through the Woods*	Teenage theme
Wodehouse, P. G.	Any titles	Humorous
Wren, P. C.	Any foreign legion titles	Adventures
Wyndham, J.	Any titles	SF

List compiled from survey of teenage readers in Walsall Public Library, 1969.

Appendix C

Boston Public Library. Branch Library Meetings For Young Adults. Oct. 1972.

Young Adult Chess Tournament for ages 10–18.
Fall Fashions. Clothing modelled by girls from the Library Youth Council, a speaker on today's fashions, and a book talk.

Film Program. 'The Stanley Cup 1970' and 'Big Moments in Sports'.
Young Adult Council Meeting.
Film Program. 'Nobody Waved Goodbye', 'Black Pirate', 'Son of the Sheik'.
'Pante Rhei', 'Syrinx', 'David' and 'Angel'.
Young Adult Book Club.

New York Public Library. Teenage Book Talk.
Oct. 1972. Four broadcast unrehearsed discussions of books and reading with teenagers, authors and others from the publishing field.

1. *In Search of Ghosts* by Daniel Cohen. Guest author Daniel Cohen.
2. *Real Plastic Magic* by Lawrence Kardish. Guest author Lawrence Kardish. Guest Moderator Emma Cohn.
3. *Walk in the Sky* by Jack Ishmole. Guest author Jack Ishmole.
4. *Not All Girls Have Million Dollar Smiles* by Sidney Offit. Guest author Sidney Offit.
Moderator: Mrs Ruth Rausen. Manhattan Borough Young Adult Specialist.

Appendix D

Alderson, C.　　　　*Magazines Teenagers Read*. Pergamon, Oxford, 1968.

Carlsen, G. R.　　　　*Books and the Teenage Reader*. Harper & Row, New York, 1967.

Chambers, A.　　　　*The Reluctant Reader*. Pergamon, Oxford, 1969.

Egoff, S. (ed.)　　　　*Only Connect*. OUP, London, 1969. (Nat Hentoff on fiction for teenagers.)

Fader, D.　　　　*Hooked on Books*. Pergamon, Oxford, 1969.

Hanna, G. R. and
　McAlister, M. K.　　*Books, Young People and Reading Guidance*. Harper & Row, New York, 1960.

Library Association　*Attitudes and Adventures*. Readers Guide No. 121, 1971. (Colin and Sheila Ray.)

Appendix E
Task force on young adult services working paper (revised July 1973)

PREFACE

Adolescence can be defined as that period in a person's development when he no longer sees himself as a child but other people do not see him as an adult. It is a period of intense intellectual, physical, emotional, and social development. To pin a specific age or grade on this individual in transition is unnecessary and impossible.

The pressures felt by a young person and the strain created between him and adults make his needs for self-development unique. In order for him to reach his full potential, it is important for him to have immediate access to specialized services and programs.

This paper represents a philosophy of library service for young adults in the 1970s. Libraries dealing with young adults should be alert and responsive to young people's needs, constitutional rights, and their roles as taxpayers and consumers.

What follows is an attempt to make explicit the background philosophy of the library's role in relating the total community resources to young people's needs. Both the philosophy and suggestions for its implementation were determined by investigation, collective experience, research, and testimony taken from young adults themselves.

I. YOUNG ADULTS ARE ENTITLED TO OPEN AND EQUAL ACCESS TO ALL MATERIALS AND SERVICES — REGARDLESS OF COST, LOCATION, OR FORMAT — AND THE RIGHT TO A CONFIDENTIAL CLIENT-LIBRARIAN RELATIONSHIP, A NON-JUDGMENTAL ATTITUDE, RESPECT, AND PARTICIPATION IN THE DECISION-MAKING PROCESS OF THE LIBRARY.

1.1 Discrimination because of age is as deplorable as discrimination because of race, sex, or class. Yet young adults are frequently victims of discrimination in libraries, being denied materials and services on the basis of youth. As emphasized in the ALA statement *Free Access to Libraries for Minors* (Adopted by the ALA Council, June 30, 1972), no library has the right to prevent a young adult from reading, seeing, or hearing anything of his choice.

1.1.1 A single type of borrower's card should suffice for all age groups, permitting borrowing of all materials.

1.1.2 Young adults should be extended the use of films, recordings, audiovisual (including videotape) equipment, or anything else available to other users, regardless of cost or fragility.

1.2 All services – whether a reserve system, interlibrary loan, or help in translating letters – should be available to young adults. The quality of service should be uniformly high, without regard to the age of the client or staff judgment as to the seriousness of a request.

1.2.1 Young adults are entitled to assurance that information about materials used or questions asked will not be divulged to any third party.

1.3 Since young adults do make up a sizeable portion of real and potential library users, they should be consulted along with other age groups in relation to library service planning.

1.3.1 Young adults should be eligible to, and should, serve on library boards. They would thus be able to advocate the interests of a group neglected in most communities.

1.3.2 Youth councils should be established in order to increase young adult participation in the development of library services to meet the needs of young people. Such councils can work with librarians in planning programs and services and building materials collections. They can sound out new ideas, act as public relations liaisons with other young adults, and be a resource for librarians and trustees in dealing with mutual concerns.

2. YOUNG ADULTS SHOULD HAVE FULL ACCESS TO MATERIALS IN ORDER TO PERMIT INDIVIDUAL DECISIONS TO BE MADE WITH A FULL UNDERSTANDING OF OPTIONS AND ALTERNATIVES.

2.1 The personal growth, formal education, social and career aspirations, and hobbies and fads of young adults are all sources of legitimate informational needs that must be recognized and provided for by libraries.

2.1.1 Because of intellectual and cultural differences, information to meet the needs created by these differences should be available in a variety of media and in varying degrees of complexity and sophistication.

2.1.2 Information services should include the provision and interpretation of materials, direction to specific facts found within materials, and referral to agencies and groups that provide other services. Information services should also include

readers' advisory services that help young people discover
books and other materials for personal development and
enjoyment.

    2.1.2.1 The first often requires the creation and updating of
informational tools, such as directories of community
resources – institutional and human – annotated lists of
recommended media, and the repackaging of information
that synthesizes information found in both formal and
informal sources. Libraries should see that these are prepared and kept current on a national, state, or local level.

    2.1.2.2 The second requires young adult specialists who have
a thorough knowledge of materials that can help develop a
philosophy of life, a sense of humor, and a creative
imagination. Such persons should relate materials to individual needs and interests and instill enthusiasm for such
materials in others.

2.2 Young adult specialists should recognize that school-assign-
ment-originated information needs may also be expressions of
legitimate personal needs.

2.3 Since personal needs may emerge after a subject request, the
young adult librarian should be a sympathetic listener as well as
a provider of information.

3. THE SPECIAL NEEDS AND INTERESTS AND THE UNIQUENESS
OF YOUNG ADULTS MUST BE RECOGNIZED IN LIBRARY
SERVICES AND MATERIALS.

  3.1 Materials

    3.1.1 Materials of special interest to young adults should be
selected by young adult specialists, with some systematic input
from young adults, regardless of where the materials will be
housed; e.g., the young adult specialists should be involved
with film, periodical, recordings selection, etc., as well as book
selection.

    3.1.2 Materials of an ephemeral nature should be represented
in library collections as a legitimate expression of the youth
culture.

  3.2 Programming

    3.2.1 Young adults should be consulted in the program
planning of the library, including those programs intended for
adults or the entire family, as well as those planned specifically
for young adults.

    3.2.2 The library should provide programming on topics of
particular interest to young adults, especially when this interest
is not met elsewhere.

3.2.3 The library should provide a showcase for young adult talents by engaging young adults to participate in dramatic and musical presentations, poetry readings, etc., and by offering display space for the products of their creativity (e.g., photography, crafts, etc.).

3.3 Library Environment

3.3.1 Young adults need a library environment that is as tolerant of their life-styles as it is of the life-styles of adults and children.

A recognition of this need does not imply a segregated teen room. It suggests that areas be provided that take into account the needs of young adults. The location and design of these

---

TASK FORCE ON YOUNG ADULT SERVICES

Penelope S. Jeffrey, Chairman
Branch Librarian, Clason's Point
Branch, New York Public Library

A. Michael Deller
Head of Programming,
Bloomfield Township Public
Library, Bloomfield Hills, Mich.

Thomas W. Downen
Assistant Professor, School of
Library Science, University of
Michigan

Marilee Foglesong
Librarian, Library for the Blind
and Physically Handicapped, Free
Library of Philadelphia

Carolyn Forsman
Doctoral Candidate, School of
Library and Information Science,
University of Maryland, College
Park

Helen L. Kreigh
Young Adult Librarian, Daniel
Boone Regional Library, Columbia, Mo.

Regina U. Minudri
Young Adult Coordinator, Ala-

meda County Library, Hayward,
Calif.

Rose Moorachian
Readers Advisor for Young Adults,
Boston Public Library

Leah K. Nekritz
Director of Learning Resources,
Prince George's Community College, Largo, Md.

Coralie A. Parsil
Assistant Director, Tucson Public
Library, Ariz.

Carol R. Starr
Young Adult Consultant, Alameda
County Library, Hayward, Calif.

Travis E. Tyer
Consultant, Professional Development, Illinois State Library

Jana Varlejs
Audiovisual and Young Adult
Librarian, Montclair Free Public
Library, N.J.

areas, as well as alternatives to conventional library furniture, require careful planning in order to integrate them within the total framework of library services. Talking, typing, and listening are some of the activities that need to be accommodated.

3.3.2 Because the process of locating information and materials in a library is complicated and confusing to many young people, the library should simplify and facilitate these processes. Conspicuous directional signs and basic explanations of library resources such as the card or book catalog should be provided to encourage independent use. Equally important are alert staff members who offer unsolicited help and one-to-one instruction.

3.3.3 A variety of attractive and frequently changed displays should be provided to help young adults discover library resources of surprising interest.

3.3.4 The atmosphere of the library and the accessibility and attitude of library staff members should enable young adults to find sympathetic adult listeners.

3.3.5 Young adults are vulnerable to adults' assumption of superiority. If a tone or facial expression in any way conveys ridicule or judgment, the young adults' requests for help or information, in effect, will have been denied.

3.4 Personnel

3.4.1 Specific responsibility for young adult service should be assigned so that the number of staff reflects the actual and potential young adult use of the library.

3.4.2 Young adult specialists should understand and communicate with young people, be able to give readers advisory and reference service, and be effective advocates for young adults in overall library service. Since young adults frequently meet other staff, it is essential that through in-service training and less formal efforts, these staff members become aware of adolescent psychology and develop a degree of ease in serving young adults.

3.4.3 In order to ensure increasing quality of young adult service, experienced young adult specialists should be encouraged to maintain their specialty and at the same time rise within the administrative structure. Greater rewards and opportunities should be built into the career ladder for young adult specialists, who should be able to combine the young adult specialty with that of unit administrator, for instance.

3.5 Budget

3.5.1 Sufficient funds should be allocated for young adult services, personnel, and materials.

4. ALL YOUNG ADULTS CANNOT BE SERVED DIRECTLY BY OR IN LIBRARIES.

4.1 Some barriers to direct library service are time pressures of school, home, job, and peer commitments; ignorance of the variety of materials and/or media available; detention in institutions; man-made barriers (e.g., highways, gang turfs, etc.); lack of transportation; architectural features of library buildings that prevent use by physically handicapped people. All young adults have the right to service, but some must be reached by the librarians' taking the library to them. Among the activities that may be taken out of the library are book talks and/or discussions, film programs, media presentations, sponsoring of guest artists and/or speakers. Collections of materials may be deposited elsewhere and problems referred to other agencies.

4.2 Publicity activities are important in extending service beyond the library's four walls.

4.3 Library representatives should not only accept invitations to come to groups and agencies, but also should take the initiative to request an invitation. They can at the same time serve the staff of these agencies and, through them, serve their young adult clientele.

4.4 Among places where young adults gather and where library representatives can meet and serve them are academic, vocational, and special educational agencies; hobby clubs; recreation centers; churches; drug rehabilitation centers; crisis intervention centers; coffeehouses; correctional institutions; homes for unwed mothers; mental health centers; and outdoors on the street.

5. LIBRARIES SHOULD DEVELOP A KNOWLEDGE OF AND ACT AS LIAISONS WITH OTHER AGENCIES PROVIDING INFORMATIONAL SERVICES. THE LIBRARY SHOULD IDENTIFY GAPS IN COMMUNITY SERVICES FOR YOUNG ADULTS AND ADVOCATE IMPROVEMENT OF THOSE SERVICES THROUGH AGENCIES, GOVERNMENTAL OFFICES, ETC.

5.1 Libraries cannot be all things to all people, but they do have a responsibility to be aware of what is going on in the community. Before library representatives serve as liaisons with other community organizations, they should be familiar with existing library services and programs. Specialized services to which young adults need access, such as career guidance centers, other types of libraries, family counseling services, schools, and crisis intervention centers, are available in many communities.

5.2 Young adult specialists should know what services are available and should keep other agencies informed of library services.

Young adult specialists should visit service centers or agencies and make personal contacts with at least one person in each, so that young adults can be referred to a specific individual who will be cooperative and sympathetic. Young adult specialists should also talk to people who have used particular agencies to discover what experiences they had. When young adult specialists discover that needed services do not exist or that existing services are not fulfilling their potential, they should initiate action toward the establishment of a needed service or toward correcting the inadequacies of an existing one. The young adult specialist can accomplish such change by working through other community groups and as part of the community planning process. In some cases the library should assume responsibility for a particular service, e.g., serving as a center for the distribution of scholarship and loan information, establishing a recorded phone message regarding young adult services, etc.

6. SUMMARY.

6.1 In the user-oriented library, clients should be able to choose which services they will use at any time in their lives. While focusing on the special needs of young adults, this paper should be considered as a part of the continuum of total library services.

References

CHAPTER I

1. Jeanne Noble. 'Generational Gapiosis.' *Wilson Library Bulletin*, Oct. 1968, pp. 134–139.
2. F. Musgrove. 'Social Needs and Satisfactions.' *British Journal of Educational Psychology*, no. 36, June 1966, pp. 137–149.
3. National Children's Bureau. *From Birth to Seven*. Longman, London, 1972.
4. Sara I. Fenwick (ed.). *A Critical Approach to Children's Literature*. University of Chicago Press, Chicago, 1967, pp. 3–14.
5. Ministry of Social Security. *The Circumstances of Families*, HMSO, 1967.
6. Elizabeth J. Goodacre. *Teachers and their Pupils' Home Background*. NFER, 1968.
7. F. Musgrove and P. H. Taylor. 'Teachers' and Parents' Conception of the Teacher's Role.' *British Journal of Educational Psychology*, no. 35, Feb. 1965, pp. 171–179.
8. A. R. Jensen. 'The Culturally Disadvantaged; Psychological and Educational Aspects.' *Educational Research*, vol. 10, no. 1, Nov. 1967, p. 13.
9. Basil Bernstein. 'Social Structure, Language and Learning.' In A. H. Passow and others, *The Education of the Disadvantaged*. Holt, Rinehart and Winston, N.Y., 1967, p. 227.
10. G. H. Bantock. *Culture, Industrialization and Education*. Routledge & Kegan Paul, London, 1968, p. 28.
11. Bantock, *op. cit.*, p. 29.
12. Bryn Jones. *Working Papers in Cultural Studies*. 2. Spring 1972. University of Birmingham Centre for Contemporary Cultural Studies, 1972.
13. Roma Morton-Williams and Stewart Finch. Schools Council Enquiry 1. *Young School Leavers; Report of a Survey Among Young People, Parents and Teachers*. HMSO, 1968, p. 174.
14. Table 22. 'Chief leisure activities.' *Social Trends*, no. 2. HMSO, 1971, p. 65.
15. Bryan Luckham. *The Library in Society*. The Library Association, 1971.
16. Charles Evans. *Middle Class Attitudes and Public Library Use*. Libraries Unlimited Inc., Littleton, 1970.
17. Susanne Langer. *Feeling and Form*. Routledge & Kegan Paul, London, 1953.
18. Roma Morton-Williams and Stewart Finch, *op. cit.*
19. Elizabeth J. Goodacre, *op. cit.*, pp. 94–97.

20. J. D. Halloran. *Attitude Formation and Change*. Leicester University Press, 1967, p. 59.
21. J. S. Zaccharia and H. A. Moses. *Facilitating Human Development through Reading; the use of Bibliotherapy in Teaching and Counselling*. Stipes Publishing Co., Champaign, Illinois, 1968, p. 23.
22. *The School Librarian*, vol. 6, no. 6, Dec. 1953, p. 393.
23. Susanne Langer, *op. cit.*
24. Estelle Justin. 'Confronting our Media Biases; the Social Dimensions of Media Theory.' *School Libraries*, vol. 21, no. 4, Summer 1972, p. 15.
25. G. H. Bantock, *op. cit.*, p. 15.
26. J. S. Zaccharia, *op. cit.*, p. 23.
27. Russell G. Stauffer. *Directing Reading Maturity as a Cognitive Process*. Harper & Row, N.Y., 1969.
28. Levin L. Schucking. *The Sociology of Literary Taste*. 2nd ed, revised and translated by Brian Battershaw. Routledge & Kegan Paul, London, 1966, p. vii.
29. Vera Southgate. 'Effective Reading at Every Age.' *Trends in Education*, no. 26, April 1972, p. 30.
30. G. Robert Carlsen. 'For Everything There is a Season.' *Top of the News*, no. 21, Jan. 1965, pp. 103–110.

CHAPTER 2

31. Dr Harry Judge, quoted in *Daily Mail*, Jan. 6, 1973, p. 13.
32. Norman Thomson and David Brazil. 'Productivity in English Teaching.' *English in Education*, vol. 2, no. 3, 1968, pp. 48–53.
33. Brian Phythian. 'English at Manchester Grammar School.' In *English in Practice*, edited by Geoffrey Summerfield and Stephen Tunnicliffe. CUP, London, 1971, p. 31.
34. David Holbrook. *English for Maturity*. CUP, London, 1967, pp. 27–28.
35. James R. Squire and Roger K. Applebee. *Teaching English in the United Kingdom; a Comparative Study*. National Council of Teachers of English, Champaign, Illinois, 1969, p. 81.
36. Joint Matriculation Board. Universities of Manchester, Liverpool, Leeds, Sheffield, Birmingham. General certificate of education. Regulations and syllabuses, 1973. Manchester, JMB, 1971.
37. G. Yarlott and W. Harpin. '1,000 Responses to English Literature – 1.' *Educational Research*, vol. 13, no. 1, Nov. 1970, pp. 3–11.
38. G. Yarlott and W. Harpin, *op. cit.*, p. 9, Table 2.
39. Denis Butts. 'Second Rate Books for Second Rate Children.' *The Use of English*, vol. XVII, no. 4, Summer 1966, pp. 296–300.
40. Stephen Tunnicliffe. 'Re-shaping the English Syllabus at Newton High School.' In *English in Practice*, edited by Summerfield and Tunnicliffe, *op. cit.*, pp. 73–74.
41. David Shayer. *The Teaching of English in Schools 1900–1970*. Routledge & Kegan Paul, London, 1972, pp. 171–172.
42. P. Doran. 'Attitudes of Teachers Concerning the Place of Contemporary Novels and Plays.' In W. B. Lukenbill, *A Working Bibliography of American Doctoral Dissertations in Children's and Adolescents' Literature*,

1930–1971. University of Illinois Graduate School of Library Science, no. 103, August 1972.

43. W. D. Emrys Evans. 'Literature or Life.' *Times Educational Supplement*, 7 July 1972, p. 36.
44. David Shayer, *op. cit.*
45. Kenyon Calthrop. *Reading Together; an Investigation into the Use of the Class Reader*. Heinemann, London, 1971.
46. Kenyon Calthrop, *op. cit.*, p. 107.
47. Fred Inglis. *The Englishness of English Teaching*. Longmans, London, 1967, p. 147.
48. S. F. Bolt. 'Unqualified Readers.' *The Use of English*, vol. XVII, no. 3, Spring 1966, pp. 228–233.
49. Douglas Barnes, Peter Churley and Christopher Thompson. 'Group Talk and Literary Response.' *English in Education*, vol. 5, no. 3, Winter 1971, p. 75.
50. Glenn on thematic English teaching. In Lukenbill, *op. cit.*
51. Cyril Poster. 'The Comprehensive Curriculum.' *Secondary Education*, vol. 1, no. 3, Summer 1971, p. 14.
52. W. H. Burston and others (eds). *Handbook for History Teachers*. Methuen, London, 1972.
53. Norman Thompson and David Brazil. 'Productivity in English Teaching.' *English in Education*, vol. 2, no. 3, Autumn 1968, p. 56.
54. Squire and Applebee, *op. cit.*, p. 109.
55. G. R. Hanna and M. K. McAlister. *Books for Young People and Reading Guidance*. Harper, N.Y., 1960, p. 101.
56. James I. Ellis. 'The Responses of Adolescents to Selected Passages on a Theme of Violence.' *Research in Librarianship*, vol. 13, no. 3, Jan. 1970, pp. 5–6.
57. Mary H. Beavan. 'Response of Adolescents to Feminine Characters in Literature.' *Research in the Teaching of English*, vol. 6, no. 1, Spring 1972, pp. 48–68.
58. Fred Inglis, *op. cit.*, p. 146.
59. Peter Young. *Data on Reading*. Schofield & Sims, Huddersfield, 1970, p. 80.
60. Charles G. Spiegler. 'Give Him a Book that Hits Him Where He Lives.' In A. H. Passow and others. *The Education of the Disadvantaged*, *op. cit.*, pp. 407–415.
61. J. Capenhurst. 'Organized Reading in a Comprehensive School, Years 1–3.' *The Use of English*, vol. 23, no. 3, Spring 1972, pp. 203–205, 211.
62. Daniel Fader. *Hooked on Books*, *op. cit.*
63. Squire and Applebee, *op. cit.*, p. 108.
64. Advisory Centre for Education. *Contemporary Fiction and the Older Pupil*. Ginn, London, 1970, p. 8.
65. NCTE Commission on literature, language and the English curriculum. NCTE, 1968.
66. Squire and Applebee, *op. cit.*, p. 224.
67. Evans 1968 and Crocker 1967. In W. B. Lukenbill, *op. cit.*
68. Squire and Applebee, *op. cit.*, p. 106.

69. Margaret Spence. 'Towards Fiction in the Seventies.' *Education Libraries Bulletin*; supplement 15, 1972, University of London Institute of Education, p. 13.

CHAPTER 3

70. Lovell A. Martin. 'Deiches Studies of Pratt Library Examines Student Reading.' In J. S. Kujoth, *Reading Interests of Children and Young Adults*. Scarecrow Press, New Jersey, 1970, pp. 248–249.
71. Edward Blishen. 'They'll sit there just reading.' *The Bookseller*, Jan 27, 1973, pp. 240–244.
72. R. Mitson on BBC Schools Television series on ROSLA. No. 5 Resources.
73. J. Harlan Shores. 'Reading Interests and Information Needs of High School Students.' In J. S. Kujoth, *op. cit.*, p. 411.
74. J. Harlan Shores, *op. cit.*, pp. 407–419.
75. *Op. cit.*, pp. 416–417.
76. Ellen Altman. 'Implications of Title Diversity and Collection Overlap for Inter Library Loan Among Secondary Schools.' *The Library Quarterly*, vol. 42, no. 2, April 1972, pp. 177–194.
77. James R. Squire and Roger K. Applebee. *High School English Instruction Today*. Appleton-Century-Croft, Middlesex, 1968, pp. 184–185.
78. M. H. Scott. *Periodicals for School Libraries*. ALA, 1969. W. Katz. *Magazines for Libraries*. Bowker, New York, 1969. C. W. Waite. *Periodicals for School Libraries*. School Library Association, 1969. *Willings Press Guide*. Thomas Skinner Directories. Annual.
79. Alison Day. 'The Library in the Multi-racial Secondary School; a Caribbean Booklist.' *The School Librarian*, vol. 19, no. 3, Sept. 1971, pp. 198–199.
80. M. B. Smith. 'A Gloucestershire Setting for Careers Counselling.' *Times Educational Supplement*, 17.3.72, p. 62.
81. Library Association. *School Libraries and Resource Centres; Recommended Standards for Policy and Provision*. LA, 1970.
82. Paul Zindel. *The Pigman*. Macmillan, London, 1971.
83. Library Association. *School Libraries and Resource Centres; Supplement on Non-book Materials*. LA, 1972, p. 5.
84. Martin Rossoff. 'Blueprint for Library Teaching.' In C. L. Trinkner, *Teaching for Better Use of Libraries*. Shoestring Press, Hamden, Conn., 1970, pp. 219–225.
85. Martin Rossoff. *The School Library and Educational Change*. Libraries Unlimited, 1971, p. 74.
86. Eleanor Devlin. 'Thoughts on Freshman Orientation.' In C. L. Trinkner, *op. cit.*, p. 161.
87. W. Measel and C. L. Crawford. 'School Children and Book Selection.' *American Libraries*, vol. 2, no. 9, Oct. 1971, pp. 955–957.
88. C. L. Trinkner. *Better Libraries make Better Schools, op. cit.*
89. G. Wheatley. 'The Teenage Reader in Further Education.' *HERTIS Occasional Paper no. 1*. St Alban's College of Further Education, 1967.
90. G. J. Russell. *Teaching in Further Education*. Pitman Educational Library, 1972, p. 18.

91. Daniel Fader. *Hooked on Books, op. cit.*
92. James C. Grogan. 'Library Service to Youth in State Institutions.' *Wisconsin Library Bulletin*, May/June 1970, pp. 156–157.
93. Association of Hospital and Institution Libraries. *New Horizons Expanded; Readable Books For and About the Physically Handicapped.* AHIL, ALA, 1962.
94. Alison Shaw. *Print for Partial Sight; a Research Report.* LA, 1969.
95. R. Landau and J. S. Nyren. *Large Type Books in Print.* Bowker, NY, 1972.

CHAPTER 4

96. James L. Ford. *Magazines for Millions; the Story of Specialized Publications.* Southern Illinois Press, Carbondale, Ill., 1969, p. 35.
97. H. K. G. Bearman. 'An Enquiry into the Use of Books and Libraries by Young People.' In Library Association London and Home Counties Branch. *Book Provision for Special Needs*, LA, 1962.
98. James L. Ford, *op. cit.*
99. Connie Alderson. *Magazines Teenagers Read.* Pergamon, Oxford, 1968, p. 86.
100. Fred Inglis. *The Englishness of English Teaching, op. cit.*, p. 39.
101. Squire and Applebee, *op. cit.*
102. Dan Salter. 'The Hard Core of Children's Fiction,' and Keith Bardgett. 'Skinhead in the Classroom.' *Children's Literature in Education*, 8 July 1972, pp. 39–55 and 55–64.
103. Scholastic Publications Ltd. *Scoop Club News*, May 1973.
104. Beryl I. Vaughn. 'Reading Interests of 8th Grade Students.' *Journal of Developmental Reading*, vol. 6, Spring 1963, pp. 149–155.
105. Maureen White. Walsall Teenage Library. *YLG News*, vol. 13, no. 2, June 1969.
106. Derek Hanson. 'What Children Like to Read.' *New Society*, 17 May 1973, pp. 361–363.
107. Josephine S. Gottsdanker and Anne E. Pidgeon. 'Current Reading Tastes of Young Adults.' *Journal of Higher Education*, vol. 40, May 1969, pp. 381–385.
108. Ramon R. Hernandez. 'Youth Choices and Simple Processes.' *Wisconsin Library Bulletin*, Jan.–Feb. 1972, pp. 32–36.

CHAPTER 5

109. Aidan Chambers. 'Adolescent Reading and Topliners.' *Books For Your Children*, vol. 7, no. 4, Summer 1972, pp. 6–7.
110. Oliver Muirhead. *Books For Your Children*, vol. 7, no. 4, Summer 1972, p. 9.
111. Judith K. Rosenberg and Kenyon C. Rosenberg. *Young People's Literature in Series; an Annotated Bibliographical Guide.* Littleton, Libraries Unlimited, 1972.
112. Library Association, County Libraries Group. 'Attitudes and Adventures.' *Readers Guide No. 121* compiled by Sheila and Colin Ray, LA, 3rd ed., 1971.

113. Richard Peck. 'In the Country of Teenage Fiction.' *American Libraries*, vol. 4, no. 4, April 1973, pp. 204–207.

114. Nat Hentoff. 'Fiction for Teenagers.' In S. Egoff and others. *Only Connect; Readings in Children's Literature.* OUP, London, 1969, pp. 399–406.

115. John Rowe Townsend. 'Didacticism in Modern Dress.' In S. Egoff and others, *op. cit.*, pp. 33–40.

116. Sheila Egoff. *The Hornbook Magazine*, vol. XLVI, no. 2, April 1970, pp. 142–150.

117. Sylvia L. Engdahl. 'Why Write for Teenagers Today?' *The Hornbook Magazine*, vol. XLVIII, no. 3, June 1972, pp. 249–254.

118. Robert C. Ankerman. *Reading in the Secondary School Classroom.* McGraw Hill, NY, 1972.

119. American Library Association. *Minimum Standards for Public Libraries, 1966.* ALA, 1967, para. 34.

120. Janet Hill. In Library Association. *Book Selection for Children. Pamphlet No. 3.* LA, 1968, pp. 9–15.

121. LeRoy Charles Merritt. *Book Selection and Intellectual Freedom*, H. W. Wilson, NY, 1970, pp. 50–52.

122. G. R. Hanna and M. K. McAlister. *Books, Young People and Reading Guidance.* Harper, NY, 1960, p. 20.

123. Ann Kalkhoff. 'Innocent Children or Innocent Librarians?' *Library Journal*, vol. 97, no. 18, 15 Oct. 1972, pp. 3430–3437.

124. Judith Higgins. 'Great Paperback Mystery.' *Top of the News*, vol. 24, Nov. 1967, pp. 22–29.

125. E.g. Ruth K. Carlson. *Emerging Humanity; Multi-ethnic Literature for Children and Adolescents.* Wm. C. Brown, Duberque, Iowa, 1972. Library Association, Youth Libraries Group. *Books for the Multi-racial Classroom.* Compiled by Judith Elkin. LA, 1971. Boston Public Library. *The Black Experience; Reading List compiled by Ruth M. Hayes.* Boston Public Library, 1971.

126. ALA. *Minimum Standards for Public Libraries, 1966, op. cit.*, p. 38.

127. The Institute of Municipal Treasurers' Accountants. *Public Library Statistics 1971–2.* IMTA, 1973.

128. University of Illinois Library School. *Reference Services in American Public Libraries Serving Populations of 10,000 or More.* Occasional Papers No. 61, 1961, p. 9.

129. American Library Association. *Standards for School Media Programs.* ALA, 1969, p. 30.

130. Library Association. *School Libraries and Resource Centres, op. cit.*

131. G. Huws. *Provision of Periodicals; Report of a Research Project.* Leicester, Leicestershire County Library, 1968.

132. Department of Education and Science. Library Advisory Council Working Party on Periodicals. *Survey of Serials.* DES, 1971.

133. Bryan Luckham. 'Periodical Purchase and Readership; Use in the Public Library and by Adults at Large Contrasted.' *Research in Librarianship*, vol. 23, no. 4, May 1973, pp. 141–155.

134. Margaret Clark. 'Books for New Adults.' *Books For Your Children*, vol. 7, no. 4, Summer 1972, p. 8.

135. Ramon P. Hernandez, *op. cit.*, p. 34.

CHAPTER 7

136. Bryan Luckham. *The Library in Society; a Study of the Public Library in an Urban Setting.* LA, 1971.
137. Barry Totterdell. Hillingdon Libraries Project. Polytechnic of North London School of Librarianship, 1973.
138. H. G. K. Bearman. *An Enquiry into Reading Interests of Young People, op. cit.*
139. E.g. Learned T. Bulman. 'Young Adult Work in Branch Libraries.' *Library Trends*, vol. 4, no. 4, April 1966, pp. 434–439. L. Grundt. *Efficient Patterns of Adequate Library Service in a Large City; a Survey of Boston.* University of Illinois Graduate School of Library Science, Monographs Series, 1968.
140. Agnes Rutherford. *Survey on Public Library Use.* Leeds Polytechnic Department of Librarianship; Public Libraries Research Unit, 1973.
141. Roberta Bowler (ed.). *Local Public Library Administration.* Chicago, International City Managers Association, 1964, p. 246.
142. Edwin Castagna. 'A Troubled Mixture.' In L. L. Sherrill. *Library Service to the Unserved.* Bowker, NY, 1970, p. 21.
143. *Assistant Librarian*, no. 1, 1968, pp. 9–12.
144. Anne Osborn. 'How to Annihilate Library Service to Teenagers.' *School Library Journal*, Nov. 1972, pp. 28–30. In *Library Journal*, vol. 97, no. 20, 15 Nov. 1972.
145. J. G. Burke (ed.). *Print, Image and Sound; Essays on Media.* ALA, 1972.
146. Keith Evans. 'Multi-media Resources Centres; a Cautionary Note.' *Secondary Education*, vol. 1, no. 3, Summer term 1971, pp. 3–5.
147. Edwin Castagna. 'Young Adult Service in the Public Library Organization Chart.' *Library Trends*, vol. 17, no. 2, Oct. 1968, pp. 132–139.
148. Leonard Grundt. *Efficient Patterns of Adequate Library Service, op. cit.*
149. Leonard Grundt, *op. cit.*
150. Carolyn Forsman. 'Crisis Information Services to Youth; a Lesson for Libraries?' *Library Journal*, vol. 97, no. 12, 15 March 1972, pp. 1127–1134.
151. Ruth M. Kaufmann. *Wisconsin Library Bulletin*, vol. 47, no. 1, Sept. 1972, pp. 59–61.
152. Richard B. Moses. 'Just Show the Movies, Never Mind the Books.' *ALA Bulletin*, vol. 59, no. 1, Jan. 1965, pp. 58–60.
153. Margaret A. Edwards. 'The Urban Library and the Adolescent.' *Library Quarterly*, vol. 38, no. 1, Jan. 1968, pp. 70–77.
154. *Assistant Librarian*, no. 1, 1968, pp. 9–12.
155. Carol Starr. 'Youthomania; the Care and Treatment of Discipline in the Public Library.' *Wisconsin Library Bulletin*, vol. 68, Jan.–Feb. 1972, pp. 27–38.
156. New York Library Association. Children's and Young Adult Services Section. *Criteria and Guidelines in Planning for Young Adult Services in Public Library Building Programs.* Albany, NYLA, 1966.
157. Anne Osborn. *How to Annihilate Library Service to Teenagers, op. cit.*
158. Margaret A. Edwards. *The Urban Library and the Adolescent, op. cit.*

Bibliography of sources used

A. BOOKS

Advisory Centre for Education. *Contemporary Fiction and the Older Pupil.* Ginn, Aylesbury, 1970.

Alderson, Connie. *Magazines Teenagers Read.* Pergamon, Oxford, 1968.

American Library Association. *Minimum Standards for Public Libraries, 1966.* ALA, Chicago, 1967.

American Library Association. *Standards for School Media Programs.* ALA, Chicago, 1969.

Ankerman, Robert C. *Reading in the Secondary School Classroom.* McGraw Hill, New York, 1972.

Bantock, G. H. *Culture, Industrialization and Education.* Routledge & Kegan Paul, London, 1968.

Bearman, H. K. G. 'An enquiry into the use of books and libraries by young people.' In Library Association, London and Home Counties Branch. *Book Provision for Special Needs.* LA, London, 1962.

Bernstein, Basil. 'Social structure, language and learning.' In A. H. Passow and others. *The Education of the Disadvantaged, op. cit.*

Bowler, Roberta (ed.). *Local Public Library Administration.* Chicago International Managers Association, 1968.

Burke, J. G. (ed.). *Print, Image and Sound; Essays on Media.* American Library Association, Chicago, 1972.

Burston, W. H. and others (eds.). *Handbook for History Teachers.* Methuen, London, 1972.

Calthrop, Kenyon. *Reading Together; an Investigation into the Use of the Class Reader.* Heinemann, London, 1971.

Carlsen, G. Robert. *Books and the Teen-age Reader; a Guide for Teachers, Librarians and Parents.* Rev. ed. Harper & Row, New York, 1971.

Carlson, Ruth K. *Emerging Humanity; Multi-Ethnic Literature for Children and Adolescents.* Wm. C. Brown, Iowa, 1972.

Cohn, E. and Olsson, B. *Library Services to Young Adults.* International Federation of Library Associations, 1968.

Coplan, K. and Castagna, E. (eds.). *The Library Reaches Out.* Oceana Press Inc., New York, 1965.

Crosby, Muriel (ed.). *Reading Ladders for Human Relations.* American Council on Education, 4th ed., 1963.

Davis, Ruth A. *The School Library; a Force for Educational Excellence.* Bowker, New York, 1969.

Dobler, Lavinia and Fuller, Muriel (comp.). *The Dobler World Directory of Youth Periodicals*. Citation Press, New York, 3rd ed., 1970.

Egoff, Sheila and others. *Only Connect; Readings in Children's Literature*. Oxford University Press, London, 1969.

Ellsworth, R. E. and Wagener, H. D. *The School Library; Facilities for Independent Study in the School Library*. Educational Facilities Laboratories, 1963.

Evans, Charles. *Middle Class Attitudes and Public Library Use*. Libraries Unlimited Inc., Colorado, 1970.

Fader, Daniel. *Hooked on Books*. Pergamon, Oxford, 1969.

Fenwick, Sara I. (ed.). *A Critical Approach to Children's Literature*. University of Chicago Press, Chicago, 1967.

Ford, James L. *Magazines for Millions; the Story of Specialized Publications*. Southern Illinois Press, Carbondale, Ill., 1969.

Gerzon, Mark. *The Whole World is Watching; a Young Man Looks at Youth's Dissent*. Viking, New York, 1971.

Gillespie, John T. and Spirt, Diana L. *Paperback Books for Young People; An Annotated Guide to Publishers and Distributors*. American Library Association, London, 1972.

Gillette, Arthur. *Youth and Literacy; You've Got a Ticket to Ride*. Unesco/Uncesi, 1972.

Goodacre, Elizabeth J. *Teachers and their Pupils' Home Background*. National Foundation for Educational Research, 1968.

Grundt, L. *Efficient Patterns of Adequate Library Service in a Large City: a Survey of Boston*. University of Illinois Graduate School of Library Science, Monographs series, 1968.

Gunn, Alexander. *The Privileged Adolescent; an Outline of the Physical and Mental Problems of the Student Society*. Medical and Technical Publishing Co. Ltd., Aylesbury, 1970.

Halloran, J. D. *Attitude Formation and Change*. Leicester University Press, Leicester, 1967.

Hanna, G. R. and McAlister, M. K. *Books, Young People and Reading Guidance*. Harper & Row, New York, 1960.

Hechinger, Grace and Hechinger, Fred M. *Teenage Tyranny*. Duckworth, 1964.

Hentoff, Nat. 'Fiction for Teenagers.' In Egoff, S., *op. cit.*

Hill, Janet. *Children are People*. Hamish Hamilton, London, 1973.

Holbrook, David. *English for Maturity*. Cambridge University Press, London, 1967.

Inglis, Fred. *The Englishness of English Teaching*. Longman, Harlow, 1967.

Jones, Bryn. *Working Papers in Cultural Studies*. *2*. Spring 1972. University of Birmingham Centre for Cultural Studies, 1972.

Kamm, Antony and Taylor, Boswell. *Works and the Teacher.* University of London Press, London, 2nd ed., 1968.

Katz, W. *Magazines for Libraries.* Bowker, New York, 1969.

Kujoth, J. S. *Reading Interests of Children and Young Adults.* Scarecrow Press, New Jersey, 1970.

Landau, R. and Nyren, J. S. *Large Type Books in Print.* Bowker, New York, 1972.

Langer, Susanne. *Feeling and Form.* Routledge & Kegan Paul, London, 1953.

Library Association; Youth Libraries Group. *Book Selection for Children.* Pamphlet no. 3. LA, London, 1969.

Library Association. *School Libraries and Resource Centres: Recommended Standards for Policy and Provision.* LA, London, 1970, and Supplement on non-book materials, LA, London, 1972.

Luckham, Bryan. *The Library in Society.* Library Association, London, 1971.

Lukenbill, W. B. *A Working Bibliography of American Doctoral Dissertations in Children's and Adolescent's Literature, 1930-1971.* University of Illinois Graduate School of Library Science, 1972.

Martin, Lovell A. 'Deiches studies of Pratt Library examines student reading.' In J. S. Kujoth, *op. cit.*

Mays, J. B. *The Young Pretenders.* Joseph, London, 1965.

Mays, J. B. *The School in its Social Setting.* Longman, Harlow, 1967.

Merritt, John (ed.). *Reading and the Curriculum.* Ward Lock Educational, London, 1971.

Merritt, Le Roy Charles. *Book Selection and Intellectual Freedom.* H. W. Wilson, New York, 1970.

Ministry of Social Security. *The Circumstances of Families.* HMSO, London, 1967.

Moon, E. *Book Selection and Censorship in the Sixties.* Bowker, New York, 1969.

Morton-Williams, Roma and Finch, Stewart. *School Council Enquiry 1. Young School Leavers; Report of a Survey Among Young People, Parents and Teachers.* HMSO, London, 1968.

National Children's Bureau. *From Birth to Seven.* Longman, Harlow, 1972.

National Council for the Teaching of English. *Commission on Literature, Language and the English Curriculum.* NCTE, 1968.

Newsam, J. H. *Half our Future.* HMSO, London, 1963.

New York Library Association. Children and Young Adult Services Section. *Criteria and Guidelines in Planning for Young Adult Services in Public Library Building Programs.* New York Library Association, 1966.

Passow, A. H. and others. *The Education of the Disadvantaged.* Holt, Rinehart & Winston, New York, 1967.

Reid, Virginia M. *Reading Ladders for Human Relations.* American Council on Education, 5th ed., 1972.

Rosenberg, Judith K. and Rosenberg, Kenyon C. *Young People's Literature in Series; an Annotated Bibliographical Guide.* Libraries Unlimited, Colorado, 1972.

Rossoff, Martin. 'Blueprint for library teaching.' In Trinkner, C. L. *Teaching for Better Use of Libraries, op. cit.*

Rossoff, Martin. *The School Library and Educational Change.* Libraries Unlimited, Colorado, 1971.

Russell, G. J. *Teaching in Further Education.* Pitman Educational Library, London, 1972.

Schücking, Levin L. *The Sociology of Literary Taste.* Routledge & Kegan Paul, London, 1966.

Scott, M. H. (ed.). *Periodicals for School Libraries; a Guide to Magazines, Newspapers, Periodicals and Indexes.* American Library Association, Chicago, 1969.

Shaw, Alison. *Print for Partial Sight; a Research Report.* Library Association, London, 1969.

Shayer, David. *The Teaching of English in Schools 1900–1970.* Routledge & Kegan Paul, London, 1972.

Sherrill, Lawrence L. (ed.). *Library Service to the Unserved.* Library and Information Science Studies no. 2. Bowker, New York, 1970.

Shores, J. Harlan. 'Reading interests and information needs of high school students.' In J. S. Kujoth, *op. cit.*

Spiegler, Charles G. 'Give him a book that hits him where he lives.' In A. H. Passow and others. *The Education of the Disadvantaged, op. cit.*

Squire, James R. and Applebee, Roger K. *High School English Instruction Today.* Appleton-Century-Croft, 1968.

Squire, James R. and Applebee, Roger K. *Teaching English in the United Kingdom; a Comparative Study.* National Council of Teachers of English, 1969.

Stauffer, Russell G. *Directing Reading Maturity as a Cognitive Process.* Harper & Row, New York, 1969.

Thomison, Dennis. *Readings About Adolescent Literature.* Scarecrow Press, New Jersey, 1970.

Townsend, John Rowe. 'Didacticism in modern dress.' In S. Egoff and others, *op. cit.*

Trinkner, C. L. *Better Libraries Make Better Schools.* Shoestring Press, Connecticut, 1962.

Trinkner, C. L. *Teaching for Better Use of Libraries.* Shoestring Press, Connecticut, 1970.

Tunnicliffe, Stephen. 'Re-shaping the English syllabus at Newton High School.' In Summerfield and Tunnicliffe, *English in Practice.* CUP, London, 1971.

Waite, C. W. (ed.). *Periodicals for School Libraries.* School Library Association, 1969.

Weber, Olga. *Literary and Library Prizes.* Bowker, New York, 7th ed., 1970.

Willings Press Guide. *Thomas Skinner Directories*. Annual. London.

Young, Peter. *Data on Reading*. Schofield & Sims, Huddersfield, 1970.

Zaccharia, J. S. and Moses, H. A. *Facilitating Human Development Through Reading; the Use of Bibliotherapy in Teaching and Counselling*. Stipes Publishing Co., 1968.

B. PERIODICAL ARTICLES

Altman, Ellen. 'Implications of title diversity and collection overlap for inter-library loan among secondary schools.' *The Library Quarterly*, vol. 42, no. 2, April 1972, pp. 177–194.

Barnes, Douglas, Churley, Peter and Thompson, Christopher. 'Group talk and literary response.' *English in Education*, vol. 5, no. 3, Winter 1971, pp. 75–76.

Bardgett, Keith. 'Skinhead in the classroom.' *Children's Literature in Education*, vol. 8, July 1972, pp. 56–64.

Beavan, Mary H. 'Response of adolescents to feminine characters in literature.' *Research in the Teaching of English*, vol. 6, no. 1, Spring 1972, pp. 48–68.

Blishen, Edward. *The Bookseller*, 27 Jan. 1973, pp. 240–244.

Bolt, S. F. 'Unqualified readers.' *The Use of English*, vol. XVII, no. 3, Spring 1966, pp. 228–233.

Butts, Denis. 'Second rate books for second rate children.' *The Use of English*, vol. XVII, no. 4, Summer 1966, pp. 296–300.

Bulman, Learned T. 'Young adult work in branch libraries.' *Library Trends*, vol. 14, no. 4, April 1966, pp. 434–439.

Capenhurst, J. 'Organized reading in a comprehensive school, years 1–3.' *The Use of English*, vol. XXIII, no. 3, Spring 1972, pp. 203–205, 211.

Carlsen, G. Robert. 'For everything there is a season.' *Top of the News*, 21, Jan. 1965, pp. 103–110.

Castagna, Edwin. 'Young adult service in the public library organization chart.' *Library Trends*, vol. 17, no. 2, Oct. 1968, pp. 132–139.

Chambers, Aidan. 'Adolescent reading and Topliners.' *Books For Your Children*, vol. 7, no. 4, Summer 1972, pp. 6–7.

Clark, Margaret. 'Books for new adults.' *Books For Your Children*, vol. 7, no. 4, Summer 1972, p. 8.

Cornell, M. 'Therapy in disguise; a report on reading at the Training School for Boys.' *Arkansas Libraries*, Summer 1970, pp. 20–21.

Day, Alison. 'The library in the multi-racial secondary school; a Caribbean booklist.' *The School Librarian*, vol. 19, no. 3, Sept. 1971, pp. 198–199.

Douglas, J. R. 'Free-schooling; alternative education and its documentation.' *Wilson Library Bulletin*, vol. 47, no. 1, 1972, pp. 48–54.

Edwards, Margaret A. 'The urban library and the adolescent.' *The Library Quarterly*, vol. 38, no. 1, Jan. 1968, pp. 70–77.

Egoff, Sheila. *The Hornbook Magazine*, vol. 46, no. 2, April 1970, pp. 142–150.

Ellis, James I. 'The responses of adolescents to selected passages on a theme of violence.' *Research in Librarianship*, vol. 13, no. 3, Jan. 1970, pp. 5–6.

Engdahl, Sylvia L. 'Why write for teenagers today?' *The Hornbook Magazine*, vol. 48, no. 3, June 1972, pp. 249–254.

Evans, Keith. 'Multi-media resources centres; a cautionary note.' *Secondary Education*, vol. 1, no. 3, Summer term 1971, pp. 3–5.

Evans, W. D. Emrys. 'Literature or life?' *Times Educational Supplement*, 7 July 1972, p. 36.

Federic, Yolande. 'General criteria for selection and use of material.' *Illinois Libraries*, vol. 40, June 1958, pp. 504–509.

Forsman, Carolyn. 'Crisis information services to youth; a lesson for libraries?' *Library Journal*, vol. 97, no. 12, 15 March 1972, pp. 1127–1134.

Gottsdanker, Josephine S. and Pidgeon, Anne E. 'Current reading tastes of young adults.' *Journal of Higher Education*, vol. 40, May 1969, pp. 381–383.

Grogan, J. C. 'Library service to youth in state institutions.' *Wisconsin Library Bulletin*, May 1970, pp. 156–157.

Hanson, Derek. 'What children like to read.' *New Society*, 17 May 1973, pp. 361–363.

Hentoff, Nat. 'Hearing from the teenage reader.' *Wilson Library Bulletin*, vol. 47, no. 1, 1972, pp. 38–41.

Hernandez. Ramon R. 'Youth choices and simple processes.' *Wisconsin Library Bulletin*, Jan.–Feb. 1972, pp. 32–36.

Higgins, Judith, 'The great paperback mystery.' *Top of the News*, Nov. 1967.

Jensen, A. R. 'The culturally disadvantaged; psychological and educational aspects.' *Educational Research*, vol. 10, no. 1, Nov. 1967, pp. 12–15.

Justin, Estelle. 'Confronting our media biases; the social dimensions of media theory.' *School Libraries*, vol. 21, no. 4, Summer 1972, pp. 14–16.

Kalkhoff, Ann. 'Innocent children or innocent librarians?' *Library Journal*, vol. 97, no. 18, 15 Oct. 1972, pp. 3430–3437.

Kaufman, Ruth M. *Wisconsin Library Bulletin*, vol. 47, no. 1, Sept. 1972, pp. 59–61.

Luckham, Bryan. 'Periodical purchase and readership; use in the public library and by adults at large contrasted.' *Research in Librarianship*, vol. 23, no. 4, May 1973, pp. 141–155.

Lutas, K. M. 'Strangeways Prison library.' *Book Trolley*, Dec. 1971, pp. 3–7.

Measel, W. and Crawford, C. L. 'School children and book selection.' *American Libraries*, vol. 2, no. 9, Oct. 1971, pp. 955–957.

Moore, John E. 'Ingredients of the correctional school library.' *AHIL Quarterly*, vol. 3, no. 3, Spring 1963, pp. 18–22.

Moses, Richard B. 'Just show the movies – never mind the books.' *ALA Bulletin*, vol. 59, no. 1, Jan. 1965, pp. 58–60.

Muirhead, Oliver. *Books For Your Children*, vol. 7, no. 4, Summer 1972, p. 9.

Musgrove, F. 'Social needs and satisfactions.' *British Journal of Educational Psychology*, no. 36, June 1966, pp. 137–149.

Musgrove, F. and Taylor, P. H. 'Teachers' and parents' conception of the teacher's role.' *British Journal of Educational Psychology*, no. 35, Feb. 1965, pp. 171–179.

Noble, Jeanne. 'Generational gapiosis.' *Wilson Library Bulletin*, Oct. 1968, pp. 134–139.

Osborn, Anne V. 'How to annihilate library service to teenagers.' *School Library Journal*, Nov. 1972, pp. 28–30.

Osborn, Anne V. 'It's not enough to love books, ya gotta love people too.' *School Library Journal*, March 1973, pp. 78–82.

Paton, X. 'Teaching the mentally retarded to read.' *Book Trolley*, March 1972, pp. 9–11.

Peck, Richard. 'In the country of teenage fiction.' *American Libraries*, vol. 4, no. 4, April 1973, pp. 204–207.

Poster, Cyril. 'The comprehensive curriculum.' *Secondary Education*, vol. 1, no. 3, Summer term 1971, pp. 14–15.

Pugh, A. K. 'Some neglected aspects of reading in the secondary school.' *Reading*, vol. 3, no. 3, Dec. 1969, pp. 3–10.

Pugh, A. K. 'Secondary school reading; obstacles to profit and delight.' *Reading*, vol. 5, no. 1, March 1971, pp. 6–13.

Salter, Don. 'The hard core of children's fiction.' *Children's Literature in Education*, no. 8, July 1972, pp. 39–55.

Sharp, Peter. 'Philadelphia team-free library and youth study centre.' *ALA Bulletin*, April 1961, pp. 324–328.

Smith, M. B. 'A Gloucestershire setting for careers counselling.' *Times Educational Supplement*, 17 March 1972, p. 62.

Southgate, Vera. 'Effective reading at every age.' *Trends in Education*, no. 26, April 1972, pp. 29–32.

Spence, Margaret. 'Towards fiction in the seventies.' *Education Libraries Bulletin*, supplement 15, 1972.

Staneck, Lou Willett. 'The maturation of the junior novel; from gestation to the pill.' *The Library Journal*, 15 Dec. 1972, pp. 4046–5051.

Starr, Carol. 'Youthomania; the care and treatment of discipline in the public library.' *Wisconsin Library Bulletin*, Jan.–Feb. 1972, pp. 27–38.

Thomson, Norman and Brazil, David. 'Productivity in English teaching.' *English in Education*, vol. 2, no. 3, 1968, pp. 48–53.

Vaughn, Beryl I. 'Reading interests of the 8th grade students.' *Journal of Developmental Reading*, vol. 6, Spring 1963, pp. 149–155.

Wakefield, J. M. and Hofman, C. N. 'Certifiable lunacy or common sense? combining your adult and juvenile collections.' *Wilson Library Bulletin*, vol. 46, no. 6, Feb. 1972, pp. 513–517.
White, Maureen. 'Walsall Teenage Library.' *YLG News*, vol. 13, no. 2, June 1969.

Yarlott, G. and Harpin, W. '1,000 responses to English literature – 1.' *Educational Research*, vol. 13, no. 1, Nov. 1970, pp. 3–11.

C. MISCELLANEOUS SOURCES

American Library Association. Association of Hospital and Institution Libraries. *New Horizons Expanded; Readable Books For and About the Physically Handicapped.* AHIL, 1962.

British Broadcasting Corporation. ROSLA series, no. 5. *Resources.* Video-tape. BBC, 1973.

Department of Education and Science. Library Advisory Council Working Party on Periodicals. *Survey of Serials.* DES, 1971.

Hill, Janet. 'Book selection.' In Library Association. *Book Selection For Children.* Pamphlet no. 3, LA, 1968.
Huws, G. *Provision of Periodicals; Report of a Research Project.* Leicestershire County Library, 1968.

Institute of Municipal Treasurers' Accounts. *Public Library Statistics, 1971–2.* IMTA, 1973.

Joint Matriculation Board; Universities of Manchester, Liverpool, Leeds, Sheffield, Birmingham. *General Certificate of Education. Regulations and Syllabuses, 1973.* JMB, 1971.

Library Association. Youth Libraries Group. *Books for the Multi-racial Classroom.* Compiled by Judith Elkin. LA, 1971.

Rutherford, Agnes. *Survey on Public Library Use.* Leeds Polytechnic, Dept. of Librarianship, Public Libraries Research Unit, 1973.

Scholastic Publications Ltd. *Scoop Club News.*

Totterdell, Barry. *Hillingdon Libraries Project.* Polytechnic of North London, School of Librarianship, 1973.

Wheatley, G. *The Teenage Reader in Further Education.* HERTIS Occasional Paper, no. 1. St Alban's College of Further Education, 1967.

Young Adult Services Division, ALA. 'Task force on young adult services working paper' (revised July 1973). *Library Journal*, 15 Sept. 1973, pp. 2606–2608.

'Young adult service in the public library.' Whole issue of *Library Trends*, vol. 17, no. 2, Oct. 1968.

Youth Libraries Group News. Whole issue on teenagers, vol. 13, no. 2, Jan. 1969.

Index

Index